MARY W. CRAIG is a writer
is a former Carnegie schol
of Glasgow. She writes ab
live their lives buffeted by the politics and economics of the
elite. Mary also gives talks and lectures on various aspects of
Scottish and Europe history to community groups across the
country. She is the author of *Borders Witch Hunt* published by
Luath Press in 2020. Some historians are known as hedgehogs,
happily snuffling about rooting out the minutest of historical
details. Others are known as eagles, soaring on high they see
great vistas of historical events. A few are known as magpies: if
something shiny and interesting catches their eye, they will try
to capture it where possible. Mary is a magpie.

Agnes Finnie

The Witch of the
Potterrow Port

MARY W. CRAIG

Luath Press Limited
EDINBURGH
www.luath.co.uk

First published 2023

ISBN: 978-1-80425-019-8

The author's right to be identified as author of this book
under the Copyright, Designs and Patents Act 1988 has
been asserted.

Printed and bound by Clays Ltd., Bungay

Typeset in 10.5 point Sabon by Lapiz

Contents

Note 6

Introduction 7

1 The Potterrow 9
2 Witchcraft and Magic 18
3 Halting Hame 29
4 Bad Herrings 38
5 The Buchannans 51
6 Broken Legs 69
7 The King, the Covenanters
and the Cordiners Corporation 90
8 Salt 119
9 Haunting 139
10 A Witch's Gett 153
11 Imprisonment 167
12 The Trial 198
13 Verdict and Sentence 221
14 Aftermath 234
15 Epilogue 248

Acknowledgements 254
Bibliography 255
References 261

Note

ALTHOUGH THIS BOOK is based on Agnes Finnie's trial records as well as other primary source material, not every aspect of life in Edinburgh and wider Scotland in the 17th century can be known exactly. Some of the following chapters contain descriptions of reactions to the political and religious events of the century as well as events in Agnes' life; some of these descriptions come directly from contemporary records, others are imagined responses based on those contemporary records.

Introduction

AGNES FINNIE WAS a 'witch' who lived in Edinburgh during the 17th century. Her entire trial records are held in the National Library of Scotland. As such, her story can be examined in some detail. Her alleged witchcraft spanned 1628 to 1644, a turbulent time in Scotland's history. The start of the Wars of the Three Kingdoms affected people across Scotland and its consequences were possibly most intense in the capital, making the political and military machinations of the age central to understanding Agnes' life. The battle for supremacy between Royalists and Covenanters combined with the religious fervour of the Kirk impacted on ordinary people's lives across Scotland. The rising political and religious tensions of the times mirror the increasing number and intensity of the alleged incidents of witchcraft in Agnes' case.

The Scottish witch hunts occurred within five major 'panics': 1590–1; 1597; 1628–30; 1649 and 1661–2. Agnes Finnie was not arrested in any of these, but in 1644. The stereotype of a witch is of a poor, elderly healer gathering herbs in the country-side to care for a sick child. Agnes undermines that stereotype. Although not rich, Agnes was not very poor – she was a middling sort. She was not principally a healer: she was a shop-keeper. She did not live in a country cottage, but in the tenements of Edinburgh.

Most 'witches' were arrested after an accusation from a neighbour who had been the victim of their 'witchcraft'.

The accusations against Agnes finally numbered 20 and yet the initial complaint came not from one of her victims, but from another individual in the neighbourhood.

After being arrested, 'witches' were usually tried within a matter of days. Agnes spent several months in Edinburgh's Tolbooth between arrest and facing the courts. Most juries found 'witches' guilty within hours, or at least a couple of days of the trial. The jury in Agnes' case took several weeks to deliver a verdict. Few 'witches' were defended at their trials, but Agnes employed two advocates to plead her case.

During Agnes' trial, her daughter Margaret was named as having also been a witch and yet, unusually, was not arrested. The trial records of other 'witches' detail several mothers and daughters who were arrested. So, the question remains: why did Margaret not follow her mother to trial?

* * *

Agnes' story is much more nuanced and more interesting than that of the stereotypical poor defenceless woman persecuted by the Kirk. Through Agnes' story, the everyday lives of ordinary people struggling to survive are revealed. The religious and political upheaval in Scotland and the rest of the United Kingdom impacted such ordinary people as Scotland became increasingly seen as a land under threat from the Devil and his handmaidens: witches. The women and men who were accused of witchcraft were much more than the stereotypical 'witch victim'; they were real people with real lives. This is just one of their stories.

I

The Potterrow

ON 18 DECEMBER 1644, Agnes Finnie was brought into the courtroom at the Edinburgh Tolbooth to face her accusers. Scotland was in the grip of the Civil War, plague and harvest failure were affecting many and the General Assembly of the Kirk had recently passed a series of Condemnatory Acts against witches. The town was boiling with fear and hysteria: Auld Nick was stalking the land devouring all in his way. Agnes Finnie would pay the price for that fear and hysteria. A widow with a grown-up daughter but no other family to support her, it had been her own neighbours that reported her to the Kirk minister. Faced with 20 charges of witchcraft and sorcery, Agnes was in a perilous state, not least because she had confessed at her first examination before the south-west Kirk Session of Edinburgh that she had been 'ane rank witch these twenty-eight years bygane'.[1]

Standing alone and reviled in the courtroom, Agnes' trial would expose a world of social, political and religious upheaval where superstition, belief, fear and greed mingled with money-lending and murder. This was no old woman from the farmlands of Midlothian curing her family's ailments with herbs and charms. Agnes did not climb a Borders hill to sup with the Devil in the pale moonlight. Agnes was a shopkeeper in the capital city selling fishcakes, lending money and wreaking revenge on those who wronged her. But was she also a witch?

Agnes lived and worked in the Potterrow Port, Edinburgh. Less than a mile from the castle, the parliament and St Giles, it was, nonetheless, a world apart: a dark corner of the town that sprawled south of the Royal Mile running for a fair distance along the southern edge of the city wall where the working poor and the destitute rubbed along together. It was the sort of area no one visited unless they had a reason to, and certainly never after dark. But it was also home to a few middling folk: shopkeepers, craftsmen and artisans, those who thought themselves a step up from the working poor, but for whom poverty was only a wage or two away. The middling sorts who made real money left the old neighbourhood as soon as possible: Agnes was not one of those.

Part of the parish of Greyfriars Kirk, the tall tenements crowded together along the Potterrow just as they did on the Royal Mile, but for all the similarity and close proximity, life in the Potterrow was more secretive. No ministers walked along the Potterrow to go to St Giles, no advocates hurried to the law courts, no Lords of the Privy Council walked the streets as they did the Royal Mile: the Potterrow lived a life of its own, unseen, unheard and undisturbed.

Greyfriars Kirk had been built in 1620 and was one of the first new Kirks to be constructed in Scotland after the Reformation. When the diocese of Edinburgh was created within the Scottish Kirk, the parish of Greyfriars was incorporated into the new structure. Previously, the congregation had worshipped in the western portion of St Giles until it had grown too large. A new Kirk and manse were built on the site of the friary of the old Greyfriars. The new building was 'comfortable and commodious, ane true house of God'.[2] It was quickly populated by the pious members of the parish, as well as those whose attendance was motivated primarily by social standing. The lack of Potterrow inhabitants on its pews on the Sabbath was barely noted. For those that bothered to climb the hill, the new Kirk had none of the easy familiarity of old St Giles. There were no shadowy corners in which to hide and perhaps sleep through the sermon or sit and gossip with your friends. The Sabbath was the day of worship, but, for the working poor of the Potterrow, it was also their only day of rest and enjoyment.

That day of rest was needed. Life in the Potterrow was tough. A lucky few had apprenticeships as carpenters or butchers or worked as weavers, but most scraped a living as day labourers, as servants scrubbing floors at the parliament building or as messengers for merchants and shopkeepers. The local tradespeople, cordiners, tailors and bakers, were only one or two steps above them. Most of the shops were on the ground floor of the tenement buildings with the family living in the backroom which often served as the shop's storeroom. The goods sold were not high quality – who in the Potterrow could afford that? The community was relatively closed – apart from the few that worked in the High Street or the courts as cleaners, residents had little need or desire to go elsewhere. Occasionally, the children would wander down to the great expanse around Arthur's Seat to catch rabbits for their dinner. Sometimes there would be a gala day high up at the castle when someone was executed. But other than that, the Potterrow residents regularly left the area for only one thing:

attendance at the Kirk on a Sunday. But not everyone went to the Kirk; in fact probably fewer than half of those in the area did, and that was the problem with the Potterrow. Located at the very edge of the city boundary, the Potterrow was not physically close to Greyfriars Kirk.

Known as the haunt of undesirables and troublemakers, it held more than its fair share of drinking dens and mean, low shops and was barely visited by the minister at Greyfriars. Attendance at the Kirk might be the required custom, but it was barely observed in the Potterrow. Even those who did attend did so infrequently. This was partly because, for many, Sunday was their only rest day and to climb the hill to Greyfriars was quite an undertaking. In addition, the harsh life in the Potterrow was such that the majority of the residents drank heavily when they could to escape from the sheer drudgery of their lives. The Sunday morning climb to the Kirk was even less appealing when combined with a hangover. For many of the parishioners, therefore, attendance at the Kirk was not a priority. These matters were complicated by the sheer number of residents in the area. No one knew exactly how many people lived in the Potterrow. There were families with multiple children, not all of whom had been christened by the Kirk. Many of the couples in the area lived together without the sacrament of marriage. George Hickes, in his chronicle of the trial of the conventicle-preacher Mr James Mitchel, wrote that in Scotland in the 17th century there were 'more bastards born within their country [...] than in all our nation besides.'[3] Then there were masters with apprentices who slept in workshops. The tall tenements housed tenants who sublet rooms, and in some cases single beds, to lodgers who may or may not have used their real names. There were peddlers and itinerant traders who came and went with the fairs and holy days. And finally, there were the destitute that slept in back alleyways and the stairwells of tenements.[4] It was estimated that there may have been as many as 20,000 souls packed inside Edinburgh's city walls; the numbers in the Potterrow remained unknown.

In addition to the normal residents, there were the travellers that passed through the Potterrow on a daily basis. The Potterrow, with its Port, was a bustling thoroughfare which led into the city. The old medieval walls of Edinburgh were still in existence with their four 'ports' or gates into the city. Originally, the ports had towers at either side where the city guard controlled entry into and out of Edinburgh. These were still used as toll gates where traders paid a tax on their merchandise. At busy times, a queue would form as people waited to have their papers checked and their carts and goods examined. This was a prime location for pickpockets, thieves, prostitutes and others to gather to see what business could be done. It was here, beside the bustling port, that Agnes had her shop. But for all its prime location, Agnes' shop did not have the pick of the merchandise that arrived. Most traders, once their papers were checked and their tax paid, drove straight up to the High Street. Few in the Potterrow could afford their goods. Those who traded in cheaper goods, or were opportunistically seeing what was what, stayed in the Potterrow. One final class of frequent visitor to the port were those who traded in stolen or counterfeit goods. Mingling with honest tradespersons, they would hawk their wares while trying to avoid paying tax, hiding from the harassed clerks at the port and avoiding notice from the city baillies. It was probably from those sorts of traders that Agnes supplied her shop.

When the port 'closed' for the evening and after the honest traders and city clerks had left for the day there was still plenty of activity at the Potterrow. Agnes' shop traded well into the evening with plenty of customers calling to buy her goods or borrow some money.

Despite the fact that the Potterrow was in Scotland's capital city, life was a struggle for all but the rich and buying cheap, counterfeit goods or borrowing money was in many cases the only way to survive. Death rates among children were high, with around 50 per cent failing to make it past their tenth birthday. The food supply was unpredictable, with around one in every ten harvests in the surrounding area failing; harvest failures in the Highlands were even more frequent. The better-off merchants and nobility may have had food stores, but for everyone else one bad harvest could mean starvation. For the rest of the time, the population survived on a diet that left them chronically undernourished with deficiencies in several vital minerals and vitamins. Such food as was bought and sold in neighbourhoods like the Potterrow was of poor quality. In such a perennially weakened state, any illness or injury could be, and frequently was, fatal. Those doctors who existed were too expensive for the likes of the Potterrow residents and, in an era before modern medicine, had little to offer in the face of infectious diseases. Herbal remedies supplied by the mother or grandmother of the house gave some relief where they could.

Housing conditions were equally dire. There was rampant overcrowding in the tenements of the Potterrow, partly from the large size of the families and partly from the necessity of taking in a lodger or two to be able to afford the rent. The tenements had no running water and no sanitation.

The picturesque expression of 'gardyloo', the customary Edinburgh warning cry when slops were thrown from the windows into the streets, belies the realities of life with no sanitation when human excrement was thrown into the street. Night soil men, who were paid to dispose of such excrement, would not be seen until the 18th century and the streets had to be swept clean by the residents of the Potterrow themselves. Water for cooking and cleaning had to be carried up flights of tenement stairs and for those elderly or infirm living on the top floors, washing often became a luxury for high days and holidays only. There were also, of course, the other residents of the Potterrow tenements; the fleas, lice, bed bugs, cockroaches and rats. All of these contaminated water, ate food supplies and acted as vectors that spread disease and general ill health among the local population.

The houses were also cold and damp with all the mould and other health hazards that that entailed. Those who could afford it bought coal and logs, although they were in the minority. Those who could not afford coal or logs burned animal dung, but although this supplied some heat it could not fully dispense with the damp that settled on weak chests and arthritic bones and further debilitated the population. Many windows were kept tight shut to keep out the cold, increasing problems with smoke, soot and dust in the air. Lighting was another perennial problem. Other than natural light, households used tallow candles made from the fat of cows or sheep. Foul smelling, these candles gave minimal light unless several were used – which of course was too expensive for most households. The lack of lighting inside the tenements, especially in the Scottish winter, gave rise to frequent accidents.

The resulting injuries could, in turn, cause health problems if any wounds became infected or broken bones were set incorrectly, leading to permanent disability which affected the individual's capacity to work. There were also, of course, severe accidents which resulted in death.

Underlying all of these issues was the fear of destitution. The stark reality of life for almost everyone below the better-off middling sorts was to find enough money to buy food and pay your rent or risk eviction. Therefore, everyone had to work. If you could not work due to illness, injury, exhaustion, old age or malnutrition then death from starvation or hypothermia in the Scottish winter was a very real prospect unless you had a relative who would care for you. The Kirk did help in certain cases, but this was at the discretion of the minister and was generally only a matter of a few shillings that would last barely a week. Offered mostly to widows and orphans, church charity was seldom if ever available to men. The duty of church-goers to donate to the poor that had been prevalent in the Catholic church had been replaced by a strict Calvinist work ethic that condemned many to penury.

With little, and in most cases no, practical help to alleviate their living conditions, many used alcohol as a means of escape. While this initially proved a temporary solution, in the long term it increased the pressure on the family's finances. Despite this, alcohol consumption rose alongside its consequences: violence and increased ill health.

Given the living conditions in the Potterrow, the people in the area needed a shop that sold the everyday essentials at an affordable price, a means by which to borrow money when necessary and a source of basic health care. All three were supplied by Agnes Finnie.

While the poor of the Potterrow struggled to survive, the ministers and councillors up on the High Street were consumed with the ongoing religious and political turmoil that characterised the mid-17th century. When the high politics of Edinburgh and London collided, Agnes Finnie of the Potterrow Port would become one of its victims.

2

Witchcraft and Magic

WITCHCRAFT AND WITCHES were a perfectly common fact of life in Scotland in the 17th century. Despite the very loud protestations of the Kirk that they were God's Elect and that Calvinism was the purest form of Christianity, older beliefs remained stubbornly present. Belief in the power of magic was more or less ubiquitous among ordinary people and co-existed alongside their Christian beliefs. For the Kirk, magical practices performed by witches could only come from the Devil.

The world of the early Scots was a bewildering and potentially dangerous place. Events outwith an individual's control could mean life or death. The harvest might fail, disease could kill entire families, winter storms and floods could devastate whole communities. Perhaps magic could be used to help. The world of magic was shadowy. It lurked unseen in many places. A frequent sacrifice was a metal object cast into water: metal was precious and water was thought of as a gateway to the world of the gods. But not everyone could perform magic. Some were better able to make contact, some seemed to have more power to appease the gods. Magical amulets bought from such a person offered protection from the wrath of certain gods. A supplication made by such a person might gain an individual good luck.

While various peoples arrived in Scotland as settlers or invaders, these beliefs remained relatively unchanged for several centuries. By the time the first Christians arrived in the 5th century, belief in the supernatural was deeply embedded. Christianity took some time to establish itself and belief in the old gods and Christianity co-existed for some considerable time. Syncretism, the amalgamation or attempted amalgamation of different religions, allowed a blending and cross-fertilisation between the old and the new that gave the people enough spiritual solace to ensure ongoing followers for both. The festivals around the winter solstice on 21 December mixed with new celebrations of the birth of Christ. Celebrations at the rebirth of spring were subsumed into the Easter celebrations of the resurrected Christ.

Even as Christianity became more dominant, most people, especially women, continued with the magical and superstitious traditions and practices from their pre-Christian past. The church, which was male dominated, dismissed the spiritual role of women in communities. By doing so, however, they did not remove the beliefs and practices, but merely shifted them to sit underneath Christianity.

The early Christian church in Scotland had problems. The church stated that there was a single Christian God rather than several pagan gods: one God, God the Father, who was good (and male) and that there was one evil Devil. But the one God was also Christ the son and the Holy Spirit, which sounded suspiciously like three gods to the old believers. And why, if there was only one good god, would that good god create an evil devil? To add to the confusion, the Virgin Mary was human but had given birth to a god. She was not herself divine although she was in heaven and could be worshipped. Was she not a female god?

For most early Scots, although this was confusing it was not their most pressing concern. Their lives continued to be dominated by the need for a good harvest, to be free of disease and to make it through the winter. While the church was further developing its theological arguments, ordinary people continued to appease the gods for a good harvest by asking the local priest to bless the fields at spring sowing. As time went on, the belief in 'the gods' faded and belief in the Christian God became the norm, but the supernatural creatures – such as faeries and kelpies – were still there in the shadows. They could be thanked for abundant crops both in homes and the harvest thanksgiving festival at the local church. Or they could be blamed for the birth of a baby with a 'hare-lip'. As long as the community came to church on a Sunday, most Catholic priests turned a blind eye to what happened behind closed doors. In some more remote areas of the early Catholic church, and this included Scotland, the priest was not the well-educated, theologically articulate evangelist for Christ that we might expect. It was unlikely that he was literate and he probably did not speak Latin. The mysteries of the sacraments were delivered by rote. These 'Mass priests' could sing the Mass in Latin, but with no understanding of it and lived like everyone else. Thus, the local superstitions were not alien concepts to be condemned from the pulpit or ignored in a well-meaning attempt to attract a congregation, but, in most instances, were part and parcel of the priest's own life and internal beliefs. Attendance at the church on Sunday to hear the priest say mass did not stop you visiting the local witch on Monday to help a sick child. A blended, simple faith, which in some cases bore little resemblance to Rome's theological tenets, was accepted.

That is not to say that the early church did not try to stamp out superstition and magical practices. Sacrifices to the 'old gods' such as leaving offerings at Holy Wells that had previously been pagan wells, fortune telling and charming were all anathema to the church. However, it took time and effort to quell such practices. It was all very well for 'the church' to send out an edict forbidding such practices, but it was quite another matter for a local priest to do so. A single priest might have a parish that spanned the entire length of a river valley that was well-nigh impassable for at least four months of the year. What was going on in remote settlements could continue unseen for years. Local priests had to live with their parishioners. Telling people repeatedly that they must not do what their mothers and grandmothers had done for generations and that such practices were sinful and evil could cause, at best, ill-feeling and, at worst, downright hostility. The other problem was the difference between legitimate and illegitimate magic. Ringing the church bells to dispel a storm and leaving cheese out for the faeries to ensure good weather were both magical rituals, but only one was legitimate. What was and was not magic was determined by the church. The female practitioners of magic did not determine its legitimacy. Holy water was made holy, and thus able to perform miracles, by the recitation of the priest's Latin prayers. That same priest could condemn a local woman for washing a baby in water from a local spring while saying a rhyme over the child. The theological arguments behind such distinctions may have made sense to the priest, but probably not to anyone else.

This situation could not continue forever. By the 16th century, a simplistic non-questioning belief that left room for magic was no longer acceptable and the Reformation shook Europe, including Scotland, out of its religious torpor. The new faith gave primacy to personal salvation; an individual had a personal relationship with God, with no priest or bishop to intercede. The mystical element – the Latin mass, the transubstantiation of bread and wine into body and blood – was lost. But those were the very elements of Catholic faith which had, albeit unwittingly, allowed the ordinary man and woman to profess their Christian faith while firmly holding on to their belief in magic and magical supernatural creatures. The Catholic Church, under threat, reformed many of the practices that had caused Martin Luther's protest in the first place, but retained the mystery of faith in ritual. The new Protestants saw in that the work of the Devil. Neither, however, greatly changed the belief in magic and the supernatural that underpinned most people's lives. The Reformation and Counter-Reformation challenged theology across Europe; new ideas sprang up and for a brief, very brief, time in some small pockets of Europe women found their voice to discuss faith and spirituality. However, as the Protestant Reformation advocated study of the Bible, women's voices were considered to be controversial and were soon suppressed because of the edict in the Bible for women to be silent: 'Women are to be silent in the churches. They are not permitted to speak, but must be in submission, as the law says.'[5] The men in the Protestant churches dictated what practices were magical. After the upheaval of the split from the Catholic church, Catholicism itself was now viewed as diabolical, as were all other practices not sanctioned by bible teachings. After the Reformation, the Kirk fulminated against such 'diabolical' practices and thus fundamentally failed to understand the beliefs of their flock, who saw magic as a way to deal with the uncertainties of life. People had not worshipped the Devil, or any devil; they had merely understood that the faeries were capricious and, on occasion, had to be appeased. That they could help you, if you asked in the right way, to cure your child or to lay illness on your enemies.

The Protestant faith in Scotland swept away Catholicism, but in that religious zeal completely failed to see that it was leaving ordinary believers bewildered in a sea of predestination and personal salvation that did nothing to help when your child fell ill or you were too poor to pay your rent. The lack of understanding by the Kirk of the continuing belief in the magical world was one thing, but their conflation of that magical spirit world with worship of the Devil would prove disastrous for Agnes Finnie and thousands like her. The minister of Greyfriars Kirk might thunder in his pulpit about the demonic paganism of Halloween, but the few residents of the Potterrow listening in the pews would probably just nod their heads and then go home to bob for apples to divine the future and tell ghost stories by the fire. It was a clash of beliefs that could not be easily resolved. Protestant and Catholic ministers alike railed against the superstition and magical beliefs of their parishioners. Especially when those same parishioners hesitated to fully believe the Holy Sacraments. Richard Greenham, the great English puritan, wrote in the late 1600s, 'there are many who hearing in the Word of the wonderful creation, redemption, and preservation of man, and of the matter of the Sacraments, cannot believe them, yet afterwards go to witches.'[6]

But if witches were not pagans believing in the old gods, who didn't exist, and were women and so not supposed to wield power on their own, the only place the superstition and magic could come from was the Devil. The Calvinist Kirk knew they were God's Elect and as such would be attacked by Auld Nick. This meant, however, that not only did they fear witches but that they actively sought them out. What minister worth his salt would not be attacked by the Devil? The more holy one was, the more likely to be attacked. The more one was attacked, the more it proved one was holy. With this circular logic, the Scottish Kirk developed an almost delusional mindset about the Devil. The Kirk firmly believed that witches were the Devil's handmaidens; that these women had renounced their faith and had made a pact with the Devil. This was not, however, what the people thought. The separation of good and evil into two supernatural entities had never made sense to them. As human beings were flawed, with both good and bad in their characters, so too the magical world was inhabited by creatures that were changeable and unpredictable. The world of magic was more complex than the binary division of good and evil preached from the pulpit, and was more believable because of that. Navigating that world might involve wearing an amulet to protect from illness or casting a charm to ask for a successful childbirth. It certainly made more sense than the cold concept of personal salvation and was the done thing in this period. It was as natural as breathing or walking. To have their congregations wear their Christianity so lightly horrified the Kirk and further 'proved' the diabolical nature of witches through the ease with which they could undermine the faith of the people. What tripped up many 'witches' in the early interrogations was the lack of understanding of the concept of a good god and an evil devil. Practices that had been innocently pursued were given a diabolical basis to the complete bewilderment of many of the accused. They would confess that, yes, they had left an offering to the man with the black hat or, yes, they had looked in water to find stolen property. The confessions were true because these were common practices. The problem for the women was that what was a normal procedure for them, and had probably been practised in their families for generations, had become an act of evil to the Kirk.

As in all faiths and beliefs, what constituted witchcraft and a belief in the supernatural varied between individuals. Although everyone in Scotland was Christian and they were repeatedly told that Calvinism was the purest form of Christianity, how did an individual navigate the everyday when the Kirk minster was either unapproachable or less than understanding? Those who believed in the old ways of magic would attend the Kirk on a Sunday, but still seek out the likes of Agnes when their child fell ill. The Kirk was one thing, but an accommodation with the little people was the only way to survive. Many accused witches confessed to making a pact with the Devil. For some, this confession was made in order to stop whatever interrogation and possible torture was happening. In most cases, it was drawn from them by repeated questioning by the minster who held the fervent belief in the diabolic element of witchcraft and framed their questioning accordingly. For many, however, a contract with the Devil was perfectly reasonable. Their 'Devil' however, was not the evil antithesis of Christ, but Auld Nick. He was the man in the black hat who could offer help in punishing your enemies. He was part of the spirit world, one of the supernatural creatures with whom an individual could easily bargain. The Devil held a special almost, it could be argued, friendly place in the lives of most ordinary Scots. He was Auld Harry, Auld Clootie, Auld Sandy and even Auld Horny. He lived across the country in places like the Devil's brig, the Devil's dyke, the Devil's beef tub, the Devil's elbow, the Devil's lum and even the Devil's arse. With such long standing and easy familiarity, the new Kirk's obsessive focus on his malevolence was confusing. For most accused witches it was not necessarily even Auld Nick with whom they had communed. It could equally have been a charm said to the little people to help find lost property, or to one of the now-disgraced medieval Catholic saints. Prayers and offerings said to the Virgin Mary for a healthy baby were the same prayers and offerings that had probably been said for years.

Witches were special because they had not lost their links to the world of magic and so could tap into its power. If your child was ill, the witch could help; if your neighbour had wronged you, the witch could summon a punishment. These were ordinary everyday matters, but mundane though they might be, they could also encompass life and death. They were the ordinary and mundane matters that the minister in his pulpit often could not or would not help in overcoming. The minister was remote, alien and male – and in most cases unbending in his Calvinist faith. He did not live in the dirt and the poverty of the Potterrow Port, but in his 'big hoose' the manse. He did not understand the scramble for necessities that went on in the back tenements, but sat drinking good claret with members of the Privy Council in furnished rooms in the city chambers. He was a man; how could he know of the pains of childbirth or the misery of a miscarriage? The cold theology of predestination gave scant comfort to those already cast out by its reasoning. If the Christian God had already decided who was saved and who was damned, then what was the point of prayer? At least you could bargain with the supernatural beings of the magic world. Given this reality, it is little wonder that even those who did attend the Kirk of a Sunday still turned to the local witch to help them get through the working week.

For those who did visit the local witch, there was ample proof of her magical power. Most who helped with illnesses did so using herbs with a great deal of efficacy. White willow bark is a very effective pain killer. The active ingredient, salicylic acid, is found in modern aspirin. Foxglove, containing digitalis, could be used to calm a racing pulse. Camomile tea can soothe the nerves. In addition to the potions the witch might give you, she might also use some comforting words. A prayer, a supplication, a rhyme or a spell: whatever the name, it reinforced belief in the witch's power and in the potency of the potion. A similar phenomenon has been demonstrated in the modern placebo effect. Research has shown that some individuals can experience a measurable improvement in a medical condition when given an inert substance for treatment while being told it is an active drug. The authority of the doctor and the understanding that the treatment has been tested and authorised outweighs the lack of active drug in the substance. The improvement is caused by the person's expectations about the treatment.[7]

Similarly, if that witch had the reputation and power to help you and cure your illness, then she would equally have the reputation and power to harm you if she so wished. Stress is known to be a contributory factor in several medical conditions including strokes.[8] Those with an underlying condition such as high blood pressure, may, if faced with an extremely stressful situation, have a stroke. If the local witch is known to be powerful and an individual angered that witch such that she cursed them to their face, it is possible they could be 'seized with a palsie'. Trial records show multiple cases of 'witches' accused of causing palsies, loss of power in one side of the body or loss of speech.

This, then, was the world of Agnes Finnie. A world where life could be, and frequently was, precarious. A world where the authority of ministers and doctors was as alien as the world of the spirits was familiar. And a world that was increasingly under stress from the high politics of the court of the King in London.

3

Halting Hame

ON 27 MARCH 1625, James I of England and VI of Scotland died and his son Charles ascended to the throne. A very different man from his father, Charles' reign would cause political turmoil across Great Britain and strain the relationship between King and subjects. It would also heighten fears about witches and witchcraft across the country but most notably in his northern Kingdom.

His reign was barely two months old when Charles married Henrietta Maria, a French Catholic. It was a marriage that upset everyone. Charles had been raised in the Protestant faith, the Thirty Years War, fought over political and religious differences, was raging in Europe and the form of Protestant faith across Britain was still not settled. In the eyes of many, 'popery' remained a very real danger, thus for Charles to marry a Catholic princess was considered a threat to the country and an insult to the new faith. The Kirk in Scotland was outraged: as far as they were concerned the old enemy, popery, was now sitting on the royal throne. Even before his father's death, Charles' relationship with the Scottish Kirk had been extremely fraught. Raised in the hierarchy of the English royal court, Charles had no time for the presbyterian denomination north of the Borders. He had been brought up to become the defender of the faith: the Anglican faith. The predominance of the Calvinist faith in Scotland was problematic for both King and Scots. Charles could not understand why his northern Kingdom had not accepted Anglicanism and the fact that he was not head of the Scottish Kirk offended his sense of royal dignity. Moreover, Charles had been able to reconcile the Catholic faith of his wife with his own Anglicanism and he could not understand why the Kirk could not accept this. The Kirk was equally puzzled as to why Charles could not see the problem of his Anglicanism and the danger of having a Catholic wife. Unfortunately, Charles was advised by and sought support from William Laud, who would later become Archbishop of Canterbury. As an advisor to the King, Laud had little to no understanding of the Scots and even less inclination to learn. Neither Charles nor Laud understood the manner the Reformation had taken in Scotland. They failed to grasp the intricacies of Scottish life and how the battle between Catholic and Protestant had been fought on top of the existing and long-standing division between Highland and Lowland Scotland.

The unease felt in Scotland upon the King's marriage was further intensified when, shortly thereafter, he passed the Act of Revocation. This Act gave all church or royal property that had been alienated since 1540 back by the crown. This greatly alarmed the Scottish nobility, many of whom had received lands previously held by Catholic religious houses, and it was seen as a wholesale attack upon property rights. The Kirk supported the nobility in their protests: partly because members of the Kirk had themselves received land, partly because they were supported, in turn, by the nobility and partly because this early example of heavy-handed royal authority rang alarm

bells with those who knew of Charles' antipathy towards Presbyterianism. Charles, who had little knowledge of the culture
of Scotland, further antagonised both Kirk and nobility by
sending a Roman Catholic adviser, Lord Nithsdale, to enforce
the measure. The leaders of the Kirk and the Scottish nobility
closed ranks and Nithsdale had to spend several weeks coax-
ing, cajoling and horse-trading before a compromise of sorts
was agreed by both sides. Even Lennox and Hamilton, Charles'
two most loyal Scottish courtiers, only agreed to transfer the
lands their fathers had received from the church for a price. It
was an inauspicious beginning to Charles' reign. The Scottish
Kirk, mindful of its status as 'God's Elect', eyed their new monarch with barely-disguised suspicion. Was Auld Nick starting
to rise? And the Kirk had, in their own eyes, more reasons
to be wary.

In 1623, the harvest had failed across most of Lowland
Scotland. There was famine across the Lothians and the Borders, and food shortages in Edinburgh. The Divines of the
Kirk sitting in St Giles saw the harvest failure as a sign from
God that all was not well with the world. The Town Council
were more mindful of the Edinburgh mob and how easily they
could rise up when riled. For the most part, the poor of the city
would stay in their neighbourhoods and not bother the 'good'
citizens, such as merchants, but when food supplies ran low,
they could become unpredictable and violent.

The events of 1623 were compounded the following year
with an outbreak of plague in the Lothians and the Borders.
Plague could mean one of several diseases – cholera, typhoid
or even the bubonic plague – but in a time before antibiotics the name was largely irrelevant to most people. All were

equally lethal in the 17th century and, whatever the actual disease, panic gripped the city. Travellers and traders from the south were barred from the city and the city ports locked. The Town Council looked to the city baillies to keep order. The Kirk looked to their bibles for answers: many found them in the book of Revelations. Having faced famine, pestilence before the King's marriage and now a wedding to a Catholic, it was no wonder that the Kirk started to feel itself under threat from the Devil himself. And if Auld Nick was abroad then he would be calling his handmaidens, witches, to help him attack good Christians everywhere.

The King married his Catholic wife in 1625 and by 1626 witches were seen across Scotland. In March, Jonett Budge of Caithness was 'long suspected of witchcraft'.[9] Patrik Landrok, Helene Darumpill, Jonnet Pedie and Helene Dryburgh were arrested and imprisoned in the Dysert Tolbooth in April, having confessed to being witches.[10] Up in Scone, Bessie Wright was arrested in May suspected of curing sick folk by witchcraft.[11] In June, in West Wemys, Jonnet Demspart confessed 'the renunceing of hir baptisme, ressaveing of the devillis mark, and giving of hir soule and bodie over to the devillis service'.[12] By September, Auld Nick was back in Fife and Annas Munk and Elspet Nielson were tried for 'the crymes of witchcraft, sorcerie, and using of charmes and otheris divilishe practices'.[13] The year finished with a trial in Aberdeenshire when, on 14 December, Johnne Davie; Agnes Cairil; Issobell Leslie; Cummer Mutton; Johnne Propter; William Young; Agnes Forbes and her sister; Agnes Durie; Johnne Findlaw; Gowane Andersoun; Marioun Quhite; Elspet Herald; Margaret Turnour; Margaret Cleroch; Jonnet Robbie; Annabell Cattenhead; Helene, wife of Alexander Rid and Margaret, wife of Johnne McConnochie were all arrested for 'witchcraft, sorcerie and using enchantments.'[14]

And it was not just the ministers that were increasingly feeling uneasy. The residents of the Potterrow were seeing the results of the plague and famine. When the city ports were closed to prevent disease from entering, those whose business involved travel outside the city were faced with a real dilemma: continue to trade and perhaps catch the plague and die or stop trading and hope their savings would keep the family housed and fed until the plague had gone. For those that chose the first option there was also the risk of attack by the mob who blamed such traders for spreading the plague. In addition, there was the threat of arrest and fine by the city authorities which could also result in their licence to trade being suspended or removed altogether. And what then? How could they provide for their families? Some in the Potterrow chose to wait things out but for most, with few or no savings, this wasn't an option. But the Potterrow had Agnes Finnie. Slightly better off than most of her neighbours, and as a shopkeeper, Agnes had a little extra money to spare. Money she could lend out at a price. When the harvest failed and the cost of food increased, Agnes raised her prices accordingly. For those who could not pay credit would be offered, again at a price. Money-lending, continuing to trade and increased prices all assured that Agnes would survive, but it may not necessarily have endeared her to her neighbours in time of famine and plague.

There were also those who were not strictly, or legally, speaking in-dwellers of Edinburgh. Desperate to enter the city to avoid the plague and starvation that was just outside the

ports, they could not approach the authorities. The local baillies would have had them put out in an instant. They were also,
because of their status, unable to claim parish charity. Those
without friends or family willing to help had only one person
they could turn to: Agnes. Though her food, lent money or
rented rooms came at a price, at least it was something, anything, that might see them through.

By 1628, Agnes was thriving. She was possibly in her early
30s. She was widowed with one daughter, Margaret Robert-
sone. Whatever was happening in the city and wider country-
side, Agnes was taking full advantage. She was becoming well
known, if not well liked, in the neighbourhood as someone
you could go to if you were in trouble. By the end of the year,
the neighbourhood would soon also learn that if you crossed
Agnes, she would cause you trouble.

William Fairlie was the 19-year-old son of Fairlie of Braide,
a merchant and gentleman farmer from the Braids area south
of the city. William had heard of Agnes and her reputation
as a witch and nicknamed her 'Annie Winnie'. When William
passed Agnes' house, he called out 'Annie Winnie'. 'Winnie' was
a general term of abuse for older women who were 'past their
best': coming from winnowing where the good grain was sep-
arated from the chaff, a 'winnie' was a woman who was now
nothing more than chaff, no one of any substance or deserving
of respect. It was generally applied to skinny or, as was said of
Agnes, scrawny women as again, like the grain, they had little
substance about them. This was an insult Agnes couldn't let
pass. Regrettably for William, Agnes heard him and instantly
cursed him, threatening that she would make him go 'halting
hame' for his insult. Sure enough, the following day, William

felt unwell. As the day wore on, he became progressively more and more ill and by that night he had lost the power of the left side of his body. He became bedridden with 'so incurable a disease' that despite his young age his family were convinced he was dying. Nothing they did seemed to make any difference. With more money than most, the family called the doctor but nothing could be done. It was stated that the 'haill substance of his bodie ran out at his cute.'[15] It is unclear if William's family approached Agnes and asked her to stop his illness but if they did, she must have refused. William remained at death's door for another week until, finally, he died. At the later trial, the physicians would describe the cause of William's death as something 'supernatural'. The residents of the Potterrow may well have agreed.

Fairlie of Braide was not local and did not live in the Potterrow, although as a farmer he frequently brought his farm goods through the Port. He was a man of some standing and yet, despite the suspicious nature of his son's death, Fairlie did nothing. Everyone in the neighbourhood had heard the argument, so presumably Fairlie knew his son had called Agnes a witch and then been cursed. Although it is not known if he approached Agnes to ask her to lift the illness, neither did he report her behaviour to the minister, as was his Christian duty, or to the baillies. In fact, Fairlie would only accuse Agnes of having caused his son's death some years later when she was arrested after someone else complained. His behaviour remains unexplained.

To bewitch someone to death for name-calling may seem extreme to modern eyes, but to be publicly called a witch could be a death sentence for a woman in the 17th century. Many in the Potterrow would have known Agnes and her reputation, including the clerks and baillies that worked at the Port. There is, however, a difference between being known as a witch in a general sense and it being openly stated. The baillies who 'knew' that Agnes was a witch could conveniently ignore her and her activities as long as they were not too blatant, but they could not ignore the situation if people were calling her a witch in the street. Agnes would have known, like everyone else, the increasing condemnation of the Kirk against the Devil and witches and witchcraft. There were increasing numbers of women and men being brought to trial for witchcraft. As a woman alone and with a business, Agnes was potentially an easy target for those who sought to attack her for gain, spite or genuine religious zeal. She could not afford to have William Fairlie running round the neighbourhood calling her a witch. And what of his friends and family? If Agnes allowed William to defame her as a witch, then what was to stop one of his friends, when in drink, doing the same? Where would it end? The baillies could only turn a blind eye for so long. Agnes had to put a stop to William and his name-calling.

The argument between Agnes and Fairlie had unsettled the residents of the Potterrow. The increasingly uneasy times in which everyone was living may also have contributed to Agnes' response to Fairlie. After the numerous witchcraft trials of 1626, the following year had seen a further 17 'witches' brought to trial. 'Witches' were found in Aberdeen, Dalkeith, Dysart, Peebles, Turriff and Wemyss, where Margaret Hendersone was accused of witchcraft and sorcery by 'a number of hir unhappie associatis, who hes worthielie sufferit for the lyke wicked and unhappie doingis.'[16]

During 1628, there had been trials in every single month of the year with several very close to Edinburgh: Longniddry, Leith, Musselburgh, Newbattle and Cramond. There were several more trials further out in the Borders in Peebles, Berwickshire, Selkirkshire and Roxburghshire. In July in Dalkeith, Margaret Unes and Janet Schitlingtoun were arrested and 'confest the raising of the devil, the renouncing of their baptisme and the using of diverse devilish practises agaynste the loeges.'[17] The case against these women was not one of simply using charms for healing or laying sickness on a neighbour, but concerned the murder of Lord Borthwick and the wife and children of James Borthwick. Traders from Dalkeith were common in the Potterrow and stories of the 'foul wytches' and their wickedness were told and retold in the local inns. But for all the stories were exaggerated and the audience entertained by hearing of their bloody deeds and grisly end, both women were executed. It was a sobering truth that there were increasing number of witch trials in the Borders and Midlothian and along the coast. The residents of the Potterrow might be used to the likes of Agnes as a local witch who cured illness, or cursed young men, but even those who did not go to the Kirk on Sunday could not fail to sense the sea change in attitudes. The increasingly fervent sermons delivered from the pulpit by many Edinburgh ministers who had started to feel themselves encircled by the Devil and his witches did little to quell the fears of Edinburgh residents.

4

Bad Herrings

THE SUMMER OF 1630 was hot, with traders coming in from Midlothian and the Borders bringing the smell of fresh air and clean water into the city. Agnes bought fresh food and essentials such as salt and flour, selling them on at a reasonable profit to her neighbours. Life in the Potterrow, although never easy, was not overly onerous. As the summer wore on, however, the heat increased and finally the shout went up – plague. There was plague in the Borders and Midlothian. The baillies rushed to close the city ports to keep the disease out, but was it already too late? The cry of plague set off a panic in Edinburgh. The city was dependent on its hinterland for food, but traders from the south could bring disease. The city fathers knew this and the food stores were kept well stocked. But they could not last forever and when the cry of plague went up the panic that ensued put everyone at risk. Those who could afford it bought as much as they could. The poor scrabbled for what they could manage. But it was not just food that was an issue. For those with shops, like Agnes, where were they to get the goods to sell if the traders from the south were not allowed in the city? Shortages meant that prices rose. A small rise was, grudgingly, accepted, but those thought to be profiteering were attacked by the mob. Equally, those with a seemingly good supply were accused of theft or of selling plague goods. The flotsam and jetsam who normally hung around the port now found themselves unwelcome and starving. The prostitutes that were usually to be seen had fewer and fewer customers. Anyone with a Hawick or Kelso accent was likely to find themselves chased out the town if they were lucky, or stoned and then thrown in the Nor' Loch if they were not. All the time the heat continued. Tempers frayed and the baillies were hard pressed to keep the peace. Finally, in the autumn, the weather eased off and no more cases of plague were reported from the south.

But it was not just plague with which Agnes and her neighbours had to contend. In 1629, the King had dismissed his English parliament preferring to rule on his own. While this was probably of little consequence to the residents of the Potterrow, even if they had heard the news, it meant that there was now no brake on the King's actions: the Privy Council in London supported Charles in all he did, while the Privy Council in Edinburgh was too far distant to be of any use. The Scottish Privy Council was supposed to administer the country on behalf of the King while advising him about his northern Kingdom and how to conduct his business. Scots law was maintained by the Lords of Session which sat within the Council. The secretary of State for Scotland, Lord Stirling, communicated between the King and the Council. Early in his reign, Charles had removed the Lords of Session from the Privy Council and then proceeded to elect his own favourites whenever a vacancy arose. The King's councillors were the few Scots that were Anglican in practice, if not in real faith. Knowing of Charles' intense dislike of Presbyterianism, most councillors attended Anglican services in the Chapel Royal.

They were, thus, doubly set apart from the country and were increasingly seen as, and in effect were, distant from what was happening across the country. By the time Charles was ruling England without his parliament, the Privy Council in Edinburgh had been reduced to administering the country as Charles wanted but without the ability to provide feedback or advise the King how his policies affected Scotland. Although the Privy Council seldom, if ever, bothered about the lives of the poor in general, they did consider how the economic policies of the King would affect trade. Most notably, how it might affect them. With the English Parliament dismissed and the Lords of Session full of Charles' supporters, the Privy Council in Edinburgh had to enact the King's policies no matter how they affected the poor.

The King had several problems with the royal revenue, not all of which were entirely of his own making. Principally, the value of money had fallen since his father's reign while at the same time the crown costs had increased markedly.[18] On top of this, Charles' two main sources of income were both complicated and badly administered.

Import taxes which generated the majority of royal income, known as Tonnage and Poundage, were normally fixed by parliament at the beginning of each monarch's reign. The English parliament, which wanted to have a degree of control over Charles, refused to fix the rate for more than a year at a time. While Charles raged at the insult to his royal person of having to ask the parliament for money every year, it also left him short of funds.[19]

Taxation also posed a significant problem. Taxation revenues were raised via tax farmers who maintained tax records and calculated and collected the monies due. They then levied a percentage for their own profit. Charles borrowed from the tax farmers and speculated on the tax returns in advance of the actual payments. The repayments of the borrowing and the shortfall in some of the speculation created confusion and yet more financial loss.[20]

Given these problems, by the early 1630s King Charles' economic policies were starting to bite. Unable to gain the funds he wanted from parliament, Charles had tasked his advisors with finding every royal privilege and taxation right, no matter how old or obscure: produce from the foreshore, game from the Royal forests, moribund medieval rights; Charles reclaimed every one he could find. He squeezed every penny he could from the Corporations and Trade Guilds in England, which had a knock-on detrimental effect on Scottish traders.

He created two rival English patents for salt production. This increased the price of salt generating a reasonable royal income, however, the increased price was a disaster for ordinary people. Salt was essential for food preservation in an era before refrigeration. It was a staple in every home, was one of Scotland's principal exports as well as a mainstay of the home market, yet Charles' patents had skewed the European market towards English salt rather than Scottish. The King caused even more chaos when he interfered in the manufacture and trading of soap. When he restricted the use of whale oil in soap, the Scottish whaling fleet saw a good third of its trade disappear. This was followed by a doubling of the export duty on Scottish coal, which saw several mine owners recouping their losses by cutting wages in half.[21] These issues were compounded by an old debt of the King's due to the Earl of Stirling. The King had granted Stirling the right to mint copper tokens which compensated for the lack of small coins in the country. Stirling was supposed to use the profit from the coins to pay off the King's debt, but he did not. Instead, he used the tokens to increase inflation, keeping the King in debt to him while profiting from the mint.[22]

Within months, the burgesses of Edinburgh were beginning to groan under the combined weight of all of these different measures. Shopkeepers like Agnes, although slightly better off than many of her neighbours, were starting to see the takings in her shop decrease. For every extra penny she had to pay to traders, she raised her prices accordingly, but the poor of the Potterrow were finding it increasingly difficult to find those extra pennies and often went without all but the most basic essentials. While they still bought necessities like salt and soap from Agnes, their other purchases dwindled. Money was becoming a real issue, and for the middling folk and the working poor the only option was the local moneylender. Agnes, with her access to extra cash in the shop, was able to start lending. A few pennies here and there to start with, but the business grew and soon proved lucrative. But however useful a moneylender might be in times of need, it is not a profession that garners respect. It is also rarely a profession taken up by women. Money-lending was, moreover, both illegal, for individuals, and immoral. Unless you were a bank, lending money at interest, usury, was a criminal offence. In addition, as far as the Kirk was concerned, it was a heinous sin. To be a moneylender in the 17th century required a strong character. To be a moneylender required a reputation for toughness: a reputation that Agnes was slowly acquiring.

Hector Nisbet was down on his luck when he ended up renting a room from Agnes for two dollars* a quarter. An old man with no permanent work, Hector seems to have survived by doing occasional odd jobs for people for a few pennies, getting handouts from his married daughter and, when completely desperate, begging from the traders who passed through the port. The chaos in the town over religion may have passed Hector by, but the unrest made people more wary over money and less generous in their charity to beggars. By the late autumn, Hector was desperate for money. His rent was due on 11 November, Martinmas, and he couldn't pay. Hector had to find the money or risk eviction. Given Agnes' reputation and hot temper, it was more or less a forgone conclusion that she would throw Hector out into the streets. Spending a Scottish winter outdoors would be a death sentence for the old man.

Somewhat unwilling to approach Agnes, he asked his daughter, Beatrix, to speak to her. Beatrix, who also lived in the Potterrow, was married with several children and there was little space at home. Her husband may have been reluctant to take the old man in, even with the approach of winter. Older relatives with no work could quickly become a burden on a household. The combination of cramped living quarters and an additional mouth to feed was often too much for poor families to bear. Older women tended to fare a little better than men as they could help out with childcare and domestic chores. Some could even earn a little money by taking in some weaving or sewing work, but for men there was little charity.

---

* From c 1124 until 1709 the coinage of Scotland was unique, and minted locally. A wide variety of coins, such as the plack, bodle, bawbee, dollar and ryal were produced over that time.

Beatrix could not offer a home for her father, nor could she afford to spare the money to pay his rent, but she could try and ask Agnes for more time to pay. Agnes would probably have been reluctant to give Hector any leeway with regards to his rent. Elderly and out of regular work, it would have been difficult to persuade Agnes how he intended to make up the rent and any late payment or penalty she might impose. Beatrix, who did weaving work on a handloom at home and who had a working husband, was another matter. With his daughter standing as guarantor, Agnes might be persuaded to relent and give the old man a little longer to find his rent money.

Beatrix went to Agnes and explained that her father did not have the money to pay his rent and asked if he could have more time. Agnes replied that she did not care; the rent was due and she was not willing to wait for an old man who might never be able to repay her. As winter was approaching, Agnes knew that she could easily find someone else to rent the room, so had no need to be charitable towards Hector. Beatrix, desperately trying to buy her father more time to come up with the rent money, retorted that Agnes was heartless and uncaring towards the plight of an old man. Agnes was unmoved. Beatrix tried some more pleading, and matters deteriorated into a yelling match. Finally, screaming at Beatrix, Agnes cursed her and said she would 'dearly buy it'. Suddenly Beatrix was seized with a severe palsy, losing the power of the right side of her body and of her tongue. Whatever Beatrix thought of Agnes, she could no longer say it round the neighbourhood. Beatrix crawled home and Hector, distraught at the plight of his daughter, spent the next few days desperately scrabbling about for the money to pay his rent. The records are unclear as to what happened to Hector, but there is no note of him as Agnes' tenant after this and it is probable that he moved on to somewhere else. Beatrix never fully recovered and her limping presence round the Potterrow was a constant reminder to all not to cross Agnes.

The room that Hector had rented from Agnes would just have been a room in her own house which also contained her shop. Anyone with enough money to buy property, no matter how humble, would usually move out of the Potterrow. Agnes may have been 'middling folk', but she was always just a step or two above the likes of Beatrix. The room that Hector rented from Agnes may have been in her own home or, more likely, have consisted of a corner of her shop after it closed at night, where he was able to eat a little supper and sleep, possibly even alongside her shop assistant. Space was at a premium in the Potterrow and any small quarter could be rented out, particularly coming into the winter.

Alongside her money-lending, Agnes shop was also thriving. One day in 1632, Jonet Grinton came to Agnes' shop to buy a couple of herrings. Jonet and her husband lived in the Potterrow and had done all their lives. It is highly unlikely that Jonet was unaware of Agnes' reputation. Despite this, Jonet may have had little choice but to buy her fish from Agnes. For all the Potterrow was busy with traders, it had few actual shops. The neighbourhood saw plenty of goods coming into the city, but few of the carts coming from the farmlands of Midlothian and the Borders stopped locally. Even those tradespeople coming in through the port who traded in cheaper goods that the Potterrow could afford were more likely to trade an entire cartload of goods to Agnes than spend hours selling one or two items at a time to housewives like Jonet. Agnes' shop appears to have catered for all the neighbourhood's needs: foodstuffs, household goods and some basic clothing. There was no need for any other shop in the Potterrow. The fisherwives that travelled from Musselburgh and Newhaven to Edinburgh with heavy creels on their backs were only too glad to sell their entire load in one go and return home.

When Jonet asked Agnes to buy a couple of herrings, it was a perfectly mundane occurrence. Jonet handed over eight pennies and Agnes gave her the two fish. Without refrigeration, fish can easily spoil. When Jonet picked up the herrings, she said they were not fresh. She refused to take the fish and demanded her eight pennies back. Agnes could not accept that. Alongside the personal insult of rejecting her wares, a reputation for selling bad food could ruin her shop. An argument ensued, Jonet again demanding her money, Agnes again declaring the herrings were fresh. Finally, Agnes lost her temper completely, flew into a great rage and threw Jonet out of the shop, cursing her as she left, saying 'ga thy ways home, thou shalt never eat more meat'.[23] Jonet left the shop, without her eight pennies or the fish, and hurried home. That night she was seized with some sort of 'heavy sickness' and took to her bed. For several days Jonet lay ill, unable to eat or drink. The family could not afford a doctor and nursed her themselves. They had no one else to turn to for help. Despite their best efforts, Jonet remained seriously ill and finally, after a fortnight, died.[24]

Whatever had happened to Jonet, whatever the cause of her illness and death, the Potterrow continued to buy fish from Agnes. But the neighbourhood was uneasy; the argument with

William Fairlie may not have caused his death, but now there had been a second fatality. Although Agnes had cursed Jonet inside her shop it had probably been overheard. Jonet had also, no doubt, told her family about the incident when she returned home. Equally, her illness was widely known. In fact, if the illness had arisen from another cause, it is likely that Jonet would have gone to Agnes for help. But curing illness and laying illness were simply two sides of the same coin.

By this time, Agnes' reputation as a witch was well established. True, she had a temper and was not someone you would cross if you could avoid it, but that did not diminish her power. If anything, it enhanced her standing in the community. Despite Jonet Grinton's death, many continued to ask Agnes to use her magical powers to help those who were ill. What else could they do? It was not just the lack of money to pay for a doctor. The people of the Potterrow would, in the normal run of things, never think to approach a doctor. Agnes was local, female and therefore considered a natural carer, and a healer with special powers. No doctor lived in the Potterrow and there were very few doctors in the entire city. Edinburgh was better served than most Scottish cities: it boasted a few university educated physicians (available only to the rich) who treated illness; barbers who let blood, drew teeth and set broken bones, unliked and unwanted by the poor; surgeons who carried out major operations, available only to the rich; and apothecaries who sold medical preparations. Those 'doctors' who, very occasionally, visited were more likely barbers, student doctors in their final years of training at the university seeking experience, or possibly even those who had either been struck off or had never actually qualified. All of them were male, used traumatic methods like leeches and bloodletting, disregarded folk medicine as ridiculous superstition and generally made their patients feel uncomfortable and humiliated. In addition, few of their treatments were any more successful than the likes of Agnes' herbal cures. Agnes was the *de facto* doctor for the Potterrow Port, no matter how hot her temper or how evil her reputation.

During all of Jonet's illness and eventual death, and despite the public knowledge of her being cursed by Agnes, the local baillies took no action. The rough and tumble of daily life in the Potterrow was never a real concern of the baillies unless it tipped over into actual criminality. The neighbourhood was predominantly a very poor one and had all the associated ills. There was daily drunkenness and domestic violence. The area beside the port itself was home to prostitutes, thieves and pickpockets. The goods that arrived daily were a mixture of farm produce and artisan goods of high and lesser qualities alongside the stolen property, illegal weapons and downright counterfeit goods that various individuals tried to move without detection. Had Jonet been attacked and stabbed in the street, the baillies may have taken some action, but their main priority was always the smooth movement of trade goods up to the rich folk in the centre of Edinburgh and the detection and confiscation of illegal goods. The squabble of two women in a shop in the Potterrow was none of their business. The death of Jonet had not been reported as anything suspicious and her burial in Greyfriars Kirk had been routine. No baillie, doctor or minister had heard report of anything untoward. Therefore, there was no reason to take any action against Agnes, but suspicions may have started to spread.

The death of the likes of Jonet was a daily occurrence in the Potterrow. While the King embellished his palace in White-hall and his master architect Inigo Jones set out his grand plans for London as the foremost city of Europe, the tenements of Charles' northern capital had barely improved in a hundred years. The contrast between the grandeur of the royal court and the lives of Edinburgh's poor was stark. The King owned several 'wonderful beasts' in his various palaces: menageries were a common feature of royal life in the 17th century. One of these beasts was a camel which was housed in a magnificent stable to the west of Edinburgh. The camel ate the best of food and had a warden and two grooms who cared for it daily. The camel was taken out for walks every day except the Sabbath when, like all good Christians, it rested. Anyone could go and look upon the wonder free of charge.[25] It is not known if any-one from the Potterrow ever visited the camel. It is doubtful they could spare the time, but if they had they might have won-dered at the care that was given to the animal in contrast to their own living conditions. The King received regular reports on the condition of the animal: he received no reports on life in the Potterrow.

Meanwhile, the Kirk in Leith brought one Marion Mure to trial for witchcraft. Marion had allegedly 'confessed her-self a witch', and was arrested under warrant by the minister, William Wishart. When she was brought to the Tolbooth in Leith, she appeared to be 'addled in her wits', something that her parish minister did not appear to have known previously. The court ordered Marion to be examined by a doctor, Dr Gel-lie, who found her to have 'symptomes of hypochondriak dis-tractioun'.[26] The law in the 17th century recognised two main forms of mental illness: madness, a general term for all mental illness, and those addled in their wits, who had 'grown feeble due to age' or were considered 'simple' from birth. Under the law those classed as mad or addled in their wits could not be tried for their crimes as they could not be held responsible for their actions. Under the law and with the medical evidence given, Marion Mure should not have been tried. But whatever the law said, the Kirk had other ideas. As far as the Kirk was concerned, if the madness was genuine, it had been caused by contact with the Devil and was a just punishment for her rejection of the Christian faith. Most ministers, however, suspected that witches feigned their madness and this was further proof of their wickedness. In Marion's case, Mr Wishart overruled Dr Gellie. This was accepted by the examining magistrates and Marion stood trial, was found guilty and was executed.

5
The Buchannans

LIFE CONTINUED TO be precarious for those living in the Potter-row. One bad harvest, one outbreak of illness and even those middling sorts like Agnes could easily find themselves reduced to poverty, if not destitution. Moreover, the threat of diabolical Catholics lurking in corners had not gone away and the Kirk was becoming increasingly shrill in its condemnation of Auld Nick and his wicked handmaidens: witches.

As if proving that the Devil was indeed roaming abroad, the autumn of 1635 brought plague and harvest failure together. The city ports were, again, instantly closed to prevent the entry of the plague, but unfortunately this time the cry of plague had coincided with the harvest, when the city fathers brought in the food supplies to feed Edinburgh over the winter. That year the harvest was poor and food supplies from the Borders and Midlothian were sparse. The few supplies that entered the city before the ports were closed would not feed the city over the winter. The Edinburgh mob panicked and the city fathers imposed a curfew while sending riders out, as safely as possible, to buy food from wherever it could be found. The curfew, however, did not dispel the mob but rather increased the sense of panic. The usual rabble-rousers and trouble-makers continued to whip up panic; the more zealous in the Kirk announced the arrival of the apocalypse and the city baillies arrested anyone they could find. Although the city was short of food it was not completely bare and new supplies were quickly brought in from West Lothian and Fife. However, several unscrupulous shopkeepers had increased their prices and made themselves both a pretty profit and a nasty reputation. The mob continued to roam the streets, with several running battles with the baillies in Edinburgh's High Street; 'ruffians' from the Potterrow were among the many that were arrested. Food shops were looted of the few sup-plies they had, while opportunists among the mob also found time to steal clothing from other shops. Several thefts of 'guid leather boots' were reported to the baillies. Although many of those arrested may have been looting shops in the High Street, others were arrested for stealing to feed their families. As it was noted that the Town Council had not gone hungry, this increased ill-feeling among the city's poor. Amid the chaos, which lasted for several weeks, the rich either left the city for their estates or barricaded themselves indoors, the middling sorts saw their savings greatly depleted, the poor went hungry and the destitute starved to death.

In the Potterrow there was simmering resentment that, yet again, their livelihoods had been badly affected and the heavy-handed actions of the baillies had not helped matters. The sight of the dead bodies of those who had succumbed to starvation being removed from the tenements was a further point of anger. The absence of the minister, who had seldom been seen in the area, was also noted and it was said that sev-eral locals were openly 'murmuring' the said minister.[27] The city was only saved from open revolt by the severe winter that set in, finally forcing the mob indoors in search of warmth. The worst of the trouble-makers had either been arrested or gone to ground. The plague had been chased away by the cold, and the prices fell in most shops as the city's supplies were replenished. Despite the calm that had started to descend, this incident had offered a stark warning: the general unease across the country was growing and could be easily inflamed.

By the spring of 1637, the city had more or less settled down. The harvest of 1636 had been good and food supplies were back to almost normal levels. The plague in the Borders and Midlothian had been, for the most part, kept out of the city and trade was starting to recover. Life in the Potterrow went back to its normal rhythm. Yet the calm was not to out-live the summer; the King decided to impose the Anglican service on the Scottish church. His Kingdom would have his faith. Despite all the advice of his counsellors to leave well enough alone and despite the very vocal opposition by lead-ing members of the Kirk, Charles would not be dissuaded. His own father, James VI/I, had even cautioned him against such a move. Although James had been in favour of a uniform faith across his entire Kingdom, he had also realised the disruption it would cause in Scotland and felt the fight not worth the candle. Unfortunately, Charles was not the politician his father had been. He was determined to enforce Episcopacy on the stubborn Scottish Presbyterians. On Sunday 23 July 1637 in St Giles in the High Street, James Hannay, the Dean of Edin-burgh, began to read the Collects, part of the Anglican service. Jenny Geddes, a market-trader, allegedly threw her stool at the Dean and yelled, 'De'il gie you colic, the wame o' ye, fause thief; daur ye say Mass in my lug?' This was instantly followed by several more insults and missiles before developing into a riot in the church which soon spread onto the streets.

After Jenny Geddes threw her stool, a riot broke out in the Kirk with most of the congregation screaming abuse and throwing Bibles, stools, sticks and stones at James Hannay as he ran from the pulpit. Amid the chaos, the Provost, Sir John Hay of Lands, sent for the baillies who charged at the rioters and forced them out of the church and barred the doors. After a few moments, Hannay shakily resumed the service to a depleted congregation. The rioters hammered at the doors of St Giles, threw stones at the windows and incited others to join them. By the time the service was finished, the Edinburgh mob was in full swing. Some were, no doubt, genuinely angry about the attempted imposition of the Anglican service on them, others were merely enjoying a good day's ruck. Either way, Sir Hay and the other city magistrates along with James Hannay and the rest of the King's supporters barely made it through a hail of stones, rotten vegetables and other more pungent missiles, to the City Chambers where they found themselves besieged. While those in the mob for the fun of it periodically threw stones at the City Chambers' windows, the more sober among them negotiated with the besieged magistrates. The Lord Advocate, Thomas Hope, suggested the creation of a committee known as The Tables to discuss the matter with the Privy Council. Although some discussion did take place, King Charles rejected outright The Tables demands for the withdrawal of the Anglican Liturgy. On hearing this, more riots ensued, with the baillies of Edinburgh barely able to keep order in the city. The problem for Charles was that genuine ill-feeling against the imposition of the prayer book had been building for weeks and news of what had happened at St Giles had quickly spread across the country. As a result, rioting against the imposition of the Anglican Liturgy had spread to other cities and was becoming more organised. This was no longer a mindless mob riot; this was a coordinated protest.

Although Jenny Geddes may not have actually existed, as definitive evidence on her is lacking, many of the congregation sitting in St Giles that day had been waiting to see if Charles would actually dare go through with his 'Anglican insult' and were well prepared. The town had been talking about nothing else for weeks. In fact, the event was so eagerly anticipated and a confrontation so widely expected that at least two of Charles' councillors made sure that they were unable to attend the service. Archibald Campbell, 1st Marquess of Argyll, was suddenly taken ill and was forced to spend the day in his bed. John Stewart, Lord of Traquair, had some urgent business that unfortunately took him out of Edinburgh that Sunday. Regrettably, neither councillor had been able to find the time to send a servant to attend in their place.

As summer turned to autumn, Charles reiterated his command that the Anglican Episcopacy should be imposed on Scotland. In addition, he was furious at the rioters' challenge to his royal authority and demanded that the perpetrators should be hunted down and hanged, and that any minister preaching support for them should be dismissed from his post.[28] Edinburgh was full of angry individuals. Since Hannay's failed sermon, speeches were being made to the crowds outside the doors of St Giles and on every corner of the High Street. In October, the King commanded the Privy Council to deal with the situation. Unsure exactly what to do, the Council ordered the city baillies to clear the streets of anyone who 'had not lawfulle reasons to be abroad'. The order backfired spectacularly and led to more rioting across the city. Those who were in the High Street listening to the speeches against the 'great Anglican insult' were further angered by this infringement on their rights. Ordinary tradespeople were harassed and demands made that they prove their right to be about. Those who were up to no good took advantage of the confusion to strike a few deals and dip a few pockets. Tempers rose and, after one of the baillies was alleged to have struck someone, a full-scale riot ensued. The Council, realising that, yet again, the Edinburgh mob was in full swing and that they were its target, tried to slip away while the baillies were fighting to restore order. Most managed to escape safely, although Thomas Sydserff, the Bishop of Galloway and supporter imposition of the Anglican Service, found himself surrounded at one point by a group of furious protestors and was in danger of being physically attacked before Lord Traquair came to his rescue. Both men fought their way out of the crowd and only just managed to reach the safety of Lord Traquair's coach.[29]

While the rioting was going on in the High Street, the Potterrow was benefitting from the absence of the baillies. The affairs of the rest of the town that took the baillies away were welcomed in places like the Potterrow. Those trading in dubious goods could relax somewhat as the baillies at the port were called up to help their colleagues in the High Street. Those who needed to borrow money from Agnes or repay her could slip into her shop while no one was about to see them. In other words, the Potterrow could get on with its own business without the interference of the authorities.

It was around this time that Agnes had a series of altercations with the Buchannans. John Buchannan and his wife Bessie Currie had lived in the Potterrow all their lives. John was a journeyman weaver and Bessie was a home weaver. Agnes' trade in all sorts of goods, no questions asked, may have been thriving, but the continued disruption to ordinary trade from the situation in the town was placing an increasing strain on ordinary workers.

The Buchannans had become victims of this disruption and money was scarce. Finally, in desperation, the Buchannans turned to Agnes who agreed to lend them money with the usual warnings as to what would happen if she was not repaid on the due date. Despite the economic disruption, the Buchannans were known to be good workers and there was little risk to Agnes.

Agnes was due to be repaid at Whitsunday, 15 May, another of the Scottish quarter days. But this was also when the Buchannans' rent was due and Bessie's work and income were not secure. Nevertheless, just after the Whitsunday holiday, Bessie came to Agnes to pay her. The Buchannans had scraped together the money. Bessie handed over several coins, one of which was a sixpence. Agnes, however, was suspicious. She looked at the sixpence and declared it was counterfeit. Bessie was outraged. She and John had worked hard to earn the money to repay Agnes, but now her honesty had been called into question. The usual insults were thrown back and forth until Agnes grew into a great rage and threatened Bessie that she would 'gar the Devil take a bite of her'.

Around Lammas day that same year, Agnes fell out with Bessie Currie again, this time over a cake. Lammas, which fell on 1 August, was a holiday. Bessie Currie wanted to buy a twelvepenny cake to celebrate the holiday and, with nowhere else to go, went to Agnes' shop. Unfortunately, Bessie, didn't have the money. Perhaps hoping for some of the holiday feeling to have rubbed off on Agnes, Bessie asked for the cake and stated she would pay at the end of the week. Holiday or no holiday, Agnes refused, probably due to the earlier argument over the sixpence. Being refused credit by one shop could have serious consequences. What if other shopkeepers heard about it and, thinking you were a bad risk, decided not to offer credit either? For those living day-to-day, a reputation as a bad risk could make the difference between eating or not. In any case, Agnes was adamant she would not sell Bessie the cake. An argument ensued with insults thrown back and forth as before, with Agnes loudly screaming that Bessie was a bad housewife for not having enough money to pay and was a bad risk and so would not be given credit.

Being labelled a bad housewife was a common, but nonetheless weighty, insult. No matter how little your husband earned or if he drank his wages away, a woman who could not manage her household and could not pay her bills was a disgrace. Managing the house was her role in life. If her husband did drink all his wages, that was also frequently blamed upon the wife for having chosen such a poor specimen to marry in the first place. It was mostly wives that had to deal with angry landlords when the family could not pay the rent. It was mothers who were blamed if their children were in ragged clothes. Although the women of the Potterrow all worked as home weavers, cleaners, or laundresses, their primary role was still the management of the household.

The issue of being a bad risk was, in many ways, an even greater insult than that of a bad housewife. Much of 17th century society rested on trust. When you bought a pint of milk you were trusting that the shopkeeper was selling you good milk and that it had not been adulterated in any way. When you sold someone a pair of shoes, they trusted that the shoes were well-made and of decent leather. That much was the basic standard. But more than that, when you rented a house, the owner trusted that you would pay the rent when it was due. When you accepted work as a home weaver, you trusted that you would be paid for the cloth you produced. This trust extended to all aspects of life. When a man gave evidence in court, you trusted his word. When a woman said 'I do' at a wedding, you trusted she was free to marry. If you asked for credit, the shopkeeper had to trust that you would pay at a later date. But if that trust was broken, then all of the structures of society were undermined. Much of the tension in the town had been created, initially, by the breakdown of trust between the King and his subjects. If the word of the King could not be trusted, then anyone's word might not be true.

Bessie left Agnes' shop without her cake but carrying the weight of Agnes' insults. With questions raised around her abilities as a housewife and her trustworthiness, her very reputation was at stake.

It is not clear why Agnes refused to give Bessie credit. The earlier issue over the counterfeit sixpence seems to have petered out. Bessie lived locally and both she and her husband John Buchannan were in work. The amount that Bessie wanted credit on was not a large sum of money. The couple had lived in the Potterrow all their lives and had a generally good reputation.

Neither was known as a heavy drinker and they had only one, or possibly two, children dependent on them: the records are unclear. But with two wages coming in and a small family, they should have been a good risk. They were even one of the few families in the neighbourhood that was known to attend the Kirk reasonably regularly. Had Bessie merely caught Agnes on a bad day? Was the situation of the sixpence still unresolved? Was she perhaps unlucky and had been the third or fourth person to ask Agnes for credit that day? Or had the growing atmosphere of distrust that pervaded the town influenced Agnes?

When Bessie arrived home, she told her husband John about the argument and the insults Agnes had offered her. Immediately, John walked round to Agnes' shop and demanded to speak to her. Defending his wife's reputation, John threatened to throw Agnes down the tenement stairs and have her burnt as an old witch unless she instantly withdrew her insults and apologised to Bessie. Agnes, undaunted by John's threats, retaliated: she told John that she had no intention of doing any such thing and, furthermore, as he had begun with witches, so he should end with them, the implication being that his own mother had been a witch. In 1628 a general direction had been posted that 'witches, sorcerers, necromancers and seekers of answers' be tried.[30] The records for that period are incomplete, but it does appear as if two women from the Potterrow may have been questioned during that time. John Buchannan's mother may have been one of them. The rumour in the neighbourhood may well have been that his mother was a suspected witch, albeit not one that was ever arrested by the authorities.

The argument continued, with Agnes and John exchanging more and more insults. Finally, with nothing resolved, he left the shop and went home. That night John lay unable to sleep, ill with a fever, despite having been perfectly well during the day. As the night wore on the fever grew worse and Bessie later said he was 'lyke to melt away in sweiting'. The next morning, John remained ill but refused to be cowed by Agnes and went round to see her again. The situation over Bessie's reputation had still not been resolved and he was suspicious over the cause of his fever in the night. Going into the back room of the shop, Agnes and John sat together talking and drinking ale. Matters started to grow heated again until John told Agnes that if he was ill for another night 'all the toune should hear of it'. Agnes knew she had met her match and 'lifted' the illness from John. She also kept her tongue in her head where Bessie was concerned.

It is interesting that, when she was challenged by John, Agnes backed down. She was not afraid of the other women around the neighbourhood and the likes of William Fairlie had not troubled her, yet John Buchannan was somehow different. Was he a physically fit young man that would indeed have thrown her down the tenement stairs? Agnes was a middle-aged woman and no match for a man's strength. Had his mother indeed been a witch and that stayed Agnes' hand in some way? Had the continuing sermons from the Kirk about witches and their fate cooled her temper? Agnes could not have been unaware of the dangers of being labelled a witch. Or had John simply brought the ale and the two had patched up the quarrel over a drink? Whatever had happened, the quarrel seems to have been soon forgotten and indeed when the Buchannans needed help for their child they turned once more to Agnes.

Young John Buchannan was ill and the Buchannans couldn't afford a doctor. Agnes, whatever her temper, certainly had some sort of magical healing power. Indeed, they knew her as a witch. What else could they do?

John had been ill since birth. He had been born with some form of weakness or palsy in his legs. He was a small and generally sickly child. Over the previous months, he had become progressively more frail and the Buchannans decided to approach Agnes for help. When Agnes arrived at the Buchannans, John was in bed with yet another sickness and it appears that the palsy in his legs was also getting worse. After examining at the child for a few moments, Agnes told the parents to go into the next room and pray to God to help heal their son while she worked with young John. The parents left the room and Agnes approached the bed. Bessie and John left and went into the next room to pray. After praying for a short time, they waited, but, hearing nothing from the room next door, went back to their son. They found Agnes had gone. Approaching the bed, they found young John even more ill than previously. The child was unable to move and appeared to be in some pain. He was extremely pale and was sweating profusely. His parents lifted him in the bed in an attempt to make him more comfortable and he cried out in acute pain. Turning young John over, they found a large open wound on one of his buttocks. About the size of an adult's hand, it looked as if a collop of bacon had been sliced out of him. For the next eight days John lay unmoving and unresponsive in the bed. He had a fever and the wound did not heal. Given the unsanitary living conditions in the Potterrow, it is likely that the wound would have become infected, despite the best efforts of his mother. In a world before the discovery of antibiotics, a severe wound on an already weakened and ill child was almost bound to lead to death. Bessie nursed John continuously, but on the eighth night after Agnes' visit, he died.

John and Bessie were devastated. For once, the minister, Andrew Ramsay deigned to come down to the Potterrow. The Buchannans had been semi-regular members of his congregation and when he had heard of the death of their son, he made one of his rare visits to the Potterrow. Ramsay prayed over young John and helped the Buchannans arrange a funeral for the child. He was buried in a modest grave in the corner of Greyfriars Kirkyard. No mention was made to the minister about Agnes and the parents' role in asking for her help.

This macabre tale has two interesting elements. Agnes, although Christian, firmly believed in and practised magic. While she instructed John's parents to pray for their child, Agnes would be saying the magical rhymes and charms that would hopefully effect a cure. It was a simple blending of superstition and faith which made sense in the world of the Potterrow and neighbourhoods like it, but was entirely the work of the Devil as far as the Kirk was concerned. If the minister had instructed them to pray for their child's health then that was acceptable, but if a local woman did so it was not. In the Catholic faith, the priest interceded between parishioner and God, but the Reformation had done away with such 'nonsense' as Calvin had labelled it. Parishioners could commune directly with God. So, Agnes' prayer should not have been a problem. The complication with Agnes' instruction was that her prayers were tainted by her belief in magic. She may have said 'pray to God' and the Buchannans may well have done so, but as a 'witch' those prayers were probably meant for whichever supernatural being could help. Agnes may have meant the faeries who, with their affinity for children, may have helped the child, she may have meant the 'Virgin Mary' or a being that was an amalgam of the virgin and some other supernatural being or she may just have meant some generic being that could help. In the eyes of the Kirk, however, all prayers emanating from a witch could only be meant for the Devil. The Buchannans would have known those prayers to be at the very least irregular in the eyes of the Kirk, coming as they did under instruction from a witch. Although they were regulars at Greyfriars, the Buchannans also believed in magic and that is probably why they did not speak of Agnes' visit to Andrew Ramsay.

The cutting of the collop from the child's buttock was a gruesome event. Why had Agnes done so? Why had the Buchannans not reported this apparent assault on their child? The boy had been seriously injured, and by a known witch. Bloodletting, leeches, lancing boils and opening wounds were all common medical practices at the time among physicians, barber-surgeons and local healers. In the case of an infected wound where some of the tissue had become necrotic, a barber-surgeon would cut the dead tissue away, but also, in some cases, some of the surrounding healthy tissue would also be removed to try to ensure a clean wound. In the case of 'palsie', treatment was also to cut at the top of the offending muscle or tendon.[31] It was thought that spasticity in muscles could be relieved by cutting the tendon that attached the muscle to the bone. Tenotomy, the surgical procedure of cutting or dividing an affected tendon or muscle, is still occasionally used today as a treatment for those with muscular spasticity due to cerebral palsy. Given this background, Agnes' actions seem less horrific. It may be that, by cutting the child's buttock, she hoped to relieve the tightness in his leg muscles. The problem then became the reaction of the parents. From their later complaint, it appears that they had been unaware that Agnes was planning to cut their child. Agnes may not have told them, as she did not know what treatment she would use until she saw the child. She would also, as a matter of routine, keep many of her methods and treatments secret, partly because she did not want to alert the authorities to her activities, but mainly because magic was intrinsically a 'secret art' performed under cover. The efficacy of magic was greatly diminished if it was widely spoken of or exposed to non-practitioners.

After she had cut the collop from the child, Agnes took the piece of flesh away with her, presumably in order to 'remove' the palsie from the child. However, a collop is approximately the size of a modern rasher of bacon and to discover such a wound on their son must have been horrific for the Buchannans. Despite the mutilation of his son, however, John did not feel the need to challenge Agnes. The child lay ill for eight days before dying. John had ample opportunity to see Agnes and indeed 'throw her down the tenement stairs', but did not do so. Bessie was constantly at their son's bedside for those eight days, but John would still have had to go out to work. Why did he not speak to Agnes? Did he believe her treatment might work? Or was he so scared of Agnes and what she was capable of that for all his previous bluster he was, in reality, too frightened to actually challenge her?

It is also curious that at no point in the eight days during which their child lay ill in bed from the effects of Agnes' treatment did the Buchannans think to approach a doctor of any kind, although this may well have been for the practical reason of a shortage of money. They had, presumably, already paid Agnes, so to have to find the money to pay a doctor was probably beyond their means. After the death of young John, they also had to find the money to pay for a funeral.

A full church burial, even for a child, was not cheap. A basic coffin could be made relatively inexpensively, but the family also required a mortcloth (from the Latin *mors* meaning death). A ceremonial cloth that was draped over the coffin (or just the corpse if the family were too poor to afford a coffin), a mort cloth was an absolute necessity at any funeral. Barely any ordinary families had their own mortcloths and they were normally hired from the Kirk. The monies raised from hiring out the mortcloths went into the parish poor fund and as a result their hire could be expensive. It is unlikely that the Buchannans would have had enough savings to cover such an expense at the time. They were unfortunate in that they were not poor enough to be able to claim a pauper's funeral for their son, but neither were they rich enough to be able to pay for his entire funeral, no matter how basic, themselves. They may have used what savings they had and then borrowed the rest from sympathetic friends and family. It is unlikely they would have gone to Agnes to borrow any money at the time. But there was certainly no extra money in the household to pay for doctors.

The Buchannans may also have been worried in case the doctor asked how the child had received such a wound, potentially leading to the revelation that they had consulted a witch, which was a criminal offence. The law was very clear, and the minister even clearer: witches were to be put to death but so were those who consulted them. The Witchcraft Act of 1563 stated that:

> forsamekeill as the Quenis Maiestie and thre Esta-
> tis in this present Parliament being informit that
> the havy, abominabill superstitioun usit be divers
> of the liegis of this Realme be using of Witchcraf-
> tis, Sorsarie, and Necromancie, and credence gevin
> thairto in tymes bygane aganis the Law of God:
> and for avoyding and away putting of all sic vane
> superstitioun in tymes tocum; It is statute and
> ordanit be the Quenis Maiestie and thre Estatis
> forsaidis that na maner of persoun nor persounis
> of quhatsumever estate, degre, or conditioun thay
> be of tak upone hand in ony tymes heirefter **to
> use ony maner of Wichcraftis, Sorsarie, or Necro-
> mancie:** nor gif thame selfis furth to have ony sic
> craft or knawlege thairof, thairthrow abusand the
> pepill; Nor that na persoun seik ony help, response,
> or consultatioun at ony sic usaris (or abusaris) for-
> isaidis of Wichcraftis, Sorsarie, and Necromancie,
> under the pane of: dead asweill to be execute agan-
> is the user-abusar, as the seiker of the response or
> consultatioun.And this to be put to execution be
> the Justice Schireffis, Stewartis, Baillies, Lordis of
> Regaliteis and Rialteis, thair Deputis, and uthers
> Ordinar Jugeis competent within this Realme with
> all rigour, having powar to execute the samin.[32]

The Potterrow might understand and forgive those who con-sulted Agnes; the law would not. The Buchannans' neighbours might well accept their behaviour; a doctor from outwith the area might well not.

While Agnes was increasingly terrorising the Potterrow, the only authority that might have been able to stop her, the Kirk, was more or less missing in action. The ministers of Greyfriars were nowhere to be seen in the Potterrow. Following the lead of James Hannay in St Giles, on the 23 July James Fairlie of Greyfriars read the new service book in Greyfriars Kirk. Just like in St Giles, the congregation were ready for the 'gross insult', rose up and started shouting at the minister. Fairlie, however, was made of stronger stuff than Hannay and did not run away, but stayed in his pulpit and continued to preach while exchanging curses and insults with several of the women in the congregation.[33] The following week, Fairlie was berated by several leading Kirk elders for having used the new 'popish' service book and for abusing his congregation. The bishop of Edinburgh supported Fairlie and the imposition of the service book, but, in order to stem the growing tide of discontent in the city and any confrontation with the leading Kirk elders, offered Fairlie the Bishopric of Argyll. Fairlie accepted and left the parish of Greyfriars within the week. His co-adjudicator, Andrew Ramsay, was then asked to do the reading of the Anglican service book. Ramsay refused and was called before the bishop who demanded he do the reading. Ramsay again refused and, despite being supported by the elders, was put to 'silence' (refused permission to preach) by the bishop.[34] To all intents and purposes, Greyfriars had no minister. The parishioners in Greyfriars parish could attend another Kirk, or not, as their conscience dictated, but for the ordinary residents of the Potterrow with no one present in the Kirk there was no one they could turn to for help. No one who could combat Agnes' growing power and temper.

6

Broken Legs

DESPITE THE BEST efforts of the King and his authorities, the initial riots in Edinburgh in 1637 had spread nationwide. Charles continued to state that he would not withdraw the Anglican service. The affront to his royal majesty would not stand. Tensions rose. The Kirk was appalled and several ministers started preaching on the 'evils of Catholicism' and the 'foolishness of the King'. Charles reiterated his command that Anglican Episcopacy should be imposed on Scotland and, as he felt himself personally insulted, demanded that the perpetrators of the riot should be hunted down and hanged. In addition, any minister that preached support for the rioters should be immediately dismissed from his post. This merely served to further anger the Scots. On 20 February, the King's loyal Scottish Lords met in Stirling and issued Charles' proclamation which stated that the King believed the actions of his council in Scotland to be 'more derogatory to our authority than conducive to the true quiet of the country'. Their only hope of obtaining the royal mercy was in 'complete submission'.[35] Two days later, the proclamation was read out at the Mercat Cross in Edinburgh to a barrage of insults. The leading opponents of Episcopacy made a series of speeches which were all but drowned out by the Edinburgh mob, who were in danger of attacking the King's herald. After the mob had their fun, those opposing Episcopacy met and, on 28 February 1638, they drafted the National Covenant of Scotland which was initially signed in Greyfriars Churchyard in Edinburgh. Copies were made and circulated round the country where they were signed by thousands of ministers, Kirk elders and ordinary Scots, including some from the Potterrow. The fact that the Covenant was initially signed in Greyfriars rather than St Giles was a huge cause for celebration and pride for Andrew Ramsay. His church, his parish, was at the forefront of Scottish religious life. What they thought of this in the cold, dark tenements of the Potterrow is not recorded.

The initial signing of the Covenant was celebrated as the 'great marriage day of the nation with God' and Edinburgh erupted into a day of festivities. The city merchants held great feasts in their town houses. The more sober Covenanters spent the evening in exultant prayer. Ordinary members of the Kirk toasted each other, while the people in the Potterrow, Kirk members or not, took the opportunity to get as drunk as possible.

The Covenant repeated the King's Confession: the anti-Catholic statement of James VI, signed in 1581. It then listed the parliamentary statutes that defined the polity and liturgy of the Kirk in Scotland. It finished with a bond committing the signatories to stand together to maintain the nation's religion and oppose any changes to it. The subscribers engaged by oath to maintain the Presbyterian religion while also professing loyalty to the King, although it was widely understood that this loyalty did not extend to showing obedience to an 'ill-advised' King.[36] As the Covenant swore loyalty to the King, most ordinary people thought that the document would be enough to persuade Charles to leave the Presbyterian faith alone. However, Charles saw the signing of the Covenant as yet another insult to his dignity and authority, and political opportunists and religious radicals on both sides used the Covenant to stoke up more ill-feeling. The Marquess of Argyll and six members of Charles' Scottish Privy Council backed the Covenant; copies were made and were circulated round the country. Ministers preached the signing of the Covenant as a literal and symbolic act of faith. Andrew Ramsay, minister at Greyfriars saw his congregation markedly increase over the spring and summer as genuine believers celebrated the victory of their faith over the attempted 'pollution' of Episcopacy. Others went along partly from fear, partly from curiosity, and were swept up in the general enthusiasm of the re-invigorated Kirk services. Some of the flotsam and jetsam of the Potterrow might also have attended the Kirk, although this may have been due to the possibility of some Christian charity from the better-off merchants who attended Greyfriars rather than any sense of piety. The drafting and signing of the National Covenant had unleashed a wave of religious excitement across the city. A group of religious zealots marched down the High Street singing psalms and chanting. By the time they had reached the Holyrood Chapel, they had been joined by a mixed crowd of the religious and the unruly. The latter soon whipped everyone up and the Chapel was broken into and several windows smashed.[37] Several of the city's baillies were called to restore order, including John Elies from the Potterrow, with several Potterrow residents arrested for affray. Fortunately for them, so many had been involved in the rioting across the city that the Tolbooth was full and most had to be released.

While the rougher elements in the Potterrow were having fun, life in the neighbourhood was becoming increasingly fraught. By the late 1630s, Agnes' temper seems to have been out of control on an almost daily basis. Arguments with her neighbours and customers were becoming more frequent and more violent. In addition, the national, political and religious tensions were seeping into life across the country and the Potterrow was no exception. The outside pressures may well have contributed to increasing anxieties in the Potterrow, giving rise to more frequent arguments.

On Lammas Day, 1 August, Euphame Kincaide, who owed Agnes some money, couldn't pay. The problem was that Euphame was a drinker. Alcohol was readily available in the Potterrow, as it was in the rest of Edinburgh. Alcohol was one of the few items that Agnes did not sell, yet while not available in many local shops, there were at least three taverns at the Port itself that did a brisk trade in ale and cheap whisky. In addition, there were the unofficial howffs, drinking dens, where the cheapest of alcohol could be bought, no questions asked. A quart of ale could be bought and taken home to drink for less than the equivalent quantity of milk. There were also several housewives that still brewed their own ale. Brewing, as a domestic task, had been dominated by women until the 14th century when men took over, producing for the growing markets in taverns. Yet some women, especially in poor areas, continued to brew for their families, selling any extra ale to neighbours for a few pennies to supplement the family income. The water supply in the Potterrow was of dubious quality and the ale was probably safer to drink. Everyone, including children, drank on a daily basis. However, with so much cheap ale and whisky available in the neighbourhood, it was no difficult task for someone to tip from the era's normal daily drinking into becoming a drunk. For the desperate, old sourmash could be also be bought from some of the traders that supplied it as pig feed.

Euphame was a widow with at least one child, but without a husband to support her she was struggling to pay her bills. She may have been known round the neighbourhood for being a drunk. As a woman, the Kirk Session would have censured Euphame for her behaviour, especially as she had a child to care for. There is no note in the Kirk records of her being offered any help from the poor fund. She may not have asked or she may have been refused on the grounds that was a drunk; the poor fund was reserved for the 'deserving' poor.

She probably worked as a weaver on a handloom at home but, due to her drinking, she may have been making mistakes or been late in handing in her work. As a result, she would have been offered less work and work of more basic quality, producing 'rough weave', basic cloth for general use, rather than good wool for clothing. The production of rough weave was paid at a lower rate than 'fine finish' and, combined with her declining customer numbers, Euphame was earning less and less money. This would obviously be stressful and, for someone with an existing drink problem, would most likely lead to increased alcohol consumption. While none of this can be known with absolute certainty, it was a familiar tale across the working poor of the time.

This downward spiral increased Euphame's money worries and had led her that spring at Whitsunday, 15 May, to borrow some money from Agnes hoping, possibly, to earn enough over the summer to pay her back at Lammas. The money was probably for her quarterly rent payment. Unfortunately for Euphame, when Lammas came around she didn't have the money to repay Agnes. Yet again, there was another argument. Euphame asked for more time to pay, Agnes refused and demanded her money. The argument grew heated and Agnes called Euphame an old drunkard. Euphame then lost her temper and called Agnes an old witch. Agnes replied instantly, 'If I am one, you or yours shall have better cause to call me so.'[38] Euphame, no doubt instantly regretting what she had said, fled home. The debt was still unpaid. Two days later, Janet Fairlie, Euphame's youngest daughter, was playing with her friends near Agnes' house. As they were playing, a large wooden joist sitting between two beams on a nearby building suddenly swung loose and fell, landing on Janet's leg. One of the other girls ran to tell Janet's mother about the accident. Euphame started to run down to where her daughter was lying. As she passed Agnes, Euphame saw her standing leaning against the jamb of the shop door, watching and 'laughing heartily'. Janet's leg had been crushed by the joist and several bones were broken. The girl's leg was so badly injured as to be rendered almost useless for the rest of her life.

Despite this recent example of Agnes' power and the obvious consequences of non-payment, not everyone seems to have learned the lesson of Euphame's daughter and her broken leg. Around the following June, Agnes had yet one more of her great arguments, this time with Isobell Atchesone who was also struggling to repay her debt. When Isobell visited Agnes in her shop to explain that she couldn't pay, Agnes, described as being in a 'great rage', screamed at her, 'the de'il ryde about the toun with you and all yours.' Isobell did not reply and hurried home to get away from Agnes and her temper. The next day Isobell was returning from a visit to Dalkeith. She may have been visiting her daughter, possibly to borrow the money to be able to pay Agnes. Travelling from the south, she had covered the ten kilometres from Dalkeith up to Edinburgh perfectly safely when, on entering the Potterrow Port, the horse she was riding stumbled. Isobell fell heavily and broke her leg. Agnes had been out of her shop at the Port when Isobell had fallen and yelled at her, 'Sie that ye say not that I have bewitched you, as other neighbours say.' There is no note of Isobell ever repaying Agnes, but equally there is no record of any more arguments between the two women. Had Agnes considered the debt repaid by the broken leg? The 'accident' did not benefit Agnes financially, but it certainly enhanced her reputation and reminded those who owed her money of the consequences should they fail to pay.

What is interesting to note is Agnes' request to Isobell not to say she had been bewitched. In none of her previous encounters with her adversaries had she asked for their silence. Many of her arguments, where she had threatened to call on the Devil to attack people, had been public. Was it the word 'witch' that was worrying her? Calling on the Devil to 'get' a neighbour in the midst of an argument might just be acceptable, but the accusation 'witch' was becoming more dangerous. There were increasing numbers of witchcraft trials taking place across the country. Had Agnes noted what was going on and wanted to keep a low profile? And there were certainly rising levels of political and religious tension, especially in the capital.

Agnes had not asked Euphame to keep quiet about her daughter having been bewitched. Why the change from the previous year? The Solemn League and Covenant had focussed minds on the one and only correct form of worship allowed in Scotland, and Agnes' beliefs and use of magic were increasingly under threat. Was Agnes worried that Isobell's accusation would reach the ministers ears?

Luckily for Agnes, Isobell held her tongue, possibly because she was more concerned about her broken leg and its consequences for her ability to work in the future. It was a bad break and, despite the best efforts of the barber, the bone did not set straight leaving Isobell permanently lame. Crippled workers were often offered less work even if they were capable, the thinking being that if they were lame they would be less capable of physically demanding tasks such as weaving. She had needed to pay the barber to set her leg, as she could not, obviously, go to Agnes for any treatment. It is not known where she got the money to pay the barber and, as she was short of money, it is unlikely she could afford a good bone-setter which may have contributed to her leg being left permanently damaged. Moreover, Isobell still had the outstanding debt owed to Agnes and may have remained silent because that was still to be repaid. She was probably also frightened by what more Agnes might do to her if she were to speak out.

Given Agnes' reputation, it is likely that a fair few of the residents in the Potterrow knew or guessed that she had been the cause of Isobell's accident. Isobell may well have kept quiet, but the neighbourhood gossips could not be entirely silenced. Whatever Agnes' hopes over the incident, she could not ensure everyone would mind their own business. Even if they had, it was unlikely she would be able to hold her temper in check for long.

One curious note is that in all of these incidents no one from the Potterrow sought any help from the minister at Greyfriars. The situation at Greyfriars was complicated: a relatively new church, it had two charges (ie two ministers), but the main issue was that the parish straddled both rich and poor Edinburgh, being attended by the merchants from near the top of the High Street and the destitute in the stairwells of the Potterrow. It was obvious who was saved and who was damned, so why bother with those already damned by God? Greyfriars was also closely linked, both geographically and spiritually, to St Giles, the pre-eminent Kirk in the land. Any minister worth his salt kept one eye on the prize of becoming a minister at St Giles.

* * *

On 4 May 1638, Edinburgh Town Council appointed Alexander Henderson, the compiler of the Covenant and leader of the church, to the second charge at Greyfriars in succession to James Fairlie.[39] The congregation of Greyfriars was served by two ministers until 1840, known as the first and second charge. While this was good news for the Covenanters' cause, it did little to help the Potterrow. Greyfriars now had two fervent Covenanters as its ministers, neither of whom were particularly interested in their parishioners. Andrew Ramsay in its first charge saw his poor parishioners as a mere nuisance that were, at best, to be tolerated. Henderson, whose appointment was contested by the crown and indeed many in the Kirk, was a career minister who, his opponents said, had not even been a true Christian when he had first become a minister in 1612. Once he had written his three sections of the National Covenant in 1638, he became Moderator of the Glasgow Assembly of the same year. With the success of the Covenant, he was then offered the ministry at St Giles which he accepted instantly, abandoning Greyfriars where he had been a minister for less than a week. When he died in 1640, he was buried in its graveyard – as was his right as an ex-minister of Greyfriars – despite never having delivered a single sermon. This left the second charge at Greyfriars empty; it would remain vacant until 1644, with all the parish work falling onto Ramsay's shoulders in the interim, just as his mind was consumed by the great struggle for the soul of the nation. Given these circumstances, it is, perhaps, understandable that no one from the Potterrow sought any help from the minister at Greyfriars.

For those who did attend the Kirk more regularly than their neighbours, there may still have been a reluctance to approach the minister. Was a request to the minister to visit the Potterrow likely to be turned down? Or was Agnes considered more powerful than the minster in such matters? Even if the minister did come to the Potterrow and chastised Agnes in some way, what would happen when he left? Sitting safe and snug in his manse beside the Kirk, Andrew Ramsay wouldn't be around if Agnes wanted to wreak revenge on someone who had complained about her. The more powerful Agnes appeared, the less likely the residents were to seek help from the authorities in curbing her temper. In turn, the lack of any authority that could rival and chastise Agnes increased her power in the neighbourhood. The only way to stop Agnes was to ask for help from another witch but that was a dangerous path to tread, for who was to say the two witches would not join together – they were sister witches after all – and terrorise the Potterrow even more.

During the spring and early summer of 1638, tension between the King's supporters and the Covenanters continued to rise. In June, Charles decided to send a Commission up to Scotland to sort matters out. He appointed James, Marquis of Hamilton, to travel north and demand the withdrawal of the Covenant. If this was done the King would, temporarily, suspend the use of the Anglican prayer book. Hamilton was also given the power to dismiss disloyal members of the Scottish Council and arrest anyone who protested. Charles wrote an official letter to Hamilton that stated, 'if there be not sufficient strength within the Kingdom to force the refractory to obedience, power shall come from England.'[40] When Charles had written to Hamilton, it is not known if he intended the contents of the letter to be become widely known.[41] Hamilton, however, confident in his own abilities and the rightness of the King's cause, had not kept the letter to himself. For the Covenanters, the phrase 'power shall come from England' was enough to send them to every gunsmith and armourer they could find.

Consequently, by the mid-summer, the Potterrow Port saw a steady increase in illicit arms being smuggled into the city. As the south port of the city, the Potterrow allowed access to goods coming up through the Borders and Midlothian, including material that could not be legally or safely unloaded at the Leith docks. These goods could arrive at Berwick-upon-Tweed and then make their way to the capital. English naval ships were patrolling the east coast of Scotland and rumours abounded that the King was planning to seize control of the port of Leith. Although the rumour came to nothing, those who had seen the opportunity to make money by selling weapons used Berwick-upon-Tweed as their trading base. The arms, which were bought in the Low Countries, were shipped to the north English port, avoiding Charles' navy. Although an English town, the majority in Berwick-upon-Tweed were sympathetic to the Covenanter cause. The arms then travelled up through the Borders and Midlothian in barrels of fish that were deliberately left unsalted.[42] The late summer was particularly hot that year. Most of the baillies and clerks on duty at the Port knew what was going on and were either Covenanters or were reluctant to search for contraband through barrels of rotten fish. This allowed those of a mercenary turn of mind to facilitate the trade by renting out fish barrels on the carts of ordinary goods that they were bringing in, or to bring in their own illegal items also hidden under rotten fish. Although the entire length of the Potterrow stank of fish that summer, trade in Agnes' shop was brisk as most goods were being bought and sold without having paid duty at the Port. By the end of the summer, almost every Covenanter in Edinburgh was armed in some fashion.

One of the problems Hamilton faced was that many of the King's councillors were either openly professed Covenanters or were sympathetic to the cause. While this mindset caused tension to rise among political and religious leaders, it also affected the ordinary people of Edinburgh. The talk of the town was the Council's defiance of the King and Charles' response. Although Scotland was not a modern democracy, neither was it a medieval autocracy. The policing of everyday life in communities such as the Potterrow was carried out by consent. Everyone knew their place and, in general, knew the law. There was good, there was bad; there was right and there was wrong. If you stole, then the baillies would chase you. If you got caught, you would get sent to the Tolbooth. These laws were made by the King via the Privy Council, were enforced by the Town Council via the baillies and the moral imperative to accept, and hopefully obey, those laws was enforced by the Kirk. But what happened when the Kirk no longer respected the King, the Privy Council was divided and the King threatened the land with force? What was the law? And why should those in the Potterrow obey it?

In August, while Agnes and the rest of the Potterrow were trading as fast as they could before the storm – which everyone knew was coming – broke, 'ane great sensation' took place at Greyfriars Kirk. Thomas Abernethy had been a Jesuit priest until that summer, when he had suddenly seen the error of his 'popish wayes' and had converted to Calvinism. Standing before the minister and full congregation in Greyfriars, Abernethy publicly declared his rejection of the Roman Catholic faith and desire to enter the Calvinist fold. Under the patronage of Andrew Ramsay, Abernethy was encouraged to preach from the pulpit in Greyfriars where he gave dire warnings about the dozens of Catholic priests that were secretly working across Edinburgh spreading their 'filthy popish wayes' and presiding over the abominated mass. Abernethy had named the priests to the Kirk assembly to avoid prosecution just before his conversion. Each week his sermons and warnings grew more fantastical: there were hundreds of masses said every week in London, there were thousands of priests working in England, Pope

Urban VIII had seen and approved the Anglican service book that the King was attempting to force on the Scots.[43] Although the assertion about the pope was completely untrue, it did create 'ane great sensation'. The gullible believed it instantly and completely, while the more discerning members of the congregation did little to calm their fears, instead using their panic to further demonstrate the perfidious nature of the King and the rightness of the Covenanter cause. The story ran the length of the town and for several days after Abernethy spoke the baillies had a hard time keeping the peace. Any stranger trying to enter at the Potterrow Port was instantly assumed to be a rampant Catholic priest intent on some 'devilish popery mischief'. Yet again, Greyfriars Parish was at the heart of the religious turmoil of the day.

There was more than one 'great sensation' to be seen that summer. After the excitement of Abernethy's statements had died down, a young woman appeared wandering up and down the High Street outside St Giles. The daughter of an obscure Edinburgh minister, Margaret Mitchelson claimed to have seen 'Covenanting Jesus'. She wandered the High Street periodically falling into trances and then making great declarations: that the Covenanting cause was the only true cause, that the National Covenant had been made in Heaven and that she could see the heavenly hordes riding forth. At first, she was just one of many who were caught up in the religious excitement of the Covenant, but as her trances became more frequent and her declarations more visionary, she drew crowds who pressed forward to hear her prophecies on a daily basis. The crowds were again a mixture of the pious and those looking for some amusement. As Mitchelson continued, the crowds grew in size and, on occasion, became rowdy. Children from the Potterrow and the tenements down the back wynds of the High Street arrived, cheering and yelling as the mood took them. Those of a more pious nature started to bring her small gifts until the situation grew out of hand. The baillies could not keep order in the High Street and watch what people were up to in the Potterrow at the same time. Appealing to the Town Council for help, Archibald Johnston, Lord Warriston, a leading and fervent Covenanter, took the situation in hand and volunteered to move Mitchelson into his Edinburgh townhouse. The baillies and Council were glad to be rid of a problem: Warriston was glad to have gained some more authority.

Several leading members of the Covenanters visited Warriston to hear Mitchelson's prophecies and declared them sent by Christ himself.[44] The same Covenanters who railed against witches and condemned their ability to talk to spirits as emanating from Auld Nick were nevertheless quite happy to listen to Margaret Mitchelson's prophecies and repeat them in their Sunday sermons and speeches. This was especially true when she declared that the King was attempting to undermine the Covenanters by trying to force them to sign the old Confession of 1580. His actions were, according to Margaret, as damned as the document itself. Just like Abernethy before her, Mitchelson's pronouncements were exactly what the Covenanters wanted to hear. Both John Leslie and Archibald Campbell visited Warriston on several occasions specifically to hear Mitchelson speak. Several Kirk ministers, including Ramsay at Greyfriars, used Mitchelson as an example of a pious woman, holding her up as an example against whom all other women were to be measured. Sermons were built round her as a warning to others to seek out women like Mitchelson, but to beware of those devilish temptresses, witches.

While Margaret was being feted by the leading Covenanters in Edinburgh, in Fife they were arresting witches. In Kirkcaldy an 'intimation to be maid in all pulpetts anent Marion Grig who is detained in Dysart for witchcraft', was declared by the reverend George Gillespie. When Marion was 'challengit upon sundrie poynts of witchcraft: denyed it all.'[45] This was followed three months later by an announcement that 'Cristian Wilson and her dochters compeiring for some poynts of witchcraft alledgit aganest hir, they are ordeaned to be wardit.' Cristian and her daughters were also under investigation by Gillespie.[46] Two months after that, the presbytery stated that 'Mr Georg Gillespie, minister at Wemys, declaired to the brethren sundrie presumptiouns of witchcraft aganest Janet Durie in Wemys.'[47]

The witchcraft trials that took place in Scotland tended to happen during specific 'witch panics' such as those of 1628–31, 1649–59 and 1661–2. They also tended to occur in specific areas with specific ministers. It may be that some ministers thought themselves so godly and so pious that they would never be attacked by the Devil and so never encountered an actual witch in their parish. For others, like George Gillespie, they may have thought that their very godliness made them a target for Auld Nick and so actively sought out and prosecuted witches. Whatever Gillespie's reasoning, his zeal in prosecuting witches in Fife would have ramifications for Agnes.

While the Kirk ministers were catching witches, the radicals among the Covenanters had raised an army and were preparing to defend the Calvinist faith. The Covenanters had 'beat the drum' through the streets of Edinburgh to levy troops in the name of National Covenant. There was a moment's hesitation as the Scots realised that they were literally preparing to fight their King for their faith. The zealots urged everyone on and the army was mustered with many of the moderates possibly assuming, and probably hoping, that the King would surely now back down in the face of this show of strength. However, Charles continued to hold that he had no intention of making any concessions. When the National Covenant was signed and the Covenanter army was mustered, the Marquis of Hamilton advised the King that there was no alternative to war.[48] Edinburgh was at fever pitch. Parties were held all over the town to toast 'God's army'. Cakes and ale were bought and there was a flurry of activity across the neighbourhood as the pious prayed, the enthusiastic hoped to take part in some way and the cynical wondered how much money they could make from the situation.

Completely confident in his own abilities as a strategist and in the righteousness of his cause, Charles decided to reassert his authority by force. An English army of 20,000 men would march from the south and advance on Edinburgh, while a secondary force of 5,000 led by the Marquis of Hamilton would land in Aberdeen and join with the forces of the Marquess of Huntly. Meanwhile, an Irish army led by the Earl of Antrim would invade the west of Scotland and link up with the MacDonalds and other Royalist clans.[49]

The plan was overly complex and was hampered by a lack of funds and the sympathy that many in England had with the Covenanters and their grievances. At the time, however, all the people of Edinburgh knew was that they were at war with their King. The Potterrow Port was buzzing with rumours and gossip. Food supplies in the city were quickly gathered for the troops and prices in the shops rose. But while prices rose the weavers and cordiners were busier than ever with orders for the army. Young men without jobs or responsibilities looked to join up and the local prostitutes did a roaring trade. Yet for all the benefits to trade, there were many who reckoned that, as the capital city, Edinburgh would be under threat. The great and the good looked to secure their homes, the not so great and the definitely not good looked to avoid the influx of soldiers that seemed to be on every corner and the ordinary people in the Potterrow tried to keep their heads down and get on with their lives. Andrew Ramsay at Greyfriars was bustling about with self-importance, making sure his Covenanting principles were on show while avoiding any hint of actually having to fight.

The reverend needn't have worried; the 20,000 trained English troops who were supposed to muster at Berwick-upon-Tweed failed to materialise. Some 15,000 men had been conscripted, but the vast majority were untrained men from the northern militia bands. Few had any experience with military weapons and the army itself was poorly equipped. To compensate for this, Charles recruited foreign mercenaries from the Spanish Netherlands. The use of foreign Catholics 'proved' the case against him as far as the Covenanters were concerned and further weakened support for the King among the English. Meanwhile, Alexander Leslie, leader of the Covenanter army marched his 16,500 men to Kelso and Charles joined his troops at Berwick-upon-Tweed. Now that a battle was imminent, neither side was actually keen to fight and instead negotiations started which ended on 19 June with an agreement that all the disputes would be referred to the General Assembly for resolution. The truce would hold while the disputes were being discussed; meanwhile, both sides continued to prepare for any future military action.[50]

Although the armies had declared a truce, tensions remained high across the country. Royalists and Covenanters eyed each other suspiciously. Within the Covenanter camp, the moderates tried to instil patience and faith in the negotiation process into their zealous comrades while the zealots watched for any signs of weakening from the moderates. In the Potterrow it was, on the surface of things, business as usual, but the port was not immune to the national situation. There were now soldiers posted at the port alongside the usual clerks and baillies. The Town Council, taking the opportunity to rid themselves of trouble-makers, was 'encouraging' their baillies to round up any youngsters with a bad reputation and 'recruit' them into the army. A common ploy by Scottish councils, the youngsters would find themselves caring for horses, making camp and generally acting as dogsbodies for the soldiers. The lucky ones might find themselves trained up to actually become soldiers themselves; the unlucky ones were killed or injured when battles turned into a rout.

The local prostitutes in the Port may have been faring well, but the thieves and pickpockets were all keeping a low profile. Those trading in goods of a dubious origin or nature had to be doubly careful in how they went about their trade. For those who bought from such suppliers, times were lean. Things were compounded further when it was announced, in late October, that the General Assembly of the Kirk was going to meet in Glasgow. Although the Assembly occasionally met outside Edinburgh, its absence was always a disappointment to shopkeepers whose trade increased with the arrival of out-of-town visitors. Due to the situation between the King and the Covenanters, this Assembly was anticipated to be well attended and to bring even more hangers-on than usual, all of whom would need food, drink, tobacco and anything else they could be persuaded to buy. Now, all of that extra trade was lost to Glasgow.

Hamilton had hoped to have the Assembly declared unconstitutional, but when that failed, he returned to Edinburgh and attempted to persuade the constable of the castle to hand it over to him in the name of the King.[51] The news of this attempt caused outrage and threats were made against Hamilton's life. Gangs of men openly carrying weapons became a common site on the city streets. Those who could not obtain weapons legally, or for that matter were allowed to own firearms, headed for the Potterrow. Agnes' shop would have possibly been very busy.

The General Assembly of the Kirk met in Glasgow and expelled the bishops from the Kirk, putting it on a full Presbyterian basis.[52] The Covenanters were exultant: the King was furious. Charles issued a proclamation annulling every act made or to be made by this 'Assemblage of traitors'.[53] This was duly repeated by every zealot in the Kirk.

The leading Covenanters started to prepare the draft. Long lists were drawn up detailing the responsibility for each parish in each presbytery. Everyone would have a role to play: the parish of Greyfriars was no exception. But to draw up the lists of who could afford to send men and who could afford to arm them required the baillies and the taxmen to assess each presbytery.[54] As a shopkeeper, Agnes was better off than many of her neighbours, but not by much, and therefore her contribution towards the draft was yet another significant expense. The Potterrow had to endure the questions and inspections of the taxmen, protected by the baillies. Those whose lives at the Port were carried on in the shadows were not happy. Those whose sons were in danger of being drafted were even less so.

7

The King, the Covenanters and the Cordiners Corporation

WHILE THE STALEMATE between the King and the Covenanters held, the zealots in the Kirk were in a frenzy. The country stood on the edge of war. This could mean only one thing: the imminent arrival of the Apocalypse. The previous years had seen famine, plague and death and with war on the horizon this was surely the work of the Four Horsemen of the Apocalypse. The Book of Revelation tells of Four Horsemen. The first, on a white horse, invoking pestilence but also the Antichrist; the second, on a red horse, is the creator of war; the third, on a black horse, brings famine; the fourth, on a pale green horse, brings death.[55] This was part of God's final judgement at the end of days. The Four Horsemen were harbingers of the Last Judgement and the final battle between God and the Devil. As part of this, so reasoned the Kirk, Auld Nick would release all of his hellish minions across the world, including witches. Although not everyone in the Kirk believed they were witnessing the end of days, everywhere they looked the evidence seemed to corroborate their more zealous brethren's beliefs. Between 1600 and 1640 there had been five separate instances of plague in Edinburgh's hinterland, at least four harvest failures, the King had married a Catholic and tried to impose bishops on the Kirk and now the country was literally divided into two armed camps on the brink of war. And if that was not enough to convince them, in the three years since the King had tried to impose the Anglican services on them there had been over 25 'witches' brought to trial across the country, with more cases arising every year. Isobell Malcom in Botayre, had charmed two women for the bairne bed'.[56] Janet Durie was 'challangit anent sundrie poynts of witchcraft' by James Keddie of Wemys.[57] 'John Patowne being wardit in the stepil of Dysert for suspicion of witchcraft'.[58] 'Gilbert Robisone, a noted warlock, Isabel Cutbertson, Lillian Bertram and Malie Mcwatt were charge with witchcraft before the Presbytery of Peebles.'[59] Katherine Craigie stood before the courts for the 'foul cryme of witchcraft'.[60]

The list seemed endless and yet there was no end in sight to the country's woes as the King was marching north with his army. By March 1639 he was at York and although all of his advisors could see the hopelessness of the case, he was determined to press on. In the meantime, in Edinburgh, even those remaining loyal to Charles were wavering. On 21 March, the castle was 'won' by a small band of Covenanters under the command of Alexander Leslie. Just after that, another small band led by John Leslie attacked Dalkeith Castle where the crown jewels of Scotland were kept. Traquair, who held the castle for Charles, managed to hold the attackers at bay while apparently failing to guard the window through which several young Covenanters entered. Traquair was also 'unable to stop them' from leaving through the main door while carrying the crown jewels and the castle's entire supply of arms.[61] John

Leslie and his men rode with the jewels and arms to Edinburgh. That evening, the city was a strange mixture of celebration for what had been achieved but also misgivings, from some of the more sober-minded, about what such victories meant for the rule of law and respect for authority.

The Calvinist faith had always stressed discipline: self-discipline as well as respect for the discipline of the Kirk. If men like Traquair could allow the crown jewels to be stolen and if Edinburgh Castle, the symbol of Royal authority, could be taken so easily, what message did that send to those living in places such as the Potterrow? Even without the Calvinist division of people into the saved and the damned, it was obvious that not all Scots were equal. The lower orders, the Edinburgh mob, were easily swayed and barely a whisker away from breaking out into violence. For those with no work and no money, a good afternoon riot broke the monotony of their lives. While the educated Kirk ministers could accept and understand Traquair's actions within the religious and political turmoil of the times, the lower orders might just see such activity as an excuse to ignore the rule of law. For the ordinary folk in the Potterrow, events were equally confusing. If they stole, they were arrested by the baillies, but if those such as Traquair and Leslie 'stole' they were lauded for their enterprising expedition: what did that mean? Did it mean that there was no rule of law and any action was acceptable? This idea was firmly squashed by the Sunday sermons that followed both exploits. The excuse that this was God's war and these actions were acceptable made sense, but in their own way raised more fears than they calmed. If this was God's war then the opponent might be, must be, the Devil. And the presence of Auld Nick also meant the presence of witches. For a woman such as Agnes, with her reputation, her existence was becoming increasingly unwelcome in the Potterrow.

While the Potterrow worried about the 'witch' in their midst, the Covenanters took the strategic stronghold of Dumbarton followed by a triumphant entry into Aberdeen. Charles was in York drafting up lists of the traitors that would be arrested the moment he reached Edinburgh. Once that was complete, Charles told Hamilton to blockade the port of Leith. Once again, Hamilton did not keep his instructions to himself and although the blockade was never successfully complete the news of the King's orders had two unintended consequences. Blockading the capital city's port convinced the Covenanters that Charles was in the grip of evil papist, and thus diabolical, advisors. For the moderates, this was a reason for them to talk with the King and guide him away from such advisors. For the zealots, this was 'proof' of the rightness of their cause and that Charles had to be 'removed' from his wicked advisors by force.

For the Edinburgh and Leith merchants, whether Covenanters or not, the worry was for trade. The town officials at Berwick-upon-Tweed seized the opportunity and offered their port as an alternative. Now it was much more than just illegal arms that was landed at the southern port and travelled through the Borders and Midlothian to arrive at the Potterrow Port. The amount of goods coming into the Port increased, but with no reciprocal increase in staff to handle the matter, the Port clerks and the baillies were overwhelmed. Those trading at the margins of legality had a field day and Agnes' shop was busier than ever.

When Hamilton did attempt to enforce the blockade, he was thwarted by the fishing communities on the East Lothian coast who stopped any of his ships' companies putting ashore for fresh water and by an outbreak of smallpox among his crew.

In June, the gossip in the Potterrow, like the rest of the country, was all about King Charles who was camped just below the border outside Berwick-upon-Tweed. The Scots troops, under Leslie, were at Kelso. Charles ordered his troops, led by Lord Holland, to advance and engage with the Scots. When Holland reached Kelso, he took one look at the Scots troops and turned and fled. Not a shot had been fired. When the news reached Charles, he was furious; when it reached Edinburgh there were celebrations in the streets. The King's closest advisors pleaded with him not to fight the Scots; with all advising against war, and as he had no money to pay or feed his army, or buy any equipment, he reluctantly agreed. Peace negotiations started on 11 June. Charles agreed to attend the Scottish Parliament to discuss their concerns and that a General Assembly of the Kirk would be held in the autumn. The First Bishop's War, as it became known, was over. On 24 June, Hamilton read out the proclamation of peace at the Mercat Cross in Edinburgh and received the keys of the castle on behalf of the King. The Edinburgh mob was on hand to welcome Hamilton with cries of 'traitor', as word of the King's statement that the Glasgow Assembly and its acts had been unlawful were already widely known.[62] The zealots among the Covenanters had made sure that a good supply of ale had been distributed to the mob, along with the wording of the King's statement, well in advance of Hamilton's arrival. The good feeling which had greeted the bloodless win over the English troops disappeared almost overnight. The ministers were back in their pulpits preaching of the works of the Devil and his witches. Traquair and Hamilton were already involved in a plot to undermine the upcoming parliament and Assembly. The ongoing discussions between the King and the leading Covenanters were also dissolving into mistrust and, in the end, Charles went back on his word, refused to attend the Scottish parliament and returned to London. The sermons from the pulpits became ever more shrill and everyone started to be on their guard against the witches that were surely in their midst.

The town was awash with rumours and discussion. The moderates talked down the prospects of war while the zealots screamed about Auld Nick as if he was round every corner. Unfortunately for the moderates, many of Charles' councillors seemed unable to understand the effects that their talk of 'war' and the need for a 'firm hand' would have on Scotland. Viscount Wentworth, despite not being in Scotland or having any knowledge of the situation in the country, pontificated that the Scots needed to be utterly defeated in war, then crushed under the yoke of a strong administration and that the administration should be run by an Englishman.[63] As Wentworth was a close advisor to Charles and a personal friend of Archbishop Laud, such statements did little to calm nerves in Edinburgh. Wentworth went further, stating that the economy of Scotland should be reorganised to benefit the Crown. For those who thought that war was a remote possibility, the idea of Scotland being used as some sort of cash cow for Charles was quite another matter. Edinburgh merchants became nervous, as did shopkeepers such as Agnes and the suppliers that came in at the Potterrow Port. Wentworth's statements were followed by the news that he had brought a series of prosecutions before the Court of Castle Chamber in Dublin in July. Several of the cases involved Scottish landowners who also had land in Ulster and who had signed the National Covenant. Wentworth had them arrested on the charge of treason. All were found guilty and their lands in Ireland were forfeit to the crown.[64] The more hot-headed in the Kirk could barely contain themselves with this 'affront to the National Covenant' and the Edinburgh baillies noted that tempers were running high, with arguments and fights breaking out in many areas of the city, including the Potterrow.

Tension continued to rise and news soon reached the city that several Scottish soldiers, loyal to the King, had returned from the German states where they had been fighting as mercenaries. They had fought with the Elector Palatine, Charles' own nephew. They met with the King at Newcastle where they were instantly arrested and put in prison.[65] Charles was convinced that they were disloyal and about to join the Covenanters; the soldiers, despite their initial loyalty to the King, did indeed join the Covenanters on their release after months in prison, in part because of the way they had been treated. The news was discussed in the inns and taverns of Edinburgh for its display of the King's instant suspicion of anyone Scottish. Loyalty to the King, which in previous times would have been absolute and unquestioning, was starting to unravel. If King Charles viewed every member of his northern Kingdom as potentially traitorous, what did such distrust mean for the bond between ruler and subject? For the politically minded, this was contentious; for the religiously minded, which was the majority of the population, it was an unsettling development. It was an upset of the natural order: was it the work of the Devil?

This constant talk of traitors, war, political arguments and rumour and counter-rumours ratcheted up the tension in the Potterrow on an almost daily basis. The area was not home to anyone of any importance and so every piece of news that was heard was at least second hand. Exaggeration, scaremongering and trouble-making all combined to leave the Potterrow awash with rumours of Catholic atrocities, popish plots, war on their doorstop and, of course, courtesy of the Kirk, the presence of Auld Nick. All of this extra tension was in addition to the normal day-to-day pressures of living in a poor area in the 17th century.

On 12 August, the General Assembly of the Kirk met in Edinburgh. Lord Traquair and the Marquis of Huntly opened the Assembly 'in the name of the King'. The usual procession along the High Street was marred by several members of the crowd yelling insults at Huntly who, in addition to his major creditors, had outstanding debts with several Edinburgh merchants and wholesalers in Midlothian and the Borders. The Town Council had granted him temporary immunity from arrest in the city to allow him to attend the opening of the Assembly, but they could do little to stop the abuse.[66] Several of those in the crowd making sure that Huntly knew of their displeasure were Midlothian and Borders wholesalers from the Potterrow Port.

When the Assembly convened on its first day, the members confirmed all their previous decisions which were then also ratified by the Scottish Parliament. Traquair, who was in attendance on behalf of the King, objected and attempted to suspend the parliament in the 'name of the King'. The parliament responded by declaring Traquair's action *ultra vires*, beyond

his authority, ignored his ongoing protestations and continued to sit. The parliament then passed a series of acts which
included the Tri-annual Parliament Act as well as making the
signing of the National Covenant compulsory for all holders
of public office.[67] Although it was well within the power of
the parliament to pass such acts, without the previous knowledge and consent of the King they were, in fact, unconstitutional. This was a serious insult to the authority of the Crown.
Charles was furious and swore that he would bring the Scots
to heel, even if it meant war.

The Covenanters celebrated the authority of the Assembly
and the Parliament, and for a moment the country started to
relax. Summer was turning into Autumn and the fighting season would soon be over for the year. It was hoped that Charles
would listen to more reasonable advisors over the Autumn and
Winter and, in combination with the laws just recently passed,
matters would calm down and tempers cool. Unfortunately, it
was at this point that personal differences within the Covenanter camp came to the fore. Argyll, the darling of the hot-
heads and the victor of various battles, wanted Scotland to be
run by a patriarchy of men similar to himself alongside the
Kirk. Montrose, favoured by the moderates, wanted to see
Charles in his rightful place on the throne of Scotland, but ruling with the Kirk. Montrose was an old-fashioned royalist at
heart. He had never had any argument with Charles personally
and had always felt that the King was merely badly advised
rather than genuinely distrusting of the Scots. Remove the advisors and Charles' opposition to the Kirk and the National Covenant would fall away: such was his thinking. The hot-heads
were having none of it, and while Montrose spoke to moderate

men in the inns at the top of the High Street the hot-heads wandered in and out of the taverns in places like the Potterrow, whispering that Montrose made some sort of deal with Charles at Berwick and was no less than a traitor to the Covenant. The rumour spread throughout the city and, after several days, a note was pinned to his front door which read, '*Invictus armis, verbis vincitur*' (Unconquered in arms he was conquered by words).[68] It is extremely unlikely that anyone in the Potterrow would have known any Latin, but the rumour did its worst and tension rose, again. The atmosphere became even more febrile when the news went round the town that Charles had aided some Spanish – that is, Catholic – ships in a standoff against the Protestant Dutch.

* * *

Every day in the Potterrow, more and more rumours ran through the streets. The weekly sermon at Greyfriars Kirk was about Auld Nick and his tricksy ways. Tempers frayed and arguments were becoming ever more commonplace. Agnes' quick temper and ready tongue were causing more disquiet. Times were becoming uncertain: families needed money and somewhere to buy cheap food. There were more customers in Agnes' shop looking to borrow money. For every person she 'helped' with a loan, there were many more she did not accommodate and even for those not needing or wanting to seek her out, her reputation as a witch was becoming less of a familiar piece of neighbourhood knowledge and more a reason to be wary of her.

Agnes' daughter Margaret was married to Robert Pursell, a cordiner. One day Robert was called before the Deacon and brethren of the Cordiners' (shoemakers) Corporation. As a member of the Corporation, Robert had the right to work as a shoemaker within the city bounds. This membership had been granted after he had served his apprenticeship to a master Cordiner. Moreover, membership of the Corporation gave customers a guarantee that his work was of a certified quality. As such, Robert had to act as befitted a member of the Corporation. He had, however, been accused of 'riotous behaviour' and was brought before Robert Watt, the Deacon of the Corporation, and the other Master Cordiners to answer for his actions. After a fractious meeting, Robert Pursell was found guilty of having acted in a 'riotous and foolish manner' and was admonished by Watt and fined. This was a serious matter. The City Guilds and Corporations were very protective of their reputations. Any bad behaviour was not tolerated and was immediately acted upon. If Robert could not act in a matter befitting a city cordiner he was in danger of losing his position in the Corporation and being unable to work in the city. Of those 'journeymen' who left their hometowns and cities to seek work, a good few were those who had actually lost their positions within their respective corporations.

The Cordiner's Corporation had evolved from one of the old medieval guilds of the city and protected the rights and status of their members. By the 17th century, many of the older rules had fallen away but the primary purpose of the corporations still stood: affording members an increased status and giving them support if they could not work due to injury or illness. The rules preventing apprentices from marrying until they had reached journeyman status still held, as did those preventing the lower ranks from trading independently of their master until they themselves had reached master status. Reaching master status was extremely difficult and depended strongly on how well a journeyman was regarded by his master and his master's peers. As a journeyman cordiner, Robert could, therefore, ill afford a bad reputation.

When Margaret told her mother that Robert had been called before the Corporation, Agnes grew angry and went to see Watt in his house while he was holding a meeting of the Corporation. This was a bold move. Women were not allowed to be members of any Corporation at the time and Deacon Robert Watt was a man of some considerable standing in the community. Yet Agnes not only challenged him, but choose to do so in his own home and in front of the Masters of the Corporation. This was probably deliberate on Agnes' part, although it is possible that she intended to confront Watt alone and the presence of the other masters upon her arrival was a mere coincidence. Outraged that Agnes had dared to confront him, Watt ordered her out of his house. Agnes refused. A full-blown yelling match ensued, with Agnes demanding he withdraw the fine from her son-in-law and Watt equally demanding she leave as she had no business to speak to him like that in his own home and in front of the Corporation. The argument became heated and then violent. Watt lashed out at Agnes, grabbing and tearing the cap on her head. This was much more than just damaging a piece of clothing. Wearing a cap on the head showed a woman's respectability. An uncovered head was indicative of loose morals. Whether Watt intended to tear Agnes' cap or not, it was a grave insult. Agnes exploded and screamed that Watt had grown arrogant with his greed and that it should be his downfall. She cursed Watt and all the other members of the Corporation present and condemned Watt to never earn another penny before storming out of the house. The curse seems to have worked. Within weeks, Watt's business fell away. The argument between Agnes and Watt had been heard by all the Masters of the Corporation who, presumably, went home to their wives and families and spoke about the row at the meeting and the fact that Agnes had cursed all of them. Within days, the whole of the Potterrow, including Watt's usual customers, had heard all about Agnes and her curse. Did those customers then avoid Watt's shop? Who would want to buy shoes from a cursed man? Who would want to incur the wrath of Agnes by being seen going to Watt's shop? Whatever the reason, over the next several months his shop saw fewer and fewer customers. Within a year of the argument at the meeting, Watt was no longer Deacon of the Corporation; Agnes' reputation, meanwhile, continued to grow.

For a woman to challenge the male authority of the Deacon of a Corporation was almost unheard of and spoke to Agnes' character. Although her son-in-law had not denied his riotous behaviour, Agnes reaction was astounding. It was not unknown for mothers to ask to speak to Deacons on their son's behalf: pleading for leniency, asking for 'one more chance', or making promises of good behaviour. What was extremely rare was for a woman to storm into a Corporation meeting and challenge the authority of a Deacon. The position of a Deacon depended on several factors: his length of time as a Master, the quality of the work he produced and his reputation and standing within the Cordiner and wider communities. Watt had followed all of the Corporation's own rules in bringing Robert before them to account for his behaviour and it was Agnes who had flouted social convention by coming to the meeting in his house. It was Agnes' behaviour that had damaged his credibility among his fellow Cordiners. The fact that she had not baulked at going to Watt's home and invading a Corporation meeting, whether intentional or not, was shocking. Her disrespect was obvious and very public. Watt's authority as a man and as a Deacon was badly damaged.

Several years later, Agnes and Watt had a chance meeting in her godson's house. Agnes asked him if he remembered breaking her cap. She reminded him that he had been reduced to poverty since and would continue so until she 'got amends of him'. The insult of the damaged cap had not been forgotten. Watt made his apologies and even refunded Robert the original fine he had paid. Watt and Agnes were somewhat reconciled. There were no more arguments and Watt's business improved, although there is no note of him ever becoming Deacon of the Corporation again.

* * *

While Agnes was challenging the authority of the Cordiners Corporation, the King was increasingly outraged at the challenge posed by the Scottish Parliament. In November, Charles, with Wentworth at his side, decided that the Scottish Parliament in Edinburgh should be dismissed. On 8 November, he wrote to Traquair ordering him to prorogue parliament: to terminate a session of parliament by royal prerogative. On 14 November, Traquair entered the city chambers and attempted to prorogue the parliament. The Scottish lords flatly refused to accept either Traquair's authority or his actions.

Traquair left Edinburgh and hurried down to London to inform Charles;[69] yet again, rumours ran round the town that the King was attempting to subvert the National Covenant and the Kirk denounced everyone and everything they could as the work of the Devil.

The constant refrain that Auld Nick was abroad, roaming at will and dragging good Christians to their doom, was now a constant background threat. The presence of evil, wickedness and sin pervaded every aspect of life. At any moment he might appear or send one of his witches to ensnare you. There were no dissenting voices. The moderates in the Covenanter camp continued to hope for a peaceful settlement with the King but had, by this point, accepted that the Devil was indeed abroad in the world of men. On the other side, the Royalists were equally convinced of the presence of Auld Nick: what else could explain the insults to King Charles and flouting of his authority? Voicing the opinion that the country was not under attack by the Devil made no sense. In a world of total belief in the Christian God, and as Scotland was Calvinist and the people were 'God's Elect', then the only entity that could be responsible for the chaos was the Devil. Fear of Auld Nick had become the guiding emotion in people's lives. For those who were not soldiers, for those who lived in the Potterrow, this constant stress and anxiety had nowhere to go: alcohol intake, domestic violence and street fights increased in frequency and intensity. Developing a siege mentality, the Potterrow turned in on itself.

Over the winter tempers rose and fell as Covenanters and Royalists argued in Edinburgh's inns and taverns. Talk of war made everyone jittery and, combined with the usual reduction of fresh food and increased need for fuel, added pressure to those living and working in the Potterrow. While the Kirk ministers continued to trumpet the National Covenant and warn their congregation to be ever vigilant about the presence of the Devil, the reality of life for many was increased prices and a cold and hungry winter. By February 1640, the moderates in Edinburgh were in the ascendancy. There had been no incidents over the previous months – proof, they said, of the King's good nature and genuine feeling for them. A delegation left Edinburgh and travelled down to London to see Charles and the moderates talked of the new peace that would follow. The delegation reached London on 20 February and asked the King to accept all the legislation of the Assembly and the Parliament. Charles refused.[70] After rejecting the pleas of the delegation, Charles wrote to Ruthven, the commander of Edinburgh Castle, ordering him to prepare his armaments as if for war and to fire on the town if and when he thought necessary.[71] Although the King had written privately, the sudden preparation of the castle's cannons soon became common knowledge across the town and raised feverish speculation. All of the previous goodwill cultivated by the moderates disappeared and armed men were becoming a common sight in the city once again. It was an offence to carry arms in the street unless for a very good reason and with the permission of the Town Council. However, the rules became nearly impossible to police. The city baillies, in addition to their normal tasks, were almost overwhelmed by increasing numbers of fights as tempers rose. They themselves were only armed with heavy cudgels and were facing armed men of rank. The baillies could cope with a street fight in the Potterrow by – literally – hitting people over the head, but when faced with groups of men armed with swords and small pistols they retreated. Many of those who were carrying arms were followers of Argyll or Montrose and had their weapons supplied by their lord. For those without a patron who were keen to arm themselves but were unable (or unwilling) to do so through the legal gunsmith shops of the Royal Mile, the Potterrow Port beckoned, where arms could be bought with no questions asked.

While illicit arms were being traded in the Potterrow, in London the King was determined to have fully armed and properly trained troops for his spring attack on the Scots which was intended to bring them to heel. Obviously, he needed money for troops and arms, and was convinced by his advisors to recall the English Parliament in order to obtain the funds. In addition, Wentworth asked the Irish Parliament for funds. Despite strong opposition, in March the Royalists in the Irish Parliament approved an army of 9,000. In April, Charles asked the English Parliament for funds. The English stated that they would not agree to any subsidies until Charles addressed their grievances. Some of the English Parliamentarians were sympathetic towards the Covenanters and were threatening to bring the 'Scots question' to the house for debate. The King refused to listen to any of the grievances, the Parliament refused any funds and after three weeks of stalemate, Charles dissolved Parliament on 6 May 1640.[72] He would have to fund the war against the Scots himself.

While Charles was falling out with his English Parliament, the Covenanter leaders were mustering their regiments. The country was on the brink of war, yet again. In June of 1640, the Scottish Parliament met in Edinburgh. A commission of 'fire and sword' against Royalist areas was set in motion. Five-thousand troops moved across a large area of the west. They then seized Dumbarton Castle, preventing the Irish troops from landing as the castle gave control of the river Clyde and so allowing the main Scottish force to focus on the threatened English invasion.

Despite Charles' best intentions, the English troops he had mustered were no better than the last time. They were mainly southern English militiamen who were as poorly equipped as they were poorly trained and, generally, unenthusiastic about the war. In addition, other than their officers, most were unpaid and the quartermasters had few supplies. Although armies frequently live off the land in enemy territory, the English militia had been reduced to looting the areas they passed through in England on their march north, creating widespread disorder and ill-feeling among the locals and militia themselves. By the time they reached the north of England, they were tired, hungry and less than keen for the fight. The Scots troops, led by Leslie, crossed the border and headed for Newcastle-upon-Tyne which, as the centre of the coal trade with London, was a valuable prize. By the time the Scots reached the city, morale among English troops collapsed and Charles was forced to sue for peace.

While everything was, apparently, going well for the Covenanters and the Presbyterian faith in England, it was a different matter at home. Edinburgh Castle had been held for the King by Sir Patrick Ruthven with some Scottish Royalists and a few English troops. There, in the Covenanter's own back yard, was an embarrassing Royalist stronghold. When Charles had been told of this, he had been ecstatic and had sent men and supplies to last six months.

While the King was confident that he would be victorious in subduing the Scottish malcontents before the six months was up, the Kirk was furious and the Covenanters that were not fighting in the west or threatening Newcastle proceeded to lay siege to the castle. But how? There were few troops or heavy artillery left, they were all in the west or in England, and the castle was, as everyone knew, extremely difficult to take. Moreover, since the old days of the Wars of Independence an entire city had grown up around the castle. The maze of wynds and courtyards on the High Street were home to hundreds. There was also the Scottish Parliament building, the Law Courts, St Giles – it was an impossible situation. There was only one thing that could be done: a siege. At the end of May, the castle was blockaded. The city was in an uproar.

Life in the Potterrow was benefitting from the confusion. The baillies on duty in the Potterrow were overrun as more and more Covenanters and their followers filled the city. Young men from Midlothian and the Borders were streaming into the city, anxious to join the Covenanting army. Those of a more dubious nature, who had no intention of enlisting, seized their chance and entered the city without being challenged by the overwhelmed baillies. The mustering of an army always held opportunities for trade, legal or otherwise. Every week the ministers of Edinburgh climbed into their pulpits and spoke of 'God's War' and God's Army' and all donations were sent straight to army headquarters. Most gave freely, but even those not completely convinced by the cause handed over what they could rather than be publicly shamed.

Traders were still coming and going as normal and the usual petty squabbles between neighbours went on, but all the time the Covenanters were sitting beneath the castle esplanade waiting out Sir Ruthven rather than at the city ports assisting the baillies and clerks. Even the Kirk seemed to have forgotten about the ordinary people. By the end of July, the Kirk held its General Assembly in Aberdeen. This was partly to avoid the chaos that was in Edinburgh, but also to send a strong message to the Royalists who were more numerous in the north of the country. But while the Kirk appeared not to care about the ordinary lives of the Potterrow residents, their obsession with Auld Nick and his handmaidens continued. On 29 July, the Assembly passed a Condemnatory Act against witches and charmers.

> The principal acts of the generall assembly, conveened at Aberdene, July 28, 1640.

> Sess. 2, July 29, 1640.

> The Assembly ordaines all ministers within the Kingdome, carefully to take notice of charmers, witches, and all such abusers of the people, and to urge the acts of Parliament to be execute against them; and that the commissioners from the Assembly to the Parliament shall recommend to the said supreme judicatory the care of the execution of the lawes against such persons in the most behoovefull way.[73]

Unfortunately for the General Assembly, Auld Nick and his handmaidens didn't seem to be too perturbed by the Condemnatory Act. From July until the end of that year, the situation became so bad that some records merely list 'several witches' rather than register yet another long tally of names.[74]

Given the continued onslaught from the Devil, one year later the Kirk petitioned the parliament 'that the actis of parliament anent chermers, sorcerers and consulters with witches be renewed, and a solid way takin how the same acts may be put to execuтun.'[75]

The Kirk's obsession with Auld Nick was becoming an *idée fixe*. The more the Kirk convinced itself that it was under attack by the Devil, the more any incident was perceived as such an attack. The more pious the Kirk, the more likely it was to be attacked. The more attacks it received, the more the Kirk's righteousness was 'proved'. It was becoming a self-fulfilling delusion. Every action of the King and the Royalists was interpreted as the 'work o' the De'il'. Previously, when the King was active, the eyes of the Kirk had been firmly fixed on Royalists. Then, when the immediate physical danger was past, the Kirk cast around for where Auld Nick was hiding and found witches round every corner.

The Covenanter army was continuing to arm itself by whatever means it could, legal or otherwise, and those traders at the Potterrow Port who normally spent their day avoiding the eye of the baillies as they sold their dubious goods now found themselves with a new market. The army needed much more than just muskets and swords: clothes, boots, saddle bags, tents and all the other paraphernalia that an army needs on the march were all being bought up at any price. Tents were a particular problem until a few enterprising wives of the leading Covenanters donated bedsheets to be made into tents.[76] This started a trend, with those who were reluctant to part with a good piece of household linen quickly shamed into changing their minds. Most of the housewives in the Potterrow did not own any bedsheets or, if they did, they were certainly not going to give them up for the army. Nevertheless, a thriving trade in stolen sheets soon developed, with several young entrepreneurs allegedly chased out of windows as they attempted to help themselves to what bed linen they could find. In all of this, Agnes' shop was open both night and day as she traded in whatever she could. Town Council records made special note of several traders in the city who were under suspicion of trading in illegal goods. There is no note of Agnes in the records, although the records are incomplete. There were, however, so many traders and so few baillies that no action appears to have been taken against anyone.

The blockade of the castle continued over the summer and into early autumn. The Royalists inside were becoming increasingly hungry as their food supplies dwindled. The Covenanters outside were becoming increasingly confident of victory; there had even been one or two cannon shots fired into the castle, and the Edinburgh mob was becoming increasingly vocal in their derision of both sides. Traders coming in at the likes of the Potterrow Port might well profess their loyalty to the National Covenant, but when prices were deflated and some of their customers were holed up in the castle and unable to buy, it was difficult to show much enthusiasm for the siege. The early profits from supplying the army had quickly dwindled and there was a glut of food and other supplies on the market which depressed prices. This was good news, for a change, for those living in the Potterrow, but was one more reason for Agnes to be in a foul temper.

Up at the castle, the King's supplies had not lasted long. It was said that for every extra load of supplies that was smuggled into the castle, half were stolen on the way and the other half were rotten by the time they arrived. Charles' secret letter to Ruthven to open fire on Edinburgh if he thought it necessary had not stayed secret for long. Although Ruthven had denied any ulterior motive while he had prepared the castle's cannons, the contents of the letter had finally become known and had outraged many of the Scots cooped up in the castle confines, proving their worst fears to have been correct. The few castle staff with Covenanter sympathies allegedly took to 'pissing in the water supply'. A cannon shot from the town had landed on the castle well at the end of July rendering it useless and the castle inhabitants had been relying on rainwater for weeks. Unfortunately, it had been a hot summer with little rain. Several of the Royalists had died and the others were weakened from lack of food and clean water. The bodies of the dead had been piled up as few had the energy to dig graves in the hard ground. The situation had become so bad that Sir Ruthven had fallen seriously ill. Leading by example, he had rationed himself as severely as his men and had developed scurvy.[77] Plagued with fatigue and pains in his arms and legs, he had lost most of his teeth and had become deaf.

Whether the Covenanters had really taken to 'pissing in the water supply' or not, by 15 September Sir Ruthven and his men could take no more. He negotiated a surrender with the Town Council and was allowed to leave the castle, riding down the Royal Mile accompanied by the English troops and the usual barrage of insults and missiles from the Edinburgh mob.[78] The lifting of the blockade was celebrated across the city and trade in the Potterrow went back to its usual mix of legal trading and illicit deals.

A treaty was finally agreed in October between the Scots and the English Royalist troops whereby the Scots were paid £850 per day and allowed to occupy Northumbria and County Durham until final terms were agreed. Charles was forced to recall the English Parliament that November, but the tension between the King's supporters and the English Parliamentarians who were agitating for more powers remained. Both sides distrusted the other and factions were developing within both the Royalist and Parliamentarian camps.

Argyll and Montrose were now openly quarrelling, with loyalties between Charles and the Covenanters becoming entangled in the old feuds of the Highlands. Things were not much better in the Royalist camp and were not helped when, in his speech at the opening of parliament on 3 November, Charles had called the Scots 'rebels' and told the English Parliamentarians their first duty was to provide the money for him to fight the Scots. Those Parliamentarians friendly to the Covenanters made sure the news of Charles' opinion of the Scots reached Edinburgh as soon as possible. The delegation of Covenanters who travelled down to London in the hope of discussing terms to end the war had not been influenced by the moderates, but had taken their cue from Argyll and the other leading zealots.

In Edinburgh, the Covenanter victory and confirmed primacy of the Presbyterian faith was the main focus of everyone's attention. The Kirk, confident that it had seen off the Royalist threat, now turned its attention to the Devil and all his works. The problem for the Potterrow was that the Kirk, for all its Presbyterianism, gave primacy to ministers and elders before ordinary parishioners. The Kirk concentrated on its 'good' saved parishioners rather than those who were already damned: this was, after all, a church that firmly believed in predestination. God had already decided who was saved and who was damned. Given that certainty, the likes of those living and working in the tenements of the Potterrow were, therefore, at the bottom of the pile, physically and spiritually. If they were already damned, they were not worth the minister's time. Although who was damned and who was saved could not be known for absolute certainty, it was fairly self-evident which side of that divide most of the residents of the Potterrow lay. In addition, the parish of Greyfriars Kirk only had Andrew Ramsay as its minister, who was like, any true Covenanter, anxious to 'prove' his worth. This meant being seen at meetings to root out potential weak links in the Kirk or sitting in judgement over those members of the Town Council that were found wanting. Arguments between Agnes and her neighbours were of no interest to Ramsay.

The atmosphere in the town was becoming increasingly strained: Covenanters and Royalists were at each other's throats, trade was affected and money was becoming ever scarcer. But it was the heightened state of mania in the Kirk that was important in the case of Agnes. In December 1640, Archbishop Laud had been stripped of his position by the English Parliament and the news had been greeted by the Kirk in Scotland as 'proof' of the righteousness of the National Covenant. However, despite or possibly because of the victories of the Covenanting army over the King's troops and the fall of Laud, the Kirk had now passed from simple belief in the Presbyterian faith to an almost ecstatic frenzy. Every defeat was the work of the Devil; every victory was a victory over Auld Nick. Almost all of the moderate voices had been drowned out as the clamour of zealots became even louder. Faith had become absolute. Everyone had worked themselves into a complete hysteria over the presence of the Devil. Those who did not see his hand in everything were, no doubt, in league with him. No deviation could be tolerated. Any criticism, no matter how mildly expressed, was instantly condemned as it had, obviously, a diabolical basis. A claustrophobic atmosphere developed across Scotland, but especially in Edinburgh where every political event, no matter how trivial, no matter how distant, was scrutinised. Those who had even the whisper of the word 'witch' said against them were increasingly in danger. Agnes' reputation in the Potterrow was putting her more and more at risk. At the same time, two interlinked events were keeping her relatively safe. First, was the lack of concern by the Greyfriars' minister as to what was happening in the Potterrow and, second, the fact that Andrew Ramsay, the first charge of Greyfriars, left in early 1641 and was not immediately replaced. This left the parish temporarily without any minister at all as the second charge was still vacant and under the care of the minister of St Giles. However, it was to St Giles that Ramsay had moved and in his new and elevated position he had no time to worry about the Potterrow. As a result, Agnes' reputation as a witch may have been growing, putting her under threat from the rising national feeling, but she remained undetected due to the lack of attention from the Kirk.

In February 1641, the English parliament had voted an extra £300,000 towards the expenses of the Scots army in the north of England. As a result, the army in England started to buy supplies in the north of England. As the market for army supplies developed in the north of England with material being bought in bulk at lower prices, the army in Scotland also started to buy their supplies south of the border. Demand for leather goods and cloth fell in Scotland, glutting the market and causing prices to fall. This in turn had a knock-on effect on other trades and Agnes' livelihood was increasingly under threat.

Edinburgh had fallen into an uneasy calm, as the continuing row between Charles and his English parliamentarians had little effect on Scotland. Suddenly, in May, the calm was broken as Argyll made his move. Montrose, the leader of the Scottish Royalists, was summoned before the Committee of Estates on the 27th and charged with various intrigues against Argyll. On 11 June, he was imprisoned in Edinburgh Castle. Even many of the zealots in Argyll's camp were shocked. This news was quickly followed by a rumour that the King was coming at the head of an army to free Montrose and finally subdue the rebellious Scots. King Charles had intended to come to Edinburgh to open the next session of the parliament in the late summer and, combined with previous letters Charles had sent to Montrose, the rumour soon gained traction. Arguments and street fights broke out across the town yet again as people prepared for the arrival of the King's army, the presence of the Scots army in the north of England being temporarily forgotten. The few moderates left, as usual, appealed for calm while the zealots and general trouble-makers gleefully stoked up as much anxiety as possible. Rumours of witches were noted in Fife, Lanark, Midlothian, East Lothian, the Borders and Edinburgh.

On 14 August, Charles arrived in Edinburgh. Disappointingly for the zealots he did not arrive with an army and, in fact, had reviewed the Scottish army at Newcastle and even dined with Leslie, their commander. On 17 August, the town turned out to watch as the King led the procession to Parliament House to formally open the next session of the parliament. While Edinburgh held its breath and Montrose remained locked up in the castle, Charles listened to several debates in the parliament and attended church in St Giles. On 28 August, he ratified all of the previous year's legislation and, most importantly, gave his formal assent to the abolition of Episcopacy in Scotland.

After this initial positivity, matters soon deteriorated as the King and the parliament started squabbling over appointments to the Estates. The Estates was a sister institution to the Scottish Parliament. It comprised the clergy, the nobility and the burgh commissioners. The Estates could not pass legislation except that covering taxation, but could undertake investigations into the conduct of the nobility and was thus extremely politically influential. Things quickly deteriorated further on 29 September when Lord Ker, a staunch supporter of the King and a young hot-head, accused Hamilton of being a traitor. Ker was instantly called to appear before the Estates. Unfortunately for Charles, Ker decided to appear before the Estates at the head of several hundred armed men. Arriving through the Potterrow Port, Ker and his men had marched up to the Estates through the centre of Edinburgh. As they were armed 'with no just cause', Ker and his men should have been stopped at the Port by the city baillies, but there was little the two or three baillies could practically do in the face of several hundred armed men. There had been increasing number of men openly carrying arms in the town in the preceding months, but none that had come in the form of an armed force. The Town

Council called for an immediate ban on anyone carrying arms on the streets and closed the city ports for 24 hours.

The town was then gripped with a bizarre rumour. The King was staying at Holyrood and a convoluted kidnap plot spread round the town: Charles, or his supporters, were going to lure Hamilton and Argyll to the King's rooms and then kidnap them. Although the rumour was more than likely completely untrue, both Hamilton and Argyll left Edinburgh as a precaution – but not before they made sure everyone in Edinburgh had heard the rumour in great detail. Despite Montrose still being imprisoned in the castle, he was heavily implicated in the plot. On hearing the rumours, Charles overreacted from fear of repercussion at the hands of the Edinburgh mob and when he next visited the Parliament he did so accompanied by several armed retainers. However, this merely served to 'prove' the plot and, in combination with the earlier arrival of Ker with his armed followers, gave the zealots all the ammunition they needed against the Royalist cause. Worse news was to come when Charles was told of the rebellion that was brewing in Ireland and, after negotiating for the release of Montrose on surety, Charles left for London on 18 November.

The year ended in a snow storm with Royalists, Covenanters, ministers and 'witches' all hunkered down for the winter.

8

Salt

ON 3 JANUARY 1642, King Charles decided to act. The Attorney General, Sir Edward Herbert, acting on the King's behalf, accused John Pym, Lord Mandeville, John Hampden, Arthur Haselrig, Dezil Holles and William Strode of high treason. On 4 January, Charles arrived at Whitehall at the head of a large group of guards. Entering the House of Commons, Charles' idea to appear as a man of action and arrest the traitors himself failed. Pym and the others had been forewarned and were not there. This piece of public theatre backfired on Charles as he was left looking foolish having been so easily outwitted. The entire affair was soon reported across the country. In Edinburgh the radicals on both sides used the incident as 'proof' of the intransigence of the others, while the moderates were left embarrassed that matters had deteriorated to such a dangerous degree that the King should attempt such an act in the parliament. In the Potterrow, the nuances of the matter may have been lost but the gravity of the situation was not: members of the House of Commons were traitors, but the King was unable to capture them. Where was his royal authority? It was an obvious and very public breach between Charles and his parliament; a breach that few could see a peaceful way of mending. While the political situation in London deteriorated, the weather in Edinburgh was particularly harsh and the death rates among the poor and the destitute from exposure, malnutrition and the usual winter diseases rose. The Town Council reported on the need for casual labourers to be employed to help the baillies clear away the bodies of the dead for 'common decency'.[79] Several churches also needed help to bury the bodies and complaints about the amount of land given over to pauper's burials were heard among some of the Edinburgh merchants. Food supplies, always somewhat precarious in the winter months, were also running low; squabbles over supplies and prices became commonplace.

Meanwhile, the increasingly bitter arguments between Covenanters, Royalists and English Parliamentarians consumed the Kirk of Scotland, the Privy Council and the Town Council. Deaths in the Potterrow were not their priority. The Privy Council saw a looming war approaching, the Town Council saw unrest and the chaos that war might bring to the streets, while the Kirk saw Auld Nick's hand in everything from the actions of the King to the ungodly poor that did not attend the Kirk as they should. In late January, Charles inflamed matters even more when he wrote to both Covenanters and Royalists in Scotland for help in his struggles with the English. The zealots in the Covenanter camp screamed about the King asking for help after all of his insults while even the moderates failed to understand why he should write to both Argyll and Montrose, who was still *persona non grata* as far as most of Edinburgh was concerned. The Privy Council offered Argyll to act as an advisor to the King, but avoided answering the question of help.[80]

The rebellion in Ireland had turned into a bloody war of attrition and refugees were soon arriving in Scotland. Stories of atrocities, real or exaggerated, were soon spread through the Potterrow. Initially the Kirk had welcomed the refugees fleeing 'ane unjust persecutun', using their presence to fill their Sunday sermons with dire warnings of what happened when Auld Nick was given free rein. However, the welcome did not extend to anything but the most basic of Christian charity and the destitute Irish soon drifted to the poorer parts of the town, living a hand-to-mouth existence at the Potterrow Port.

Finally, by the end of March the weather turned. Temperatures rose and the early stocks of fresh food started to arrive from Midlothian and the Borders. The death rate fell and before long the Port was as busy as usual and Agnes' business was thriving.

One day, Christian Harlaw came into Agnes' shop and ordered some salt. Agnes' assistant delivered the salt to Christian at the end of the day. The following morning when Christian checked the salt she was dissatisfied with the quality and the quantity. The salt was either damp or had been adulterated with sand, a common trick with some shopkeepers to make salt go further. Whatever Agnes had done, Christian went back to the shop to return the salt and complain. Agnes was not there, but her assistant was and Christian told her that the salt was not worth the price she had paid and that she wanted her money back. The assistant accepted the return of the salt and Christian received her refund and went home. Later in the day, Agnes returned to the shop and her assistant told her about the situation with Christian and the salt. Agnes was furious. This was yet again a damaging insult to Agnes' reputation as a shopkeeper. And in this case, it was very serious. Salt was essential in 17th century homes as it acted as a preservative for foodstuffs. In a time before refrigeration, salt preserved food by drying it out and also by killing many of the microbes that cause food to spoil. In addition, it enhanced the flavour of many foodstuffs, especially the cheaper foods that would have made up the staple diet of most in the Potterrow. Whether the salt had been adulterated or not, Agnes started by screaming at her assistant for her stupidity in returning Christian's money and meekness in accepting the insult over the salt. Once she had finished with her assistant, Agnes turned her anger back to the absent Christian, and loudly and vehemently cursed her saying it would be 'the dearest salt she ever saw'.

That night Christian fell ill with 'severe sweatings'. Her family, having heard all about Agnes' curse, instantly knew the cause of the illness. The sweatings continued into the next day and the family, by now desperate, called for the doctor. The Harlaws were probably a middling family, so the 'doctor' was more likely an apothecary. The appearance of this medical man in the Potterrow ensured that the entire neighbourhood soon knew what was happening but, despite all his best efforts, the 'doctor', whatever his actual status and knowledge, could do nothing to relieve Christian. The sweatings continued into the next day. Fearing that Christian was on her death-bed, the family called Agnes to come and see her. The family pleaded and begged Agnes to lift the curse. She finally agreed, but only after receiving payment of a significant sum of money and an apology from Christian for her slander over the salt. The apology was, however, somewhat begrudging, as Christian told Agnes that if she was ill after that she would come and get Agnes. Christian knew, as did everyone else in the Potterrow, that if illness was visited upon you Agnes was the cause. Begrudging or not, within a day Christian recovered completely – much to the disbelief of the doctor.

The entire incident had proved to everyone, if proof were needed, the power of Agnes Finnie. This sequence of events was particularly terrifying for the neighbourhood as Christian had not even been present to hear Agnes' curse. Most of those living in the Potterrow knew something of how witches worked: spells and incantations worked best with the inclusion of a physical object. Curing a sick child often involved mixing some of the child's hair into an ointment. Easing the pain of childbirth might require a piece of the expectant mother's nail clippings for the spell to work. If a body part could not be obtained, then a piece of some clothing of the person would be sought. Material would often be mixed with clay or straw and fashioned into a doll or a poppet that could become the focus of the magic. Witches were powerful, but for their magic to be effective it almost always required some physical object, or at the very least the subject of the magic to be present. If Agnes required neither the individual nor some personal item belonging to them to be present to work her magic, she would be seen as an increasingly dominant force in the Potterrow. To cause illness without even being near the individual was a demonstration of real power. To the Kirk, that power could only come from one source: Auld Nick.

These beliefs were strengthened by news from Ireland. The Scottish parliament had sent troops to Ireland, less to support the King than to bring the 'Godless Irish' to heel. Initially the troops had won several early victories but for every rebel troop they defeated another appeared to spring up. Prisoners were seldom taken and wounded Irish soldiers and camp followers were killed. By May, the army was exhausted with the fighting and slaughter when the weather turned. Several weeks of high winds and bitter cold rain blew in and devastated the Scots' camps. Tents blew away or were shredded in the severe winds, rising numbers of soldiers died of exposure overnight and those that did not die were weakened by days of drenching cold rain. Proof of Irish witchcraft.[81] When the news reached Scotland, every minister of the Kirk was in his pulpit preaching about the 'witchcraft of the Popish Irish'. Those Irish traders who had lived and worked in Scotland for years suddenly found themselves hounded wherever they went. The refugees who had initially been welcomed were chased down the street, whether Protestant or Catholic. There are several notes in the official records of the Edinburgh baillies rescuing those with an Irish accent from the Edinburgh mob. The Potterrow Port, with its daily movement of people, was a particular hotspot for trouble.

While the situation in Ireland remained bloody and the situation in England continued to deteriorate, matters in the Highlands were also troubling. A new Justiciary Commission was established, headed by Argyll.[82] Officially, the Commission had been set up to deal with disorder and control the Highland clans, but, of course, had the added bonus of being able to clip the wings of Montrose and his allies. Tales of the 'wyld, wykkd Helandmen' were a staple fare in Edinburgh. Catholic in religion, wild in nature, foreign speaking, the Highland clans were feared by those in Lowland Scotland who had seldom, if ever, met a real Highlander except when fully armed and striding the town following Argyll or Montrose.

Trouble in the town arose, however, from a different and unexpected sector. While the Covenanters had looked to Ireland

and the north, the Royalists had been working on a petition in favour of Charles against the parliament. Several hundred armed Royalists arrived in Edinburgh, many of them from Midlothian and the Borders, streaming through the Potterrow Port. Armed Covenanters arrived from Fife. Rumours of attacks and plots circulated, the Privy Council were put under guard and the Kirk ministers preached war, death and destruction. The city's ports were closed and yet again life in the Potterrow was disrupted. No traders were allowed in or out, shops had no goods to sell and tempers rose. Just when things reached boiling point, the Covenanters put forward a counter petition which the Council accepted while rejecting that of the Royalists. Everyone held their breath and then the Royalists backed down.

The constant pressure from the threat of war with armed men on the streets from the different factions and the almost ubiquitous cry from the pulpits of Auld Nick's presence must have put a strain on everyone living in the Potterrow. The local records note the arrests of individuals found drunk and fighting in the streets, but do not record the arguments, the anxiety, the genuine fear that must have existed. Belief in God and the Devil was absolute. The Kirk may well have spoken of predetermination but for those living ordinary lives, theology gave no comfort when everything around them was in a constant state of tension. Even on days when there were no armed men, or when there were no plots to kill this person or that, the anxiety must have been constant. For who knew when the armed men would return? When would another plot arise? Where would the Devil strike next?

The Kirk did not have far to look. Over the summer of 1642, more and more reports were arriving from England.

Some were official reports from King Charles or from the English Parliamentarians, but most were stories from travellers and traders. On 15 July, fighting broke out at Manchester. There was no great pitched battle or set military campaign, but the confusion over what was happening in the town had quickly deteriorated into fighting. This was repeated across England with street brawls developing into armed combat with little leadership on both sides. By the end of the month, England was at war with itself. (Charles would raise the Royal Standard on 22 August.) Instantly, the King sent Hamilton up to Edinburgh to ask Argyll for his support: Argyll prevaricated. Having never fully trusted Charles, Argyll knew the Covenanters were only wanted to help the King win against the English Parliamentarians and would then be discarded. He was not willing to risk Scottish lives in 'this English quarrel' but if he had to act, he would side with the Parliamentarians. While this may have been astute politics on the part of Argyll, it was an incredible decision to the ordinary person in the street. For all the rising tension and all the talk of war, for the leader of Scotland to actually be considering fighting against the King was unbelievable. Although the Covenanters had been in conflict with the King for some time, most of the moderates still believed Charles was ill-advised. A show of strength, without any actual violence, would bring him to his senses. They could not go to war with their king. The King was anointed by God and good, bad or indifferent, was the King. To even contemplate going to war against the King was truly a world turned upside down. And yet, despite all this, actual fighting had broken out. The Council declared against the King. Soldiers were sent to the Highlands to keep watch in the Catholic clans and those with Royalist sympathies. Restrictions on all Catholics in Scotland were increased with notices posted across every town. All priests who were suspect, and that was most of them, were also detained as they were deemed to be 'crafty and politic heads and traffickers in matter of state.'[83] The baillies in the Potterrow now had to ferret out and arrest anyone they did not know in the maze of dark wynds and back closes of tenements. In late July, the General Assembly of the Kirk met in St Andrews and was attended by several delegates from Ulster who were looking for help from their Protestant brothers. However, when their presence became known it was misinterpreted by many as 'Irish Catholics' and there was rioting in Edinburgh as the rumour spread that the Assembly was under attack. Irish traders coming into the Potterrow Port were met with a hail of abuse and missiles, and John Eleis, the baillie for the Port, and his men had to battle to clear the streets.

Meanwhile, another of her neighbours was falling foul of Agnes. Christian Sympson had borrowed some money from Agnes, but when it came time to repay she didn't have the funds. Approaching Agnes in her shop, Christian explained she didn't have the money and asked for more time to pay her. For once, Agnes agreed. It was early May and the 15th of the month was Whitsunday. It was an extremely busy time at the four city ports. Landlords who normally would never be seen dead in the Potterrow suddenly appeared looking for money. Young girls who perhaps hadn't worked as hard as they should suddenly found themselves dismissed from cleaning one of the 'big hooses' up at the High Street. Apprentices who had spent their time drinking and gambling could be told they had to repeat an entire year. In some extreme cases, they might lose their apprenticeship altogether. Tenants might find their rent increased beyond their means. City tolls were raised, shop rents were demanded and loans that couldn't be repaid were rolled over at an even higher interest rate. Older workers were dismissed, youngsters jostled each other for a position or an apprenticeship.

But it was also a time when new jobs could be found. Many found a new, better position, others had retained an existing one, some had paid off an old loan, a few took out a new one. Apprentices might get promoted, some very lucky individuals might even get a raise in their wages and the even more elusive 'bonus' might be paid. Those who worked from home on piece work might receive their quarterly payment. But Whitsunday was also a holiday. There were engagements between sweethearts and general celebrations all round. Those of a charitable disposition shared bannocks and oatcakes with the destitute and most people had a day free from work. It was a day for cake and ale, but also for handing over hard cash.

It is possible that Christian was owed money for some work and this would be paid on Whitsunday allowing her in turn to repay Agnes. Whatever the situation, it was agreed that Christian could have another eight days in which to get the money to repay the debt. Agnes warned her, however, that if the debt was not paid in full in eight days, Christian would have a 'sore heart'. Eight days later the Whitsunday holiday rolled round and the Potterrow celebrated in the spring sunshine. That afternoon, Christian went to see Agnes and confessed that she still could not repay her debt. Agnes would brook no further delay and would listen to no more excuses. Another violent argument was heard along the Potterrow, with

17th century woodcut,
witches presenting wax
poppets to the Devil
© Wellcome Library

17th century woodcut,
witchesdancing with
the Devil© Wellcome
Library

17th century woodcut, woman
meeting a 'black gentleman'
and his dog © Personal Collection

17th century woodcut of Edinburgh showing the Potterrow Port © Public Domain

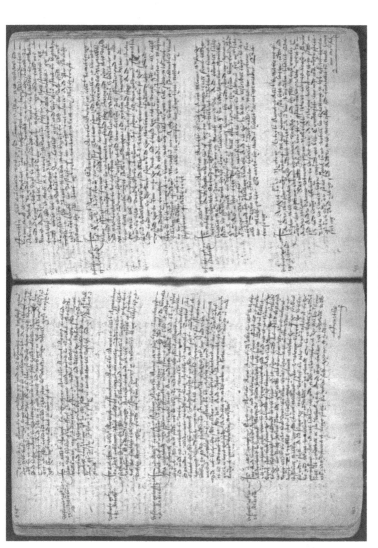

Page of Agnes' trial records © National Library of Scotland

Charles I © Public Domain

17th century Edinburgh tenement © Mike and Jessica Troughton

Greyfriars Kirk © Mike and Jessica Troughton

The Potterrow
© Mike and Jessica Troughton

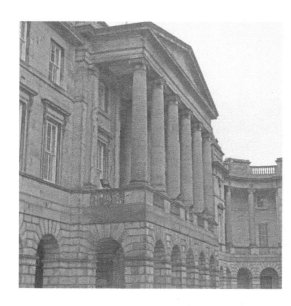

The Old Scottish Parliament © Mike and Jessica Troughton

The Witches Well at Edinburgh Castle © Mike and Jessica Troughton

The Castle © Mike and Jessica Troughton

St Giles, the High Kirk, Edinburgh © Mike and Jessica Troughton

Agnes shouting that she had warned Christian she would have a 'sore heart' if the debt was not paid. The two women continued shouting in Agnes' shop while outside everyone was celebrating the spring holiday and, probably, listening to the ongoing argument between Agnes and Christian. After a few minutes, Christian left and headed home to discover that her husband, Robert, had had an accident and had broken his leg. Robert had been carried home in extreme pain and a barber was called to try and set the bone. Over and above the obvious pain and suffering, there was a real risk that Robert might die, lose the leg due to infection or end up crippled if the bone was not set properly. As Christian did not have the money to pay Agnes, it is doubtful if she would have had the money to pay for a competent barber to set her husband's leg. Left crippled, Robert would probably have been unable to work and provide for the family. 'I'll break your legs' was a very effective piece of intimidation among moneylenders, carrying as it did the threat of loss of work and potential destitution as well as pain. For a family man with a dependent wife and children, this was a particularly chilling threat. Christian was left with an injured husband who was not earning, a barber who needed paying and still had the outstanding debt to Agnes. Despite the holiday atmosphere, the Potterrow was left with more proof of Agnes' power.

* * *

In August, the General Assembly met in Edinburgh. The new minister of Greyfriars Kirk, George Gillespie, attended. Andrew Ramsay had moved on to work within the Covenanter cause and the second charge at Greyfriars remained vacant. George Gillespie had transferred to Greyfriars from the parish Kirk in Wemyss on the Fife coast. This was a big promotion for him coming from a relatively small, peaceful parish to one in the heart of the capital and the centre of Covenanter activity. It was also a change from a small, mainly rural fishing parish to one that included local residents, travellers and traders and served some rich merchants, the middling folk and the poor of the Potterrow tenements. But Gillespie was no country fool; Fife had had its fair share of witchcraft trials in the previous years in which he had actively pursued those accused. It was Gillespie who had prosecuted the three witchcraft trials that had taken place while Margaret Mitchelson, the Covenanting prophetess, had been being lauded in Edinburgh. It appears that despite the antagonism generated by the Reformation, in matters such as this the Calvinist mindset mirrored the equally hypocritical one of their Catholic adversaries: Reginald Scot wrote of the Pope 'He canoniseth the rich for saints and banneth the poor for witches.'[84]

On 5 August, when the General Assembly voted to pass a further Condemnatory Act against witches George Gillespie was present and voted for the act.

Sess. 11, August 5, 1642:

The Assembly ... do therefore ordain all Presbyteries to give up to the Justice the names of the adulterers, incestuous persons, witches, and sorcerers, and others guilty of such grosse and fearfull sins, within their bounds, that they may be processed, and punished according to the laws of this Kingdom; and that the Presbyteries and Synods be carefull herein, as they will answer to the Generall Assemblies. And because that witchcraft, charming, and such like, proceeds many times from ignorance, therefore, the Assembly ordains all Ministers, especially in these parts where these sins are frequent, to be diligently preaching, catechising, and conferring, to inform their people thereintill.[85]

The idea from the Kirk was to stamp out the Devil. Those who were witches or consulted them would be despatched to God's judgement, while the saved could then go about their business quite safely. The war, plague and famine added to the terror of predestination. The previous Condemnatory Acts had had little effect and by 1642 the Kirk realised that they needed stronger measures against the Devil. The Kirk Session was a local church court first established in 1560 and comprising the minister and elders of an individual parish or congregation. The role of the Session was, initially, to enforce church discipline after the establishment of the Kirk following the Reformation. This role rapidly expanded to include the moral welfare of the local parishioners. By the mid-17th century, with the chaos that was engulfing the Kirk, the role of the sessions was expanded yet again but also strengthened such that every aspect of life was now under its control. The Kirk Session was everywhere, a familiar if somewhat disconcerting presence in everyone's life. An individual might live an entire lifetime without ever coming into contact with the law courts, but the Session was everywhere. The law might judge you if you committed a crime and broke the law, the Kirk Session judged every aspect of your life: how you dressed, what you ate, how you conducted yourself in public, how you spoke, what you said and even what you thought. The starting assumption was always that you were guilty of sin, it was just a matter of which sin and how corrupt you were. The Kirk Session was effectively a court that sat in judgement of sin and the 17th century was a century pervaded by sin. One of the problems was that women, by their very nature, were tainted by original sin, but as mothers were responsible for the moral welfare of their children and so were held to a higher standard than men. Women who did not dress modestly, or laughed too loudly in public were sinful and were severely castigated by the Session. Men who got drunk and beat their wives might be given a rebuke, but the wife's behaviour was also called into question: what had she done to deserve the beating?

In addition to this was, of course, the Kirk obsession that Scotland was under attack by Satan himself. To the elite of the Kirk, the Devil was a fallen angel, a spiritual entity that embodied all evil who was now enacting his evil will across the country. To the ordinary people in the Potterrow, Auld Nick was a terrifying monster that roamed the streets snatching up anyone he could find. But the Session was also roaming the streets in search of those who might fall foul of the Devil, including those who might be or might consult witches. Agnes' reputation as a witch was now a real danger not only to her, but also to those who consulted her for any reason. The feeling that you were surrounded by sin permeated the everyday. Witchcraft was just the ultimate sin in a world full of danger.

Greyfriars Kirk Session was quick to name and shame those women from the Potterrow that fell short of the expected moral behaviour of parishioners. However, once he settled into Greyfriars, George Gillespie seems to have lost his enthusiasm for chasing the Devil out of the parish, or at least those parts of the parish where Auld Nick was most likely to be found lurking. The new minister, it seems, had very quickly realised the potential for promotion that Greyfriars Kirk represented and that was not to be found in the likes of the Potterrow. Gillespie soon attracted attention for the fervour of his sermons, which were delivered from the safety of the pulpit in Greyfriars Kirk. The close proximity of Greyfriars to St Giles meant that those who wished could easily go to either church on a Sunday. Greyfriars was a newly built church sitting in a pleasant location away from the noise and smells of the High Street. For those of a religious nature, Gillespie's sermons found an eager new audience. For those of a less religious bent, the novelty of a new minister in a relatively new church was a welcome distraction. Gillespie's fulminations against the Devil and all his works must have been thrilling but also not a little frightening to the congregation.

Despite the 'best efforts' of the Reverend Gillespie to inform his parishioners of the dangers of witchcraft and witches, Agnes continued unmolested in the Potterrow.[86] The problem for Gillespie, and the Kirk in general, was practical as much as theological. If you have no money to pay a doctor and there is a local woman who can help, what are you supposed to do when your child falls ill? If you have no money to pay the rent man when he comes knocking and the bank would not even let you walk through their front door but the woman with the shop will lend to you, what choice do you have? Fetch the witch or watch your child die? Borrow from the witch or face a Scottish winter on the streets? The minister, snug in his manse and able to pay for medical treatment when needed did not live in the cold damp tenements of the Potterrow. He could preach all he liked on a Sabbath afternoon but the reality of life for the poor of Edinburgh, even those in his own parish, was practically a closed book to Gillespie. He would have been aghast had he ventured down to hear what was said openly in the streets of the Potterrow.

* * *

John Robieson, a journeyman, who had been travelling and working in the Low Countries came home to the Potterrow. John had been abroad for several years and so was probably unaware of Agnes' increasing ill-temper and malevolence. He may also have been unaware of the growing hysteria in the Kirk over Auld Nick and his presence on every street corner. During the Reformation, the majority of people in the Low Countries had converted to Protestantism, although there were still some Catholics in the south. However, their main religious influences had been Martin Luther and the Christian Humanist Erasmus rather than Calvin and John Knox, and although the Protestant church in the Low Countries were forever vigilant over the possible presence of the Devil, they were not obsessed in the way the Scottish Kirk was. The Netherlands had one of the lowest rates of witchcraft trials in Europe in the 17th century and discontinued the trials earlier than most other countries. As a result of his time living in the Low Countries, John may have been unaware of just how dangerous the word 'witch' had become in Scotland. However, he was not unaware of Agnes' reputation for sorcery. Given the later charges that were laid against Agnes stretching back several years and the fact that John had been abroad for a long time, it is interesting that on first seeing her he called her a witch.

Within a few days of his return John was walking down the Potterrow when he saw Agnes and shouted out, 'what now, Annie the witch, are ye living?' Agnes was furious and replied, 'what rack, John, what say ye?' If John did not understand that Agnes meant to 'rack' him with pain he soon found out. After walking away from Agnes, he started to feel unwell and by the evening took to his bed with 'a flux' and severe pains caused by her 'witchcraft' and sorcery. A flux was an excessive flow or discharge of fluid like haemorrhage or diarrhoea, and was probably a case of typhoid or a similar illness caused by the poor living conditions in the Potterrow.

John was a relatively young man. Unmarried, he had, like many before him, undertaken an apprenticeship although it is unclear as what. On becoming a journeyman, he had not stayed with his master. There may have been no place for him or the relationship may not have been an amicable one. In any case, John had sought his fortune abroad, most probably in the Low Countries where there was plenty of work for qualified artisans in cities such as Bruges or Amsterdam. Born and raised in the Potterrow, John may have come home for a visit or permanently, or even to fight for the Covenanting cause. He was living with his elderly parents when he first saw Agnes and it was his mother that nursed him through his illness.

The illness, whatever it was and however it had been caused, persisted up to Agnes' arrest. The continuation of this illness is interesting. Even if John had refused to apologise, why should Agnes have been so angry as to 'cause' the illness to be prolonged? Her reputation was widely known around the area and had not caused her any problems in the past. In fact, it had probably worked to her advantage with people who feared her power only too eager to repay their debts quickly. Was it the fact that John had shouted at Agnes in the street, showing no fear? Or was it the slow but inexorable rising tension in the town that was causing Agnes to be concerned? The calm after the Bishop's Wars was in a fragile state; it would take only a slight spark to ignite further trouble. The Kirk was wary. They had rooted out anyone showing less than absolute zeal for Calvinism from the Kirk and from town councils across Scotland, and now turned their attention to their parishioners. The majority were, as was obvious to any minister worth his salt, predestined for damnation, but that did not mean one should not search for the Devil and his handmaidens in the dark corners of the town.

The Reformation had, obviously, changed religious life in Scotland. The theology of belief was altered, the relationship between the individual and God was altered and the relationship between church and state was altered. What mattered to most ordinary people, however, was the relationship between them and their local parish minister. According to the new Calvinist Kirk of Scotland, Catholic priests were all at best lazy and corrupt, or at worst in league with Auld Nick himself. They sold indulgences, slept with nuns, mumbled Latin prayers they did not understand and lived off the poor. That may have been true for some priests, but what the Kirk had ignored was the fact that most parish priests came from their parishes: they did not live in grand manses. They would drink a pint of ale with you and have a joke. They did not believe themselves to be God's Elect while thinking you were preordained to damnation. They were human. They understood human frailty. They drank and gambled and smoked like everyone else. And crucially, they visited their parishioners. It was all very well for Gillespie to take up his post in Greyfriars Kirk and preach to the great and the good who sat in his pews on a Sunday but he was nowhere to be seen in the day-to-day life of the Potterrow. There were Kirk ministers who cared for the poor of their parishes, but the unbending nature of Calvinism, or at least the Scottish interpretation of it, stated that the poor were already preordained for damnation. There was a distaste for the poor, an aversion to any contact with them. The thieves, prostitutes, poor day labourers and ordinary weavers that made up the Potterrow did not appear to be in God's plan. The Calvinist faith further dictated that each person had an individual relationship with God. The average Kirk minister spent his time in solitary prayer developing that relationship. The poor of the Potterrow were expected to do the same. Calvinism was even more exacting to its ministers. If God had preordained some to be saved and some to be damned that was all very good, but how could one know for certain that one was among those who were saved? The diaries left behind by many Kirk ministers records their struggles between the absolute certainty that they were saved when they were in their pulpits preaching, to nights of self-doubt when the country faced plague or famine.

For George Gillespie, the poor and middling people of the Potterrow would have to face God alone. He was convinced of his own salvation. As the great and the good filled Greyfriars Kirk every Sunday, Gillespie received a weekly affirmation of his own righteousness. The poor in the back pews were of little consequence. An ambitious man who would go on to become the minister at the High Kirk of Edinburgh, he seldom visited the Potterrow.

While Gillespie was ignoring the Potterrow, the Covenanters were ignoring the continued pleas from the English Parliamentarians for help against the King. Argyll understood the unpredictability of war and, with the threat that the troublesome situation in the Highlands posed, he was reluctant to commit any troops to the English cause. The losses in Ireland weighed heavily on his mind. Biding his time, he hoped that the war in England might be resolved without the need for Scottish troops. Although the more sober-minded among the Covenanters agreed with Argyll, it was becoming increasingly difficult to maintain a position of neutrality. In Campveere, the main Dutch port for Scottish wool, Thomas Cunningham, a Covenanter, was arguing with Sir Patrick Drummond, a Royalist, who was using his position to raise money for Charles.[87] More and more arguments were affecting Scottish trade and the merchants of Edinburgh were becoming more vocal in their complaints. The weavers in the Potterrow saw their wages cut as merchants dealt with the uncertainties in the wool trade. In November the English Parliamentarians sent a letter to the Scottish Council accusing the King of planning to use foreign Catholic troops. Charles countered by decrying the accusation. Whatever the truth of the matter, with the Kirk seeing Auld Nick round every corner, the Parliamentarian's letter was believed; the King's denial was not and the rumour of Catholic troops about to land in Scotland ran round Edinburgh.[88] Argyll wrote to Charles urging him to speak with his English Parliamentarians and sent two representatives of the Scottish Council to Oxford to reason with him. The politicians discussed the deteriorating situation in the warm Parliament building while the poor in the Potterrow froze in their tenements. No one could see a peaceful resolution and it was a miserable Christmas for all.

9

Haunting

IN FEBRUARY 1643, the Queen, who had been in the Netherlands raising money for the war, arrived back in England. When
in York she met several Scottish Royalists led by Montrose,
Lord Aboyne (Huntly's younger son) and Lord Ogilvie (Airlie's
son). Montrose assured the Queen that the Covenanters were
not popular in Scotland, that the majority were 'for the King'
and that they were only waiting for a sign to rise up in his
name, overthrow the rule of Argyll and support Charles in his
war against the English Parliamentarians.[89] This was, of course,
untrue. There were some who opposed the Covenanters but
they were definitely in the minority; the rivalry between Argyll
and Montrose was due to the complicated politics of the Highlands and had little or nothing to do with the King's quarrels
with his English parliament. While the Scottish Royalists were
ready to fight the Covenanters at home, few if any relished a
long march to fight in the south of England. Montrose may
have been less than truthful in what he was saying to Queen
Henriette, but the visit was more a political move on his part
to prove to Argyll that he was still a force to be reckoned with.

While Montrose was politicking in York, the Potterrow
had increasing trade disruption to contend with. For every new
pair of boots or clothing bought by a Covenanter there was

a loss of trade from Royalist sympathisers who were closing up their Edinburgh townhouses and retreating to their country estates. Young girls who had worked as maids now found themselves out of work outwith the usual quarter days, when contracts were usually ended, and without having been paid. Wages that were owed were difficult to claim when the 'master' had moved to Kirkliston or Kirknewton. With little money to pay their rent, they had none to spend in Agnes' shop. For those desperate enough and with no other resources, Agnes the moneylender was approached before the money was spent with Agnes the shopkeeper.

The spring of 1643 saw the Covenanters in a quandary. While they retained primacy in Scotland, albeit with one eye constantly watching the Highland clans and their machinations, the war that had now broken out between Charles and the English Parliament was increasingly causing concern, as did the continuing politicking of the Scottish Royalists. The King remained determined to create a unified church across Scotland and England, and the Covenanters wanted the same. Charles wanted Anglican Episcopacy and the Covenanters wanted Calvinist Presbyterianism. In late April, Loudon, representing the Scottish Privy Council, and Henderson, representing the General Assembly of the Kirk, met with the King in Oxford. They presented Charles with a petition to impose a unified Presbyterian faith across all of the United Kingdom. In return for Charles agreeing to this change in religious policy they would pledge the Covenanters to fight for him against the Parliamentarians. Being slightly more honest than Montrose had been, they openly told Charles that if he rejected their proposal, they would not act as mediators between him and his parliament.[90] Charles rejected the proposal, but neither did he accept Montrose's suggestion of raising the Scottish Royalists on his behalf.[91] Hamilton assured the King that Scotland would stay neutral in his argument with the Parliamentarians. Charles believed Hamilton and also believed that the war would be over by the autumn. There was, therefore, no need to involve the Scots in the war which would have been a further expense. This was despite his previous pleas for help from the Scots. Moreover, Charles told the Scottish delegation he did not want them to even act as mediators with the Parliament. This was something the Scots had no intention of doing, but Charles wanted to be seen to reject them whatever the Scots' own intentions. The Scots returned to Edinburgh and within ten days received a letter from Charles reminding them of his goodwill towards them, how deceitful the English Parliamentarians were and how they were not to be trusted.[92] While the Privy Council discussed Charles' letter in private, he wrote in a similar vein to the Town Council. The contents of the Council's letter were widely distributed across the city causing confusion and anxiety all round.[93] Midlothian coal mine owners and traders who had been selling coal to London – Newcastle was blockaded by the Royalists – now worried that they might not get paid. They had hiked their prices for the London market and restricted sales in Edinburgh. Now they returned to Edinburgh, but sales were down. Miners were laid off and young men wandered into Edinburgh looking for work and swelling the ranks of those hanging about the Potterrow looking for casual labour. The old dislike and distrust of miners by the town folk soon spilled over into street fights. The Potterrow bore the brunt.

* * *

The main issue for Agnes was money. The war was lasting longer than anyone had imagined and was costing far more than anyone had realised. England had not been at war for many years, and the cost of equipping a modern army and paying their wages was now far in excess of what the English Parliamentarians had. Loans were raised in the banking houses of Amsterdam and their confederates in Edinburgh. While this raised money for the English it left Edinburgh short of hard cash and, as loans on the outcome of a war were a risky venture, high interest rates were levied which percolated into the city's finances. Prices shot up across the city. Agnes had to pay her suppliers more and increased her prices accordingly. Her customers, who didn't have the cash to pay, then borrowed from her at higher rates of interest. Not all could afford to pay her higher prices, not all could afford to borrow. Her business was becoming increasingly precarious, her temper ever more uncertain.

But Agnes was not the only one with a temper. Agnes' daughter, Margaret, who lived nearby, had an argument with John Cockburn, a local weaver, over some cloth he had promised her. It is not clear if John had agreed to weave some cloth for Margaret and was late in doing so or if he was lending her some cloth, but in both situations the lack of cloth was important. Most weavers worked as 'piece workers'; they were paid for the cloth they produced. But if a weaver promised to produce some cloth and did not, they could gain a bad reputation and lose potential customers to the many other weavers that lived nearby. Equally, weavers often lent out cloth to those who could not afford to buy some and to promise the cloth and then not deliver could, again, generate a bad reputation.

Rental cloth was usually of lower quality and could be loaned out several times over as a way for a weaver to supplement his income. Clothing was expensive and most ordinary people had barely more than one or two changes of clothing. There were occasions when cloth was needed but the individual could not afford to buy and so would rent. If, for example, Margaret was going to a job at one of the 'big hooses' she might have needed a temporary piece of cloth to use as a shawl. Without appropriate clothing she might not get the job she was hoping for, so for John not to produce the cloth when promised had real consequences.

Whatever John's reasons were, Margaret was furious. She stopped him in the street and started arguing with him. Angry words were yet again exchanged before John walked away from Margaret and headed home. The argument, however, was still unresolved and Margaret had shouted various insults, curses and threats as John had left. That night John was sleeping beside his wife when he suddenly woke and found that Agnes and Margaret were sitting on his bed scratching at his chest. Terrified, John called out, 'God be in this house, I see you both well enough.' At this point, John's wife woke up and saw no one. John was becoming more agitated and continued to say that Agnes and Margaret were on his bed attacking him. John's apprentice, who slept in the front shop, came through and with John's wife tried to reassure him that no one was there and that the doors and windows were all bolted shut. John continued to call out 'God be in this house' two or three more times before Agnes and Margaret finally disappeared.

While Agnes' powers as a 'witch' and her ability to cast illness on an individual were well known the length of the

Potterrow, the fact that she could now haunt people in their own homes must have been a terrifying development. Moreover, it now appeared as if her daughter was a witch as well. There are few episodes of hauntings in the trial records for Scottish 'witches'. Although not unknown, it was not a common occurrence. Whatever the nature of the disagreement had been between John and Margaret, for the two women to appear to the weaver at night in his own home through bolted doors and windows would strongly suggest that Agnes was considered so terrifying and so powerful that John could easily imagine her haunting him in his bedroom. The disagreement between Margaret and John was never fully resolved; although the records are unclear as to whether the promised cloth was delivered or not, there were no more haunting incidents.

Yet for all the fear that Agnes engendered, life in the neighbourhood continued as before. Food had to be bought, rent had to be paid and, for those with little money, Agnes was the last resort. William Smith was unemployed and needed money. Approaching Agnes, he offered to pawn some good cloth to her. Cloth, especially good quality woollen cloth, was a very valuable commodity. With the exchange of cloth for money, William was at less risk from Agnes' temper should anything go wrong, especially as the cloth were of a greater value than the money she offered. Or so he thought. However, after having handed over his cloth and receiving the money, William was no better off. He was still out of work and the money he had received for his cloth had not lasted long. He started to claim that Agnes had 'tricked and deceived him' and, by laying some 'witchcraft' on him, had reduced him to poverty. Whatever had happened, William was unable to pay back the money and redeem his cloth. Agnes kept the pawned cloth, which she was then able to sell on at extra profit to herself. While many moneylenders pawned goods in lieu of monies owed, most returned them in good faith when the debt was repaid. Most people who pawned goods and were unable to redeem them accepted their loss as part of the risk one took when pawning property. Few put the loss down to witchcraft. William could well have been the biggest spendthrift and wastrel in the neighbourhood, but with Agnes' reputation being what it was most of the locals believed William's story.

Curiously, Agnes did not seem to be bothered by William's claims of trickery and witchcraft. Was she in a rare good mood? Or had the profit she had made on the material far outweighed the insult from William? There do not appear to have been any other pawnshops in the Potterrow and so even if William was correct and Agnes had somehow tricked him there was nowhere else for the residents to go if they needed to pawn goods for money. Most pawnshops worked on a degree of trust. Taking goods to a pawnshop in an area other than where you lived raised suspicions. Were the goods stolen? Did you have the right to pawn them? Would you ever redeem the goods? Few pawnshops would accept goods from those they did not know or were not from the local neighbourhood. The Potterrow may well have believed William's story, after all most people knew Agnes was a witch, but as they had few other options, they continued to pawn their goods with her nonetheless.

King Charles was also running short of money and had offered to trade the Orkney Islands to the Danish in return for the use of their navy.[94] The plan came to nothing, but when it became known it further raised tension. Few people in the

Potterrow knew where the Orkney Islands were, but that was irrelevant. If the King was willing to trade away the islands what else was he willing to trade? And in what little regard did he hold his northern Kingdom if he was willing to trade parts of it away to wage war on his southern Kingdom?

Watching what was going on in England over the summer, the Covenanters became concerned that the war might indeed be over by the autumn and that Charles might defeat the English Parliamentarians and impose Episcopacy on the Scots. To stave off this threat, the Covenanters drew up the Solemn League and Covenant. This agreement between the English and Scottish Parliaments agreed to the reservation of the reformed religion in Scotland, the reformation of religion in England and Ireland according to the 'word of God' and the 'extirpation or popery (and) prelacy'. It did not clearly state 'Presbyterianism', which would later prove to be problematic.[95] Presbyterians were a minority in the Church of England and the religious Independents were opposed to any form of state church. At the same time, John Pym was writing constantly to his friends in Edinburgh urging the Scots to fight the King. The Covenanters finally, in late July, wrote to Pym in Westminster offering a formal alliance. They had discovered yet another plot to use the Earl of Antrim's clan to invade Scotland at Charles' behest.[96] More rumours ran round Edinburgh.

While the various factions were politicking, the Kirk was becoming increasingly wary over the actions of Auld Nick. The war in England and Ireland and the threat of the Irish invading Scotland was surely the Devil's work. The Assembly sat and passed yet another Condemnatory Act against witches: 'Sess.

Ult., August 19, 1643: The Assembly, considering [...] certain Overtures anent Witchcraft and Charming.'[97]

The problem was, yet again, no one seemed to be paying any attention to the Kirk despite the very vocal tirades of Kirk Sessions across the country. In fact, 1643 was a bumper year for Auld Nick. There were at least 40 recorded witchcraft trials across Scotland involving at least 90 accused witches, almost all of whom were found guilty and executed. For all his hand-maidens had been found and executed, Auld Nick had managed to terrorise several communities with his witches. And if 90 had been found how many more were still lurking in the shadows?

On 9 January, Agnes Grant of Elgin was described as:

> This wretchit creature hes bene euer and as yit is of ane exceeding ivill reporte, and there have bene money vehement presumptions exhibited to us that schee hes bene accessorie to diverse divilische practises.[98]

In February, Jonet Thomesone was tried in Orkney and this was followed in April, by a rash of cases with Helen Hunter, Cirstain Marwicke, Thomas Cors and Cristiane Leisk, Cristane Pollok, Margaret Raine and William Scotte, 'ane vagabond warlache' all being brought to trial.[99] These were followed by further trials in May, June and July. In June, in Dunfermline, 'Jonett Fentoun the witch died miserably in ward, and wes brot to the witches knowe.'[100] Down the road in Culross, on 8 June, Marjorie Burgess, being delated for witchcraft by John Kynnard, the self-confessed witch had 'fled the toune'.[101]

Fife seemed to be a real hotspot. Issobell Marr was arrested in August, also in Dunfermline. She was

> delaittit be the rest of her nybor witches for a witche, and being detained yrfre in the laiche thieves' hole' shoe hangit hersel and was cairyed to the witche knowe and yerdit.[102]

On 16 November, Marione Fisher of Edinburgh was dragged before the Kirk Session and accused of being a witch. After examination, it was decided that she was 'given up to be ane ordinarie charmer' and was ordered 'sit in sackcloth, in the middle of the church'. Although Marione had received a very rare light sentence, she was warned that 'if ever schoe be fund to wse anu such lyke in tym cuming, to suffer death ane real witche.'[103] Johnne Brighe of Fossoway was not so fortunate. On 24 November, he was found guilty of 'dyverse poyntis of sorcerie'.[104] The year ended with the arrest of Janet Barker and Margaret Lauder in Edinburgh. Listed as servants in the 'toun of Edinburgh' they were formally accused before the Kirk Session of being witches. Both women denied the charge. Under interrogation they still refused to confess and the Session brought in James Scobie, the witch brodder. Witch brodders, or witch prickers, were professional men who would stick steel bodkins into the flesh of accused witches to prove they had the Devil's Mark and thus were witches. Scobie brodded the women and found the Devil's Mark on both of them. After a brief trial they were both found guilty and were worriet to death and their bodies burnt.[105] To be worriet was to be strangled to death.

While this misery and mayhem was continuing in the Potterrow, George Gillespie was nowhere to be seen. There had been an Irish rebellion in 1641 which had terrified everyone with tales of Catholic atrocities repeated and embellished by Protestant ministers across Scotland and England, 'proof' of the evils of popery, they said. The division between Charles and his Parliament had deteriorated into open warfare. Although this had initially been confined to the south of England, by the autumn of 1643 the Covenanters were growing increasingly worried as the fighting grew closer to Scotland. These worries were confirmed as Royalist and Covenanters were now openly brawling in the streets of Edinburgh. The drinking dens in the Potterrow were frequently visited by the baillies trying to separate drunken men arguing and fighting.

In August, the English Commissioners, sent by Pym, arrived in Edinburgh. The Solemn League and Covenant was drafted within ten days and sent down to Westminster. The Scots Estates then drafted a further order for all able-bodied men to stand ready at 24 hours' warning. When Charles read the Solemn League and Covenant, he condemned it outright and forbade any and all of his subjects from signing it.[106] In September 1643, after the year's harvest had been gathered, the order from the Town Council went out across Edinburgh: all men aged between 16 and 60 were called to the colours. They were to come with 40 days' worth of provisions and no exceptions were to be made. Edinburgh Town Council announced it would provide 1,200 men not only with their 40 days of provisions, but also fully kitted out with uniforms and small arms.[107] The announcement made a great stir across the city. The Covenanters celebrated that they were at last to go to war and bring the King back to the right faith; the Royalists quietly discussed their fears. For the ordinary people of Edinburgh and in the

Potterrow, the order was a disaster. While most young men in the city did genuinely want to join the colours, their parents often had a different view. What family could afford to lose a father or son who might be the main breadwinner? Even if only one son was to go, where was the family supposed to find 40 days' worth of provisions? Even for those with money to spare there were doubts. For all the cheering that had greeted the initial call to the colours, the reality of kitting out 1,200 men soon became apparent to the town's merchants. The tailors and cordiners might produce the uniforms, but who would pay? And once all those young men had left, how was the town to function on a day-to-day basis? The initial order had stated that no exemptions were to be made, but some merchants soon found their family doctor could be persuaded to write of their son's bad health. Forged certificates of exemption were soon being bought for an ever-increasing price. For those who could not afford a friendly doctor or a certificate, hiding in the back closes of tenements was their only option.

The Covenanters were also starting to realise just how unpopular the Solemn League and Covenant was among many of the English Parliamentarians, despite it only having been signed by them at the end of September and hailed as an oath of 'fealty and allegiance unto Christ the King of Kings'. The signing of the Covenant had been celebrated widely across Edinburgh, with Kirk ministers beside themselves with joy at the news, but this had masked the deep misgivings of many who saw it as a temporary political expedient. Oliver Cromwell, who was one of the most prominent opponents of the Covenant, had stated he would rather fight than see the Presbyterian faith imposed on England. The majority of English

Parliamentarians were chafing under the idea of the unbending Divine rule of Charles, but they were unwilling to replace it with the imposition of the iron will of Calvinist Predestination. The Covenant was put under more strain when the Covenanters and English Parliamentarians learned that the Marquis of Ormonde had made a truce in the King's name with the Irish rebels. The fear of the King's use of Irish Catholic troops in England or Scotland temporarily outweighed the concerns over the Covenant in both political camps. Not so in the Kirk.

The English rejection of Presbyterianism, the true and only faith, and the threat of Irish Catholics saw the Kirk becoming ever more vehement about the fact the Devil was roaming the land. As tensions rose across Edinburgh and the rest of Scotland, there was an increase in the number of witchcraft cases, further proving the Kirk correct. In the Potterrow there were more soldiers at the Port: some waiting to join their units, some sent out to find those who had not reported as ordered. The baillies too were out in force. Trading slowed as papers were checked and goods examined. Arguments broke out as some were seen to pass through the port easily and others less so. Bribes were offered and some taken, accusations of bribery and favouritism were daily occurrences. Arguments quickly turned violent and the baillies were kept busy arresting people and taking them off to the Tolbooth: some simply to cool off for a day or two, others, less fortunate, to be fined and kept in gaol for a week. Traders with a hint of an English accent were viewed with suspicion, their carts upset and their goods frequently spoiled. That year's Lammas day had been particularly harsh, with many landlords raising their rents in anticipation of future trouble. Those who had their contracts renewed found their wages reduced on the previous year. Many lost their positions to be replaced by younger, cheaper workers. To add to the misery, prices in the shops started to rise. It would be a harsh winter.

The situation in London was equally dire and the capital was short of coal. As an act of good faith, the Covenanters pushed Scottish miners to increase their work hours and their output, and vast amounts of coal were shipped down to London.[108] Although this helped, somewhat, to stave off some of the criticism from the likes of Cromwell, it did not endear the Parliament to the inhabitants of the Potterrow who faced a winter with a severe coal shortage and sky-high prices. The year finished with an agreement that the Scots would send an army of 18,000 foot and 2,000 horse, including artillery, to England. The English would pay for the army and both the Scots and the English would determine the peace terms with the King. This agreement was quickly followed by the death of John Pym leaving the way clear for Oliver Cromwell, with his open antipathy towards the Covenant, to take over the leadership of the English Parliamentarians. For the moment the alliance held, just. The main priority for the English Parliamentarians and the Covenanters was to win the war. The main priority for the people of the Potterrow was not to die of hypothermia.

10

A Witch's Gett

THE BEGINNING OF 1644 saw the residents of the Potterrow Port huddled indoors trying to escape the worst of the Edinburgh winter. The neighbourhood was worn down by the constant state of tension which seemed to be ratcheted up on an almost daily basis. Moreover, there seemed to be nothing anyone could do about it. George Gillespie's constant preaching that Auld Nick was roaming the land kept everyone terrified, but was also starting to pale. The same refrain had been heard for so long and yet the Kirk seemed powerless to do anything. The Potterrow was hungry, it was cold, it was tired, it was scared.

Sometime in early 1644, a woman called Janet Walker incurred Agnes' wrath over the non-payment of a debt. Janet was unmarried and lived with her sister and her sister's family. She was in the late stages of pregnancy when she pleaded with Agnes for more time to pay the debt. Agnes remained unmoved and demanded payment. Janet could not pay. As she had no husband and was possibly not working, or at least not enough to support herself, Janet was in dire straits. Although living with her sister, she was about to have another mouth to feed. Her sister's desire to give Janet a home may well have worn thin when a new baby arrived. Whatever her exact situation was, she could not pay Agnes. After yet another screaming match in the middle of the street, Agnes cursed Janet and threatened her with a variety of misfortunes and illnesses if she did not find the money from somewhere. This was dangerous; pregnancy in the 17th century was not easy. Maternal death rates were high. Although exact figures cannot be known, it has been estimated that around one in 40 pregnancies resulted in maternal death, with an even higher rate in poor areas. As most women had multiple pregnancies, the risk of death over a woman's childbearing years was considerable. Big risk factors included conditions such as pre-eclampsia, and infections which were exacerbated by poor diet and a general lack of sanitation. The other big risk factor was stress. Being cursed by Agnes when pregnant, could, therefore, have become a fatal combination for Janet and her baby. After her encounter with Agnes, Janet took to her bed with a 'grievous sickness of palsie and feaver'. In the meantime, Agnes went about her business unconcerned.

Whether Agnes' curse had been calculated or not, Janet's illness continued for several weeks and eventually her sister began to fear for her life and that of her unborn child. Finally, after several more weeks of nursing Janet, her sister came to Agnes and begged her to take pity on Janet and the baby and to take the sickness away. Some money may have changed hands. Agnes finally relented and 'lifted' the illness from Janet who made a full recovery and gave birth to a perfectly healthy baby some weeks later.

The continued strain on Scottish finances due to the war had a knock-on effect across Edinburgh and Agnes' livelihood would have been affected. Did a public argument with a heavily pregnant woman tell the world that Agnes would accept no excuses for non-payment of debts? Others in the neighbourhood may have given their customers a little credit due to the state of affairs in the town; Agnes would not.

Alexander Johnstoune was another of Agnes' neighbours. When his wife had a baby girl, Agnes decided she wanted to be named as the child's godmother. In the tradition of the Kirk, a godmother was present at the christening of the child and promised to see that the child was raised to be a good Christian. Occasionally a child would be named after their godparent. The godmother would also offer to guide the child in moral matters and could claim legal guardianship of the child as her own if anything untoward were to happen to the child's parents – a very necessary safeguard in a time where death rates were so high. But Agnes also came from the world of magic; a world that recognised the primacy of female knowledge and skill in the world of magic and magical beings. This was, potentially, a child that might follow her in the ways of magic. A child that she could teach and mould to her will. Having a godchild would also have enhanced Agnes' reputation in the magical world. Young children were often thought to be able to commune with the faeries and other spirits, and so could be of help to Agnes.

The faeries of 17th century Scotland were not the soft-winged pretty creatures of late Victorian fancy. These were supernatural beings around the size of a toddler who could be kind if you were kind to them, mischievous if the mood took then and downright wicked if they wanted.[109] Even the most gentle-natured faerie enjoyed tricking people and they could change from kind to cruel in the blink of an eye and for no apparent reason. They inhabited a supernatural world infested with beings such as goblins, elves, selkies, sprites, kelpies and the like, all of whom were generally malevolent creatures of uncertain temper. They could, occasionally, be coaxed into helping to find lost property or healing a sick child, but mostly they were the spirits that would bite and nip you in the night leaving you covered in bruises. They would trip you so that you fell and broke your leg, or they would steal your money and ruin your work as a weaver or a brewer. If you crossed these spirits in any way, they might blight your sheep and cattle. Animals that wandered too close to a faerie ring and became ill were known as 'elf-shot'.[110] And, of course, their greatest threat of all was to steal your baby and leave a change-ling in its place. Faeries had to give a teind, a tax, to the Devil every seven years and would give a human baby in place of their own. Changeling babies frequently died, but those who lived were always considered suspicious and thrawn natured. With that reputation, most people were, quite rightly, terrified of faeries and would approach the likes of Agnes for protection from them in the form of an amulet made of iron or from the twig of a Rowan tree. There were probably few faeries to be found in the Potterrow, but they inhabited places such as Arthur's Seat and the surrounding scrubland that was frequently used by folk from the Potterrow to supplement their diet with rabbit or squirrel. There were places underneath the crags where no one ventured to go; there were faerie rings that no one dared to cross.

However, for all their malevolence, faeries were known to be have a special bond with babies and very young children. It was believed that children could see faeries when adults could not and that children and faeries could communicate well. If Agnes had a goddaughter, it would make it easier to placate the faeries and ask for their help when needed. For those like Agnes, the faeries could be a real source of power and help. In the famous case of the 'witch' Isobell Gowdie, she spoke of meeting and dining with the king and queen of the faeries and declared that it was the faeries who taught her how to fly and escape from her tormentors.[111] Gowdie's case was not typical of Scottish witch trials, but the confession that she had communed with the faeries was not overly commented upon by her interrogators, partly because the interrogators were more concerned with her meetings with the Devil but also because it was a universally accepted truth that a witch should be in contact with the faerie folk.

In addition to the supernatural world, a goddaughter would also increase Agnes' status in the ordinary world of the Potterrow. To be named as a godmother was to be recognised as someone who was trustworthy, someone who was honourable, someone who was deserving of respect. Even though this would have meant a visit to Greyfriars Kirk, a very rare event for Agnes, the Christian aspect of being named godmother would probably have been minimal. What was more important for Alexander and his wife, living in the dark tenements of the Potterrow, was having someone named who would care for your child if necessary. For Agnes, with only one daughter who does not appear to have had any children her own, the child represented another potential person who might look after her in her old age.

For Agnes, the matter may have been very simple, but her request put Alexander in an extremely difficult position. To say yes was to have the local witch as his child's godmother. Was that a good thing? Surely, they would be safe from Agnes' temper? Was it a bad thing? What if she took their child away, how could they stop her?

To say no to the request was to anger the neighbourhood witch. Would that lead to trouble? Would she curse them or their child? After much thought, Alexander answered Agnes. No, she could not be named as his daughter's godmother. Agnes was furious. Everyone in the neighbourhood knew of the little girl's birth and of Agnes' request of the parents. She had been insulted by Alexander and his wife, and been humiliated round the Potterrow. By refusing Agnes, Alexander was implying that she was not trustworthy, not honourable and someone who was not deserving of respect. Agnes recognised the insult and, just as Alexander feared, threatened all sorts on him and his family. Finally, after much screaming and yelling she 'laid' a heavy sickness on Alexander and then watched as he took to his sickbed. Alexander was a fit, healthy young man and yet could not shake the illness: he was weak, had no energy and was tired all the time, his arms and legs were painful and tender, he felt queasy and could barely eat, he had a fever with intermittent chills, he had severe headaches and a rash. Those who had been foolish enough to laugh when Agnes' request to be the child's godmother had been refused were now silent as Alexander's sickness dragged on for several weeks, and then months. Whatever was said about the situation was now said behind closed doors and not within Agnes' hearing. Eventually, after six months, in which time Alexander had been bedridden and unable to provide for his wife and young daughter, he apologised to Agnes and begged her to lift the illness from him. Agnes 'lifted' his illness, although it was said that he was never again the man he had been and certainly had no more children.

Once again, Agnes had 'proved' her power. In this particular incident what might have caused a degree of unquiet in the Potterrow was that this row had been of Agnes' making. Previously, Agnes had fallen out with people because there had been an argument over herrings, or salt, or an insult. There had been some sort of interaction that had precipitated Agnes' wrath. In this case, however, Agnes had sought out Alexander. He had been minding his own business and celebrating the birth of his daughter when Agnes had thrust herself into his life. It seemed now that anyone could fall foul of Agnes no matter what they did or didn't do.

In the late summer of 1644, she quarrelled with yet another neighbour, Margaret Williamson, over money that was owed. Margaret had owed the money for some considerable time and for some reason, in this case, Agnes had even given her more time to repay the debt. When Lammas day arrived, Agnes could wait no longer but Margaret still did not have the money to pay her. Although she was due to go to Agnes' shop that morning, Margaret did not appear. Agnes tracked Margaret down at midday and there was a very public argument in the middle of the Potterrow with the entire neighbourhood watching. Agnes screamed and shouted abuse at Margaret. Finally, in a complete rage again, Agnes cursed Margaret and called on Auld Nick to 'blaw hir blind'. Margaret started to walk away, but Agnes kept up a stream of abuse. Margaret went home shaken but unharmed. Within a couple of days, however, she became seriously ill. She had a fever with a severe headache, could not eat and barely drank. Her family spent several weeks nursing her, but she failed to improve. Eventually the family managed to scrape together the money to pay Agnes what was due and an apology of sorts was even given. But this had either been too little too late, or Agnes' temper was becoming less tolerant. Unlike in previous occasions, Margaret remained seriously ill for several weeks after the debt was repaid. Her family nursed her as best they could until she finally and slowly recovered. Despite the care of her family, Margaret was left, as Agnes had cursed, permanently blind. This was a severe handicap for anyone except the very rich in the mid-17th century. Unable to work, the individual would have to fall back on the charity of their family if they had any willing to help. Many were initially cared for by their families, but would become a burden and be 'put out' of the family home. For older men who were blind and thus could neither work or help with domestic chores in any way, begging on the streets was frequently their only option. Even for those who had a home to live in, the world was a precarious place. Lighting, heating and cooking all used open flames, and burns and scalds could easily become infected and fatal. The very tenements they lived in held a hundred trip hazards and many became housebound as a result. Those who occasionally ventured out into the streets, or were abandoned by their families, ran the risk of attack. For Agnes to curse someone with the loss of sight was an horrific act. Agnes appeared completely unconcerned as to what the neighbourhood thought of her 'blinding' Margaret, probably because she was making money – lots of it. In addition, the Potterrow was reasonably quiet as winter set in and the fighting season was over for the year.

* * *

The winter may have prevented The Covenanters, Royalists, English Parliamentarians and even the Irish rebels from fighting, but it had not stopped them from talking – endlessly talking about what would happen in the spring, who was a traitor, who was the most godly, who was in league with the Devil. In Scotland, the winter lasted well into March and saw the usual deaths from starvation and hypothermia in the Potterrow. When tempers broke in London at the beginning of January over another alleged Royalist plot, the Scots army prepared to travel down to England to help their Parliamentarian friends. Young men from the poorer parts of Edinburgh, including the Potterrow, saw food and pay being offered by the army and signed up. Within days, despite the fact that most roads could only be passed with difficulty due to the snow, the Scots army was marching out of Edinburgh and down via Dunbar to Newcastle. They were halted at Berwick-upon-Tweed by a severe snowstorm and many of the youngsters who had joined suffered badly. As raw recruits and camp followers, they were poorly equipped in comparison to the regular soldiers and there were several deaths. The Scots finally crossed the border at the end of January.

At the same time, Charles had met with Montrose who planned to raise troops in the north of England and cross the border into Scotland, attacking the Covenanters in their own back yard. Randal MacDonnell, chief of Clan MacDonnell of Antrim, known as Antrim, was to attack Scotland from the west. The Scots army reached Newcastle in February, but got bogged down in besieging the city. As the siege dragged on, those Parliamentarians who were hostile to the Covenant started to raise complaints about the lack of progress of the

Scots, especially as they were paying for them. The argument over the imposition of Presbyterianism threatened to boil over when news of the great Royalist victory at Newark broke across the city. Royalist pamphleteers triumphantly blanketed the city with the news while more sober reports were received in general correspondence. Politicians on all sides discussed the implications while the Kirk in Scotland, seeing the advance of the forces of evil, redoubled their efforts in the pulpit. The start of the spring should have brought some respite to the Potterrow as the weather improved, but armed gangs were now a daily sight in the Potterrow as elsewhere and the almost constant street fights threatened to overwhelm the baillies. The news that the Scots army had divided in two, with half staying at the continued siege at Newcastle and half marching south toward Durham, did nothing to quell the worries of parents whose sons had left to fight. Those Royalists in Scotland who were not fighting started to stir up trouble at home. Complaints were heard in every tavern about the Covenanters. Who were they to forcibly enlist all the young men? Why should every 'guid man and guidwife' have to pay to supply an army to fight in England? Why should ordinary Scots be dragged into the English Parliament's argument with the King? Opposition to the Covenant remained strongest in the Highlands, but for the Potterrow the Covenant was not the issue; making a living was. At the end of April, the Royalists struck another blow as Montrose crossed the border at Gretna Green at the head of 1,300 horse. Worse still, he received a hero's welcome in Dumfries. All of Edinburgh was in an uproar. However, the northern Covenanter troops marched south to confront Montrose, Antrim failed to appear with his troops, the English troops refused to march any further north without reinforcement and, after the initial enthusiasm in Dumfries, no other Scots rallied to Montrose. The Royalist rising in Scotland was a failure.

* * *

Sometime at the end of May, Agnes' temper got the better of her again. This time, it was her daughter Margaret who started the trouble. Margaret had had a quarrel with yet another neighbour, Andrew Wilson's wife. Whatever the initial argument had been about, Andrew had become involved when he heard Margaret abusing his wife in the street. Coming to his wife's defence, Andrew rounded on Margaret and called her a 'witch's gett'. Margaret was furious and screamed at Andrew when her mother, hearing the commotion in the street, arrived to help Margaret. Agnes now took over and, cursing Andrew, called on Auld Nick to 'ryve the saul out of him'. Terrified, Andrew and his wife hurried home. That evening, Andrew had a fit. Lying shaking in his bed, he cried out repeatedly 'the Devil ryve the saul out of him'.

Calling someone a 'witch's gett', a witch's child, was a triple insult. Not only was Agnes a 'witch', but she was also a whore and her daughter was a bastard. The Scots language at that time had several words for child, the most common in Edinburgh being 'bairn'. Also used down the eastern Borders and Northumbria, it was the usual affectionate term for a baby or child. The word 'gett' had a very different meaning. A 'gett' was a child that was the result of a brief sexual act and one that was probably not between a husband and wife. A 'gett' was an unwanted child that had not come about from an act of love and so was ill-favoured and ill-tempered. By the time most children reached the age of 14 or 15 they were seldom, except in their own families, referred to as a 'bairn', but once a 'gett' always a 'gett'. Agnes was insulted as a witch and as a whore who had borne an illegitimate child and Margaret was insulted as the ill-favoured bastard child. This was more than just an insult, however. As in the case with Isobell Atchesone, publicly calling Agnes a witch was becoming increasingly dangerous. Margaret may well have been able to hold her own in the argument with Andrew, but when he publicly called her a witch's gett, he raised the stakes. Agnes had to step in to defend Margaret and herself. Agnes knew which way the wind was blowing. Everyone in Scotland knew Auld Nick and his handmaidens were abroad; she needed to try and keep herself and her daughter safe.

After that first night, Andrew had no more fits, although from that time on he avoided Agnes and Margaret and never publicly called Margaret a 'gett' again. The original disagreement between his wife and Margaret was ignored. It was unlike Agnes to forget any argument, but times were changing and ignoring Andrew's wife and letting the argument lie was probably preferable to being publicly named as a witch.

The ongoing turmoil with Covenanters and Royalists arming for battle and new orders for boots and coats had allowed many in Edinburgh to make some quick money, but, in the longer term, it had upset the normal rhythm of trade across the city. The army ordered cloth for coats and blankets predominantly from male weavers: it was thought that female weavers made too many mistakes. The home weaving carried out by many women, and men, that produced ordinary cloth was less lucrative and fewer orders were made or workers needed. Times were hard and tempers were fraying.

Perhaps it was just one time too many that Agnes had uttered threats in the neighbourhood. Perhaps it was the rising tension in the city. But after 28 years the people of the Potterrow Port had finally had enough of Agnes and her temper.

The year had seen trials across the country, with around 60 'witches' brought to trial from Shetland down to Wigtownshire. Of those, at least nine were worriet and burned on Leith Links.[112] Things were remarkably quiet in the Potterrow over the summer, but behind closed doors conversations were taking place. By the beginning of July, it was decided that the neighbourhood would put a stop to Agnes. A meeting was held and Harry Moriesoun, who lived in the Potterrow, was nominated to visit the minister at Greyfriars Kirk and lay a formal complaint that Agnes Finnie, indweller of the Potterrow Port, Edinburgh, was a witch and a sorcerer. On 8 July 1644, Harry Moriesoun left the Potterrow and climbed up to Greyfriars Kirk where he formally denounced Agnes as a witch to the minister. At the same time, the victory won by Oliver Cromwell at Marston Moor had boosted his standing, putting the alliance between the Scotland the English Parliamentarians and the Covenant itself under increasing strain. The Kirk saw their vision of a Calvinist Presbyterian faith for the whole of the United Kingdom slipping away and responded the only way they knew how: a frenzied condemnation of Auld Nick and his hellish handmaidens, witches.

The denunciation of Agnes as the Potterrow witch raises two interesting points. Firstly, why had it not been made earlier over the death of young John, or any of the many other deaths attributed to Agnes? Why had Andrew's fit been the final straw? Why over an illness and not a death? Secondly, why did Harry Moriesoun make the complaint rather than Andrew or one of her other victims? Most accusations of witchcraft were made by a victim, yet in none of the charges brought against Agnes is Moriesoun's name listed. He does not appear to be the father, brother, or husband of any of Agnes' victims. He was from the Potterrow, but does not appear to have had any dealings with Agnes. This remains one of the many oddities of Agnes' case.

11

Imprisonment

GEORGE GILLESPIE FINALLY had to deal with the reality of the dark underbelly of his parish. Fulminating from the safety of his pulpit was now no longer an option. After hearing Harry Moriesoun's denunciation, Gillespie had instantly written to the Privy Council for a Commission to try the 'witch'. It is not known what his initial reaction had been when Moriesoun had arrived at his door to complain about Agnes, but as a prominent Covenanter it is possible that it was a mixture of anger and disgust that a wretched witch had been uncovered in his parish. There may also have been some secret feelings of elation. If the Devil only attacked the godly, then his presence in Gillespie's parish was a very public demonstration of the righteousness of the minister. Fighting Auld Nick and his work was the very core of being a Covenanter. However, the speed with which Gillespie wrote to the Privy Council was unusual. Most ministers would take a few days to ask around their parish to determine if the initial accusation had any substance to it, or whether this was just a case of malicious name-calling. There are cases in the records where women who have accused another of being a witch have then been brought to court for slander. For all the Kirk was convinced that women were inherently wicked and would easily become the servants of the Devil, they were equally convinced that women were duplicitous liars and would accuse each other of all kinds of wickedness for their own gain, or in the heat of an argument. Authorities such as Kramer, who had written the great guide to witches and their ways, the *Malleus Maleficarum*,[113] detailed why women were more susceptible to witchcraft but also how they had 'slippery tongues' that were easily used for lying. Kirk ministers and judges agreed; the courts were not to be used in the 'cackling of women'. For someone like Agnes who seldom attended Greyfriars, it would have been expected that Gillespie would have summoned the Kirk Session to ask if anyone knew anything against her. In this case, however, Gillespie did not wait and undertake an initial investigation of the truth of the accusation. Was this because of the seriousness of the initial complaint from Moriesoun? Had the complaint concentrated on the death of young John and the others rather than Andrew's fit? Was Gillespie, as a fervent Covenanter, convinced that the Devil would attack him so the accusation must be true? Even his previous enthusiasm for witch prosecutions in Fife does not quite explain his actions in Agnes' case. He had previously known those women in his former parish and the initial accusations had come from alleged victims. If Agnes' reputation in the Potterrow was known to Gillespie, then why had he not had investigated her previously? If not, why did he not approach others for advice? The speed and certainty of Gillespie's initial reaction remains unexplained.

The day after Moriesoun went to see the minister, the Privy Council received a formal request from George Gillespie, Minister at Greyfriars Kirk, Edinburgh, for permission to form a Commission to try Agnes Finnie on the charge of witchcraft.

The request was agreed to within a few days. The speed of the Privy Council's agreement may have been due to the status of Gillespie as one of God's Elect, but it was probably also affected by the imminent execution of Sir John Gordon, First Baronet of Haddo, who had been arrested and imprisoned in St Giles Cathedral in April 1644 on grounds of treason. The area in the western part of the cathedral where Haddo was held later acquired the name 'Haddo's Hole'. Despite claiming he had the King's authority for his actions, Haddo was pronounced guilty and sentenced to death. He was due to be executed on 19 July. Haddo was one of the most high-profile Royalists to be publicly executed during the early stage of the war and the Privy Council were wary of what might happen on the day. There was every likelihood that his friends might try to stage a last-minute rescue. The execution was planned for midday at the Mercat Cross, where Haddo was to be publicly beheaded. The news of a public execution was always welcomed by the ordinary people of Edinburgh. It was a great day of spectacle. As Haddo was declared a traitor to the Covenanting cause, apprentices and those in service were given the day off, ministers fulminated in their pulpits and everyone who could walked to the Mercat Cross to see Haddo die. The baillies were on hand to keep order. With their minds concentrated on the Haddo affair, the Privy Council were paying less attention to other requests for Commissions to try witches. The situation was such that some parishes arrested and investigated several 'witches' without permission. In Culross in August, Mary Cunningham complained that she and her daughter Jonet Erskine were arrested 'under cloud of night furth of our owne hous, quhilk lyis not within their jurisdictioune, without any warrand or lawfull authoritie.' Mary and Jonet were gaoled and 'they patt on sack-loath gounes upon us and loakit our leggis in yron gaddis and wald suffer nether meat nor drink to cum to us.'[114]

Whatever was going on in Fife, in Edinburgh permission to try Agnes was approved and a Commission to investigate the allegations was formed comprising Alexander Colville, Mungo Law, Patrick Henderson and John Eleis. Alexander Colville was an advocate and a justice depute. During his legal career, he was involved in the prosecution of at least 28 witchcraft trials. He was a moderator of the assembly for the parish of Blair. He was known as a harsh interrogator and was a personal friend of George Gillespie. Mungo Law was a minister, previous moderator of the Presbytery of Dysart and a fanatical Covenanter. He had taken over the second charge at Greyfriars Kirk working alongside George Gillespie on 22 March that year. He also held a position as a member of the Commission of Assembly from 1644 until 1649. Patrick Henderson was a clerk to the Privy Council and acted as their representative during the Commission investigation. As clerk to the Council, Henderson held a junior role in the proceedings, his function primarily being to ensure that correct procedure was followed during the investigation. John Eleis was an Edinburgh baillie with responsibility for the Potterrow. He represented the secular authority on the Commission.

The direction of the investigation, the questions asked and the methods followed were under the control of the Commission, however, all four Commission members were chosen by George Gillespie. This was common practice. These were the 'guid men' of the parish and as such were capable of sitting in judgement on others. The fact that one was his friend, a second was his fellow minister at Greyfriars and the third a baillie in charge of his parish (and possibly a parishioner whom he must also therefore have known), merely made the choice easier. Few Commissioners were lawyers – in many rural areas it was rare for any of them to have any legal training: it was not considered necessary. Even in the capital where some were lawyers or baillies, the primary qualification for a Commissioner was to be a man of good character. He had to be capable, in the opinion of the parish minister, of undertaking a rigorous examination of the accused and of delivering a fair judgement. The Commissioners were chosen by the parish minister, the obvious man to be able to judge a person's worth and thus suitability to sit on a Commission. This system had developed over the centuries from the various different characteristics of local justice, clan law and family affiliations that criss-crossed the country. During the medieval period, it had delivered a reasonably rough-and-ready form of local justice. By the early modern period, it was showing signs of strain. It had become something of a closed, self-regulating system which was prone to corruption. The Privy Council had, initially, recognised this and had started to introduce some reforms, but the disruption of the early part of the century with the loss of the King to London in 1603 stalled those reforms and left the system entirely under the control of the Kirk. By the 1640s, the rise of the Covenanters saw the Privy Council, the Parliament and the Assembly of the Kirk populated by the same men.

Within days of the Commission being signed, baillie John Eleis came to Agnes' house. He was accompanied by three other baillies: Andrew Symesone, George Walker and Robert Achiesone. It is unclear why four baillies were sent to arrest

Agnes. Was she considered so dangerous it was necessary to send four men to arrest her?

After searching her house for any incriminating evidence, the baillies took Agnes to the Edinburgh Tolbooth where she was locked into one of the cells. Now that they had their 'witch' safely locked up, the Commission could start their investigations. Although on paper the Commission was independent of any authority of the minister in whose parish the investigation was taking place, most Commissions took their lead from the minister in question. It was at this point that justice for the accused started to slip away. If the minister believed the accused guilty, and why would he not as her guilt 'proved' his godliness, then the men he had chosen would surely follow suit. Why would Mungo Law dispute his fellow minister? Moriesoun had gone to Gillespie in good faith to complain, Gillespie had believed the accusation and written to the Privy Council instantly. Why would Law contradict a fellow Covenanter? This would be tantamount to calling him a liar. The Covenanters all believed themselves to be God's Elect and as such they could not err. There were battling for the very soul of the country. An alternative view was unthinkable. Alexander Colville had the same fervent mindset. With both the Greyfriars ministers in agreement, John Eleis had to go along. Even if he had not believed the accusation, if the two ministers of the parish believed it then it must be true – and even if not, why would he risk his position as baillie by opposing two senior men of the Kirk and the advocate Colville. With the dominant voices already invested in Agnes' guilt, Patrick Henderson's opinion, even if it differed, was of little weight.

In a modern criminal investigation, the authorities search for evidence and follow that evidence to find their suspect. Even where a 'prime suspect' is identified, the evidence is still followed to uncover that person's guilt or innocence. If the evidence shows the prime suspect to be innocent, that person is removed as the prime suspect and the investigation continues following the evidence wherever it leads. In the 17th century, in the case of a witchcraft trial, guilt was already accepted and the investigation looked for proof of the guilt. Evidence that proved innocence was not ignored, but the way evidence was gathered was focused on and interpreted through the initial premise of guilt. Evidence that 'proved' innocence was frequently taken as a sign of the trickery of the 'witch'.

Already convinced, as they were, of Agnes' guilt, the Commission decided to get the best evidence they could: a confession of witchcraft from Agnes. This was the one piece of evidence that guaranteed a guilty verdict and an execution. The matter would be settled within a few of days and one more of the Devil's own would be consigned to the flames. Mungo Law wrote to the Kirk Session on behalf of the Commission for permission to bring Agnes before them for questioning. Two days later, Agnes was brought before the Kirk Session of Greyfriars. The session included George Gillespie, Mungo Law and several church Elders. Also present was the Commission, comprising Alexander Colville, Mungo Law, Patrick Henderson and John Eleis, with George Gillespie advising them.

The records state that, after close questioning, Agnes confessed to having been a 'witch' for 28 years. Given everything that we know about Agnes' personality that seems unlikely. The record is not wrong, but it does not give the details of how that confession was obtained. Since the basis of any witch trial was the Kirk's obsession with the Devil and his witches, the questioning put to the accused would reflect that obsession. Agnes may have been asked questions like, 'are you a witch?' but that was an already established truth. What was much more important was the nature of her relationship with the Devil. The questioning would have reflected this. What did the Devil look like? How was he dressed? What did he say? All this and more would be asked over and over and over again, until the Commission got the answer they wanted. If Agnes, angry, confused and tired, then said something like 'he wore a black hat', that was proof she had met the Devil and therefore was a witch: she had confessed. The Commission had their confession and all that was then needed was to fully accept all the complaints that had been received from Agnes' neighbours and the trial could go ahead. She would face the flames before the end of the month. But that was not what happened; there was something wrong with Agnes' confession. In Scotland in the 17th century, several thousand women and men were executed as 'witches'. Almost all of them had confessed. There are no known recorded cases where a confessing witch was not found guilty. Those who confessed but were found to be 'addled in their wits' did not stand trial. In most of the cases with guilty verdicts, the confession was the main proof. There are several records of cases in which the confession was the only proof. So why, one week later, after allegedly confessing, was Agnes Finnie still sitting in her cell in the Tolbooth? Why was she still waiting there one month later? Why would she still be there in the autumn without having gone to trial?

The following weeks and months would see the Commission wrestle with the thorny issue of Agnes' case while the 'witch' was condemned to life in a cell in the Edinburgh Tolbooth. Prison in 17th century Scotland was not for the faint-hearted. Prisoners were given the most basic of care. Guards were only supposed to supply bread and water daily and clean hay for sleeping once a week. Everything else had to be supplied out of the suspect's own pocket, or by their friends and family if they had any to help them. In the case of those suspected of witchcraft, friends and family were often nowhere to be seen. Most were afraid of being associated with the accused in case they themselves came under suspicion. Others were genuinely horrified by their relative's alleged crimes. Either way, most left the accused to their own devices. The plight of suspected witches was occasionally commented upon, although nothing was done, and some cases were recorded where the accused were reduced to 'drinking their own piss'.[115] For those that spent any length of time in gaol, Commissioners would complain about the foul-smelling, half-naked prisoners that appeared in their courtrooms. The main issue was that their stench offended the noses of the authorities and the dignity of the court. The reason why they were half-starved and foul-smelling was immaterial.

Conditions were so bad that some suspects died in gaol before being brought to trial. Such individuals were frequently recorded as being 'witches' despite not having made it to trial and as a result their bodies were often quickly and quietly buried in unmarked graves. This gave rise to rumours of accused witches escaping justice and being 'rescued' by the Devil. Many ministers fulminated that they had not been worriet and their bodies burned as should have happened. In addition, there were many fervent Covenanters who also believed the 'witches' had defied the court and escaped justice. Gaolers would frequently be reprimanded for allowing accused witches to die. Despite the death of the accused being seen as an escape from justice, nothing was done to mitigate the conditions in which they were held.

The cells of the Tolbooth were cold and damp, even in the summer. There was little light. Some had no ventilation at all, leaving the air fetid and suffocating. Others had open windows leaving the accused exposed to the Edinburgh weather. The only bedding was a pile of straw in one corner which was supposed to be changed weekly, but usually in the cases of 'witches' was not. The accused had to use the other corner of their cell to relieve themselves. They shared their cell with fleas, lice, cockroaches and rats, as well as other prisoners on occasion. For younger female suspects, they could attract the attention of the baillies who might attempt sexual violence, although this was rare in the cases of suspected witches, partly because of a genuine disgust at what they had been accused of and partly because it was widely known that witches could shrivel your manhood. Food could be brought in for the accused if they had money or friends to bring them something, but this was also somewhat difficult. Most of the baillies that guarded prisoners were poorly paid and any money given to buy food would simply be pocketed by them. Alternatively, they would simply eat the food that was meant for the accused. For those too frightened to steal a witch's food, they would frequently spit in the food or add in gravel, or worse. The safest method of getting food was for a relative to physically bring it to the Tolbooth. Although this was no small undertaking, Margaret, Agnes' daughter, did just that. As many days as she could, Margaret would take time out of her work and daily chores to prepare some food then walk from the Potterrow to the Tolbooth. She then had to coax and persuade the baillies to let her in to see her mother. Depending on the nature of the baillie, some might simply have let her through. For others Margaret may have had to fend off their sexual advances, and a few may have simply refused her entry. After the first couple of weeks, word would have spread about 'Agnes the witch' in the city and Margaret would have been marked as a 'witch's gett' as she walked up to the Tolbooth. Although no doubt able to hold her own in the Potterrow where she had lived all her life and where her temper was well known; it would have been a different matter to walk through a different neighbourhood and be met with hard stares, whispered comments and the occasional verbal and even physical abuse day after day. Edinburgh High Street was home to traders, shopkeepers and locals all going about their business who did not want a 'witch's gett' in their midst. There are numerous entries in the Council records of baillies having to stop witch's relatives from being attacked or pelted with stones as they walked to the Tolbooth. The usual method of dealing with such trouble was for the baillies to tell them to stay away.

Margaret may also have had to take over Agnes' shop and money-lending business. The records make note of an assistant that Agnes had working for her in the shop. It is unclear exactly what Margaret worked as, but it is possible that she worked as a weaver using a hand-loom in her home. Many of the clothiers in Edinburgh employed women across the city to produce the cloth they needed, paying the women on a piece rate. Margaret's husband was only a journeyman cordiner and as such was paid a relatively modest wage, so Margaret's earnings would have been essential to keep their house going. There was little extra cash, so for Margaret to take time out of her weaving to visit her mother would have reduced the family income and would, probably, have caused tension. That tension would have increased had Margaret also taken over the running of the shop and the dangerous world of money-lending.

While Margaret was running up and down the High Street with baskets of food or news about the business, Agnes had to face a risk of her own: the constant filth in her cell. The build-up of urine and faeces was a real danger, especially in a time before antibiotics when infected cuts could be fatal. Agnes was also in danger of being bitten by the fleas, cockroaches and rats that shared her cell, each potentially carrying Weil's disease, malaria, gastroenteritis, salmonella, pneumonia and dysentery. Water for washing was almost never supplied to accused witches. Despite Margaret's best efforts, Agnes could not have been eating a normal diet, leaving a weakened system more susceptible to disease and infection.

Agnes also had to deal with the baillies. Some guards ignored suspected witches entirely, often forgetting to feed them at all, with subsequent deaths from starvation if they were incarcerated for a long time. Most did the bare minimum throwing in bread and water as necessary and only cleaning out the straw when the stench became too overpowering even for the hardened guards. Some were sadists. Possibly driven by Covenanting ideals, or at least understanding that they would not be called to account for their actions, they delighted in tormenting their prisoners. Mostly it was verbal abuse, tampering with food, bringing in friends and relatives to laugh at the plight of 'the witch' and possibly even taking a penny or two for their trouble. For a few, however, they would relieve the boredom of their time on guard duty by beating suspected witches. One 'game' that was popular was based on 'waking and walking'.

Waking and walking was a common method of obtaining a confession from suspects. A suspect would be kept awake for days and walked up and down until they confessed. Sleep deprivation was a very effective way of obtaining confessions. It led extremely quickly to hallucinations with the individual losing all control of themselves rendering them compliant to their interrogators. In their desperation for sleep and with little understanding of what was happening, suspects would give whatever reply they thought would end their torment simply in order to be allowed to rest. The accused were kept sitting on small stools and not allowed to put their feet on the ground for hours on end, or shackled standing up and doused with cold water whenever they tried to sleep while being questioned. Walking was equally brutal. The suspect would be grabbed by the arms and walked up and down their cell for hours. Every time the walkers became tired, they would be replaced by two fresh walkers. This could be continued until a confession was obtained. By the end of the walking, the suspect's feet and lower legs would be a blistered and a bloody mess, making them even more susceptible to infection.

For sadistic or bored baillies, fun could be had by keeping their 'witches' awake at night by constantly dragging them out of their straw beds or forcing them to stand on stools or on one leg for long periods. For those baillies too lazy to be bothered with 'waking' their suspects, beatings were the usual game of choice. This was usually done on the legs, partly to hide any bruises under long skirts, but also as legs already painful from walking would be more easily hurt. One area that was very seldom a problem was sexual abuse. Although some suspected witches tried to wriggle out of their trial and probable execution by 'pleading their bellies', there were few baillies that would help a suspected witch become pregnant.

Agnes was a formidable woman probably in her late 40s or early 50s; she was no frightened young girl about to be cowed by baillies. She had a reputation as someone who could take care of herself. She had family that was standing by her. She also had money that meant that she could buy herself some legal advice. But for all that, in the middle of the night, alone and in the dark, there was no one there to protect Agnes from what the baillies might do. This was, after all, a time when flogging and branding were common punishments allowed by the law for minor criminals. Any brutality that was meted out to a suspected witch would have been considered par for the course. In addition, Agnes was not a stupid woman. She knew what the usual outcome was for suspected witches. Everyone in the whole of the Potterrow knew what happened to witches. The minister at Greyfriars had been preaching about nothing else for months. The whole town was awash with stories of Auld Nick and his handmaidens. Alone in her prison cell in the night, Agnes would well foresee her fate.

By November, Agnes had been lying in her filthy, flea- and lice-infested cell in the Tolbooth for around 16 weeks. Over the summer and into the autumn she had been brought out of her cell for questioning and then returned on multiple occasions, and yet still she had not been brought to trial. By the start of November, she had had enough. She had been arrested, so bring her to trial or let her go.

Since her arrest, Agnes' daughter Margaret had been active on her mother's behalf. In addition to bringing food to the Tolbooth as frequently as she could, Margaret had employed two lawyers, John Lawtie and John Nisbet. This was no easy undertaking on her part. Although accused witches were, by 1644, entitled to a defence, there were few advocates who would take on such a case. This was partly because everyone in the middle of the 17th century knew that witches existed, everyone knew that they committed evil acts by their witchcraft, and everyone knew they were the followers of the Devil. Why, therefore, would anyone want to defend them? Even in cases where the allegation was thought to be possibly false, the fact that a Commission had been undertaken, under the influence of the local minister, meant that in the eyes of the Kirk the accused was guilty. It took a strong personality to challenge such a view. It could be surmised that the lawyers were, in effect, calling the local minister a liar. Also, if a lawyer was ambitious, would his reputation be harmed by taking on a witch trial? Who, in the future, would want to employ the sort of lawyer that would defend a witch? As most witchcraft trials ended in a guilty verdict anyway, was there any point in carrying out the work? With all of these elements in play and with the country boiling with Covenanting fever, Margaret did well to find two lawyers to take the case. Were Lawtie and Nisbet sympathetic to her plight? Or were they desperate for the money? Without any 'family name', both men were at a distinct disadvantage in the world of Edinburgh advocates. Were they taking on the case hoping to make a name for themselves? They would certainly do that. Was the plan to take the case and then, after the inevitable guilty verdict, laugh among their colleagues about how they had helped convict a witch while getting paid by her? Whatever their motivation, Margaret had at least secured her mother some legal representation.

While this was, obviously, good news for Agnes it put an added strain on Margaret. The income from Agnes' shop and money-lending had dried up and Margaret had had to supply her mother with food over the weeks of her imprisonment. Initially, the two advocates were paid from Agnes' savings but that would not last forever. Edinburgh advocates most definitely did not come cheap and even before the trial took place the advocates were working on Agnes' behalf.

On 6 November, a summons was issued in Agnes' name against the complainant Harry Moriesoun who had given 'malicious information' which had led to her arrest. The names of the baillies who had arrested her were then added. Three days later, the summons was officially lodged against Moriesoun and the baillies who had arrested her.

> Summons on 9 November against Andrew Syme-
> sone, George Walker, Robert Achiesone and John
> Inglis, bailies of Edinburgh, all personally appre-
> hended and against Harry Moriesone, also person-
> ally apprehended, to compear before the Council;
> witnesses, David Wright, messenger in Edinburgh,
> and John Peirone, post there, Richard Guthrie and
> James Grahame, officers in Edinburgh, Thom-
> as Allane messenger there. John Rowane, writer

there, John Hairt, younger, and George Neill, messenger in Edinburgh.

The summons was executed by James Grahame, court messenger. But Agnes wasn't finished and, on 11 November, she lodged yet another summons, this time against 'Sir John Smyth, provost of Edinburgh, personally apprehended; witnesses, the said Robert Achiesone and Andrew Symesone, baillies of Edinburgh, and James Cleghorne, town officer there.'[116]

Both summonses had been drafted by Lawtie, Nisbet and their clerks after meeting with Agnes. Furious that she had still not been brought to trial, her lawyers probably advised Agnes that lodging a summons against the baillies and original complainant might cause the courts to sit up and take notice. Although not a common practice in witchcraft trials, it was a well-known technique for pushing the courts into action in other cases where they seemed to be dragging their heels.

The second summons, however, is astonishing. Agnes Finnie, shopkeeper, widow and indweller of the Potterrow Port had lodged a summons against Sir John Smyth, the Provost of Edinburgh. Sir John was the highest civil authority in the capital city dealing with food shortages, outbreaks of plague and the civil war that was consuming the country – and he was now being asked to appear before the Privy Council on the request of a suspected witch to account for the actions of his baillies and the time it was taking to bring Agnes to trial. Agnes was piling on the pressure. The Privy Council might have sought to ignore the complaint against the baillies; such complaints were ten a penny, they went with the job. Nobody liked baillies, everybody complained about them.

But the complaint against the Lord Provost was more embarrassing. Not only was it against one of the most senior dignitaries of the town, it was the second complaint connected to this one case. To add to everyone's embarrassment, among those who served the summons on Sir John Smyth were Robert Achiesone and Andrew Symesone, two of the baillies complained about just two days before by Agnes. This was probably a simple mistake on the part of the sheriff's office, but was unusual and raised a few eyebrows.

Did Lawtie and Nisbet suggest to Agnes that she lay a summons on Sir John? They were advocates who lived and worked in Edinburgh. Both were ordinary lawyers without any great connections. They were already taking a great risk in defending a suspected witch; to lodge a summons against the Lord Provost of the city was tantamount to career suicide no matter how much money they were charging Agnes. To lay such a summons would bring them to everyone's attention. Was that the idea? Were they suggesting this as a way to get themselves known as fearless, bold lawyers? If so, that was a very risky strategy given Sir John's reputation for an explosive temper.

Is it possible that Agnes, in one of her rages, angry that despite lodging the previous summons was still waiting her trial, demanded the lawyers do something, anything, to get the matter resolved? Did one of them say, without really meaning to, that they could summon the Lord Provost? Did Agnes latch onto that and demand they do so?

Lawtie and Nesbit were in a bit of a bind. Whatever their motivation had been for taking on Agnes' case in the first place, they could not now back out. They were men who, like everyone else at that time, firmly believed witches were real and had some sort of power and now they were defending one. What would happen if they didn't work as hard as possible for her? Could she, would she, put a curse on them? What about her daughter? It was said Margaret was a witch's gett; if they failed to defend her mother properly, would she lay an illness on them? But what if they worked too well and Agnes was found not guilty? What would the legal establishment say? What would the Kirk say? How could they live with the knowledge they had helped one of the Devil's followers walk free? The moment Nesbit and Lawtie agreed to defend Agnes, they placed themselves in an impossible position and now they were lodging a summons against the Lord Provost of Edinburgh. To challenge a powerful man was unthinkable. To cross a powerful witch was unwise. Frustratingly there remains no record of the conversation between Margaret and Lawtie and Nesbit, so their original motivation for taking the case remains unknown. Equally frustratingly, the reason for summoning Sir John and whose idea it originally was is also missing.

Society in 17th century Edinburgh was highly stratified. Agnes may have been a member of the middling sort, but she was barely a step or two above the working poor. Had she had any sort of higher status she would have moved from the Potterrow, but would still have been way below Sir John in the life of the city. Sir John Smyth of Grothill and Kings Cramond was a wealthy landowner and merchant who served as Lord Provost of Edinburgh from 1643 to 1646. He owned two estates north-west of Edinburgh: Grothill and Kings Cramond. He had been one of the only two Scottish representatives sent to settle the Treaty of London in 1641. He was also heavily involved in the drafting of the Solemn League and Covenant in 1643. After that, he succeeded Sir Alexander Clerk of Pittencrieff as Lord Provost of Edinburgh. This was a highly political election coming, as it did, immediately prior to Scotland's involvement in the English Civil War. By 1650, although he was no longer Lord Provost of Edinburgh, he was involved in negotiating the terms of the Treaty of Breda with Charles II in which the King undertook to grant everything the Covenanters wanted. And, of course, Sir John had been the Lord Provost that had been in charge when the Jenny Geddes riot in St Giles had broken out. Given all this, a summons issued from a filthy cell in the Tolbooth was probably an unexpected and disagreeable surprise. Nevertheless, Sir John had to appear to answer the charges against him. He could not be seen to flout the law. His political opponents would have quickly made capital out of the fact that the so-called Lord Provost did not know what was going on in his own Tolbooth, that justice was not being carried out properly in Edinburgh and that a witch had not been consigned to the flames on his watch. He had to act. Although the records of what happened at his appearance are missing, it is notable that after having spent all those months in the Tolbooth Agnes was brought to trial only four weeks later.

In more ordinary times, Agnes would indeed have been brought to trial earlier. In rural areas, those arrested in the summer often had to wait until the field work of high summer and harvest was over before being brought to trial. Rural workers could not be spared to sit on a jury, but no such restrictions applied in the town. Agnes was quite within her rights to demand to be brought to trial or to be released. Unfortunately for Agnes, she faced two problems. The evidence against her and the outbreak of the Civil War. The prosecution team faced one problem: Agnes.

There were four main proofs that were recognised in the Scottish Courts of an individual being a 'witch'; having a history of bad behaviour or of having committed evils acts; being named as a witch by another witch, or 'delated' as it was known in the Scottish courts; confessing to being a witch; and being found with the Devil's Mark on the body.[117]

The first and most easily found 'proof' was a bad reputation. This could easily develop over a number of years and once an individual had such, it was well-nigh impossible to be rid of a bad reputation especially in a close-knit community. This was more than just being disliked, although that was often the start. An individual might have a history of suspicious behaviour or of practising witchcraft. Some of those arrested had been performing witchcraft for many years and some even had a previous conviction for witchcraft. In previous centuries, a local presbytery might, if the offence were thought minor, merely excommunicate the person from the Kirk. By the 17th century, however, the fears raised by war, plague, famine and death were such that a bad reputation for causing rather than curing illness would see the accused brought to trial. Although a relatively weak proof on its own, it was nevertheless the one most easily found and often the 'proof' that triggered further investigation. Much of life was lived in public and so arguing with your neighbours in the street could be seen by all. Once labelled 'a quarrelsome dame', every angry outburst, every insult shouted across a street – and Agnes shouted plenty – added to that quarrelsome reputation. Once an initial accusation was made, every argument that was half-remembered, every cross word that was exaggerated, added to that reputation

There were other situations that hugely affected an individual's reputation. Non-attendance at the Kirk, unless ill, and severely so, was unthinkable. Most of those in the Potterrow may not have attended the Kirk regularly, but they were not the one in prison. Agnes' arrest may well have prompted an increase in Kirk attendance as everyone hurried to see and be seen. In contrast, Agnes' non-attendance would suddenly be remembered and commented upon. With Gillespie guiding the Commission and Mungo Law as one of the Commissioners, Agnes' non-attendance at the Kirk was a personal insult to both ministers, and of course to God, and could not be ignored.

The death of a relative also raised suspicions. Men who lost their wives in childbirth were pitied; women whose husbands had died were viewed with misgivings. As a widow, this was yet another mark against Agnes. It is not known how her husband died, but the fact of his death alone caused gossip. As most of those who cared for the sick were women, any unusual death could result in suspicion and damage to their reputation. Many women in the Potterrow would have been widows, but Agnes was the only one known as the neighbourhood witch.

Many trial records note that the accused had a bad reputation going back over ten or even 20 years. Neighbours and ministers who reported on the suspect were seldom questioned as to the veracity of their statements and local gossip became enshrined as proof once recorded by court clerks. In Agnes' case, much of the 'proof' regarding her reputation did indeed extend back over some 20-odd years.

The second 'proof' of being a witch was the accused being 'delated' or named by another witch. This was considered strong evidence of witchcraft, although some care was taken that the accuser was not delating another from malice. Those delated seldom escaped a guilty verdict. Interrogations of suspected witches always included questions about their accomplices. Suspects would be asked who had inducted them into witchcraft, who had led them to dance with Auld Nick. Occasionally, interrogators would try to persuade the suspects that if they delated others they would receive a lighter sentence. Such promises were seldom, if ever, kept. The Kirk believed that witches were inducted into a pact with the Devil when there were others present as witnesses. Interrogators' questions followed this line of reasoning: what other witches were present when they met the Devil? Who were the other followers they met with Auld Nick? It was also believed that witches would meet together to carry out their witchcraft. They might have been servants of the Devil, but they were still weak women and needed to meet together to gain the strength to perform their magic. For others, they were under the control of warlocks who, as men, were naturally in charge of the female witches.

For those witches who worked alone there was no escape as it was believed that one witch could recognise another even if they were strangers.

The third 'proof' of witchcraft, and the one the Kirk always concentrated upon, was a formal confession from the accused of being a witch. This was usually a confession of meeting the Devil either alone or in the company of others where the accused had entered into a pact with Auld Nick and rejected Christ. The Kirk needed to prove the Devil was a liar and so the details of what he had promised and, hopefully, then failed to deliver was crucial evidence of his deceitful nature. In most cases, this point of the Devil's nature was as important to the Kirk as the events relating to the actual witchcraft. Witches were, after all, only the Devil's handmaidens: in the eyes of the Kirk, it was the Devil that was important, not the women. Confession was always sought by the Kirk and those who did not confess were not thought to be innocent, but rather stubborn liars who were arrogantly flouting the authority of the Kirk by failing to confess to all. Those who confessed and then later retracted their confessions almost drove the ministers into apoplexy with their wicked insolence. And, of course, that was exactly what Agnes would do.

The fourth and final 'proof' was the existence of the Devil's Mark. The Kirk believed that Auld Nick marked his followers to seal their pact with him by touching them on the head, neck or shoulders. This Devil's Mark was found by pricking or 'brodding' the accused with a steel bodkin on a spot such as a mole or scar. As the Devil was unnatural, so the witch would not feel pain if brodded on that Mark. Brodding was usually carried out where a suspect refused to confess and often resulted in finding the Devil's Mark and a confession at the same time. It was not used as frequently as might be suspected, partly because it was expensive – witch brodders were one of the few individuals who made money from witch trials and even the most experienced did not always find a Mark – and partly because witches were incredibly tricky and could hide their Devil's Mark. A Commission might pay a witch brodder to find a Devil's Mark which then disappeared by the time of the trial, allowing the defence to deny its existence.

With one or more of these 'proofs' in place, the 'witch' could then be brought to trial.

The problem the Commission had, in Agnes' case, was that their proofs were weak. A history of bad behaviour, being a 'quarrelsome dame', was proof, but proof of the weakest kind easily dismissed by advocates (usually on the grounds that most women were quarrelsome dames). While this generally got a good laugh in court, it did not help the authorities. Agnes' bad temper was well known, but the court needed more.

The second proof, that of being delated, was even more troublesome because in Agnes' case it had just not happened. Agnes had very loudly proclaimed they had been burning 'witches' in Edinburgh and Leith for the past 20 years and not one of them had named her. Unfortunately for the Commission, she was quite right.

And as for confessing to being a witch, Agnes had done so, allegedly, at her first interrogation by the Kirk, yet the problem was that Agnes had since retracted her 'confession' most vociferously. In no uncertain terms and with several extremely uncomplimentary remarks about the competency of the minister and his elders, Agnes completely denied having said anything about being a 'witch' of any kind. This had been a stumbling block for the Commission from the beginning. True, Agnes may have said something like 'I met the man in the black hat' which the Kirk was happy was a confession of witchcraft, but would it stand up in court?

In general trials women were not allowed to speak in court. 'My Lord Advocat alleadged that ... no woman cane be witnes because by the uncontraverted laes and pract'qs of Scotland.'[118] The inability of women to give evidence became problematic in witchcraft trials as most of the initial accusations had come from women and those who had delated a witch were themselves usually women. In both cases, the law required the women to be heard. In 1591, the law was changed to allow women to give testimony in court, but only in witchcraft cases. Given Agnes' personality and the fact that she had two lawyers who would tell her she had the right to speak, there was nothing to stop her flatly denying in open court that she had confessed to anything. Her increasingly abusive denials while sitting in her cell in the Tolbooth were one thing, but her shouting them across an open courtroom was quite another. The Commission was worried.

Interestingly, the fourth and the undeniable, definite proof of the Devil's Mark was never explored with Agnes. Were the authorities unsure of themselves? Throughout the whole of Agnes' arrest, imprisonment and trial there was a hesitancy on the part of the authorities. Was she so terrifying a witch that they were too scared to even call for the witch brodder to check her for the Devil's Mark? The evidence relating to Agnes' personality indicates this would have been no easy task. Unwillingly to submit to such a search, Agnes would probably have fought any attempt to examine her. The unedifying spectacle of the baillie's men having to wrestle Agnes to the ground, doubtless kicking and scratching and spitting and cursing, while a witch brodder tried to find a mark to brod would not have been a happy one and was never put to the test. There was, of course, also the possibility that no Mark would be found on Agnes, further weakening the case against her.

All of this made the evidence against Agnes less than robust. However, the numerous serious allegations against Agnes from her neighbours would probably have seen her brought to trial relatively quickly, weak case or not, but for the interference of a somewhat larger problem: the start of the Scottish Civil War.

In June 1644, just before Agnes' arrest, the Scottish Parliament had reconvened and one of its first acts was to condemn Montrose and send troops down to the border to deal with him. Just as the Parliament was feeling confident, news came, in mid-July, that Antrim had at last landed his Irish troops at Ardnamurchan. Although Argyll was confident that the Irish could be easily dealt with, the Kirk became apoplectic when they learned that two of their ministers had been taken prisoner. All the old fears of Auld Nick were now 'proved' correct as two of God's Elect had fallen into the hands of the 'Popish Eirish'. While Argyll pondered the best way to deal with the Irish and the Kirk screamed for action, Montrose slipped quietly over the border and joined Antrim's troops. When this became known, every minister in Edinburgh rounded on the Parliament demanding to know how this had happened and what was to be done. By the middle of August their worst fears were realised: Montrose led his loyal clansmen and the Irish to victory over the Covenanter troops sent against him and entered Perth in triumph. While Argyll recalled the Scots from the north of England, Royalists from across Scotland rallied to Montrose. The tables had turned and Edinburgh was shaken by the change. The armed gangs on the street were fighting yet again, but this time the Royalist gangs had the upper hand. Rumours ran round the Potterrow on a daily basis: the Irish were coming to slaughter them all, the King was preparing to hang every Covenanter as a traitor, those who had contributed to the army were all to be arrested and of course the Devil was everywhere.

By September, it seemed as if there was no stopping Auld Nick when the English Parliament passed a motion for the 'accommodation of tender consciences'. On the surface this motion merely allowed for non-Presbyterians to practise their faith in England but, in reality, completely undermined the Covenant: there would be no uniform Presbyterian faith across the United Kingdom. On 19 October, the Scots army finally took Newcastle. Good news for the Covenanters, it barely rallied the Kirk, many of whom were now prophesying that this was the 'end time' as predicted in Revelations. The Scots made one last attempt to force Presbyterianism on the English using Newcastle as a bargaining chip, but the bill was voted down on its first reading in the House in November.[119]

The problem for the politicians in Edinburgh was that the civil war, which had started as a relatively two-sided affair, had quickly deteriorated as factions had appeared within the Parliamentarian camp. It had become increasingly polarised with the Royalist and Parliamentarian camps almost diametrically opposed to each other on all issues. It was complicated by both Royalists and Covenanters agreeing that the monarchy was ordained by God, but disagreeing on the nature and extent of Royal authority versus that of the Kirk.[120] It was further confused by the Highland clans: some were Episcopalian rather than Calvinist while others, like the MacDonalds, contained some members who remained Catholic alongside others who had converted to Calvinism. There was also the ongoing political tension between Montrose and Argyll, both of whom were vying for dominance in the Highlands. Control of the Highland clans was of equal importance to each in the fight between Covenanters and Royalists. In addition, the Highland Gaelic-speaking clans tended to prefer the King in far-off London, who more or less left them to their own devices. The Scots-speaking Lowlander Covenanters were resented for their interference in clan matters.

The outbreak of war could not have happened at a worse time for the authorities in Edinburgh. Late August had seen another outbreak of pestilence in the Borders and Midlothian, and the city ports were closed to traders from the south. This was followed by a bad harvest that further depleted the city's food supplies. Tension had been running at fever pitch for weeks, as even the most uninformed of the city's inhabitants could not fail to have heard the rumours that arose on a daily basis. The Edinburgh mob was restless and the baillies were on high alert. It was against this backdrop that the Commission had to find their evidence against Agnes.

* * *

Whatever the reason for the delay in bringing her to trial, for Agnes to have a summons issued against Harry Moriesoun for his 'malicious information' was a shrewd move. Even before the trial had taken place, by calling Moriesoun's information 'malicious' she was already sowing doubt as to the charges against her. Claiming that she was likely to die in prison 'under the blame of so detestable ane imputatione' added to her pro-testations of innocence. While accused witches who died in prison were generally thought to have escaped justice, it was an embarrassment for the city authorities. Therefore, the last thing they needed was someone as strong-willed and noisy as Agnes drawing attention to this possibility and the fact that she had still not been brought to trial.

Following this up by naming the baillies in a summons and then the Lord Provost was also a clever move. The complainant had been summonsed, the baillies in the case had been summonsed, the Lord Provost had been summonsed, the baillies who had been summonsed had then served the Lord Provost. It was fast becoming a farce. And Agnes had still not been brought to trial.

The lack of progress on Agnes' case was starting to be gossiped about the town. The inhabitants of the Potterrow may have got rid of quarrelsome Agnes, but the matter seemed to have merely been put on hold rather than dealt with permanently. Every other day over the weeks Agnes had been in the Tolbooth, her daughter had brought food to her and then returned to the Potterrow with stories about her mother's imprisonment, her case, the lack of progress and her innocence. The Privy Council's business, the shakiness of the case, the conditions in Agnes' cell and her refusal to answer any questions were all discussed. Even those who were glad to see the back of Agnes still enjoyed laughing at the discomfort of the learned lawyers and minister who couldn't seem to sort out auld Annie the witch. The Privy Council were embarrassed and angry. What was going on?

When Agnes was first arrested, there had been a flurry of accusations and many of her neighbours and customers rushed to tell their stories to the minister and the baillies. However, although there appeared to be a wealth of accusations against Agnes there was little actual evidence. Many of the complaints of arguments and threats had arisen over money. Some of those whose families claimed Agnes had injured them had not been near her at the time of the injury. When Agnes was first arrested, the baillies had searched her house for evidence of her sorcery and found nothing. As Agnes was quick to point out, when her house was searched 'there was neither pictur, toad, nor any such thing found therein, which ever any witch in the world was used to practize.' The authorities were faced with a woman with a single, contested, retracted confession; no evidence of any familiar, or spells, or charms, or poppet found in her shop or house; and with a quarrelsome, angry nature that she was not afraid to make the most of in complaining about her treatment.

12

The Trial

SINCE THE PARLIAMENTARY victory at Marston Moor on 2 July, there had been bad blood brewing between Cromwell and Lord Manchester. On 25 November 1644, Cromwell had, in the House of Commons, publicly condemned Manchester's actions in the field. On 2 December, Manchester gave a written response. In his response, while defending his own actions, Manchester claimed that Cromwell had stated that he (Cromwell) would fight the Scots if they tried to impose Presbyterianism on England.[121] All the long-suppressed fears of the Covenanters had now been openly stated. The English Parliamentarians had only signed the Solemn League and Covenant in order to gain the Scots army in their war against the King. The news soon reached Edinburgh and caused an uproar. The Moderates within the Covenanters tried to discuss what this meant for the ongoing war against the King and their relationship with the English; the more hot-headed raged about the perfidiousness of their English counterparts and the outright zealots seethed about the obvious tricks of those who were in league with the Devil, preaching hellfire from their pulpits. Cromwell's statement, after the failure of the parliamentary bill, laid bare the English abandonment of the Covenant. As the leader of the Parliamentary troops, Cromwell's statement was final. John Pym was dead and Lord Manchester was poorly regarded. Cromwell was, for all intents and purposes, the leader of the English Parliamentarians. There was now no longer any doubt – Auld Nick had forced the English to reject the true faith.

It should not be underestimated just what a shock this was to the Kirk in Edinburgh. Although many of the leading Covenanters had been wary of the English Parliamentarians and some of the more astute among them had known the alliance between the Scots and the English was merely a means to an end, for the Kirk it was unthinkable. They had complete certainty in the rightness of their cause. They were, after all, God's Elect. How could the English fail to see that? The Reformation in Scotland had been a hard battle fought and won by the Kirk against the diabolical Catholics. The English had merely moved slowly and, according to the Scots, not nearly far enough away from Catholicism. The Kirk intended to save them from themselves. It was engaged in a battle for the very souls of Scotland and England. The English had pledged their allegiance to the Covenant; how could they now, renege on such a solemn oath? It was the most serious blow to their confidence they had ever suffered. The Devil might attack them by turning the King's head, he might lead men astray to go to war, he might unleash his witches upon the entire country, but for the English to reject the Covenant was inconceivable.

As if to drive the point home, pestilence arrived in Edinburgh and settled in for the winter.[122] Death rates in areas such as the Potterrow rose.

The same week Cromwell's utter rejection of the Covenant became known in Scotland and after some five long months of her imprisonment, the trial of Agnes Finnie finally began. There were 20 charges listed on the court dittay.

> That whereas by the 18th chapter of Deuteronomy* and the twentieth of Leviticus,** and the seventy third act of the ninth parliament of Queen Marie,*** all sorcerie is prohibit; yet the said Agnes has committed the crymes following: First article, that having Threatened Mr Willian Fairlie's son to send him halting home, because in a nickname going by her door, he called his Annie Winnie, he within twenty-four howers after lost the power of his left syde by his witchcraft, and languished in so incurable a disease, that the whole physicians called it supernaturall, and the haill substance of his bodie ran out at his cute; and the buy laid the wholle wyte of his death constantlie upon the panel:
>
> Second article is, that she laid upon Beatrix Nisbet a fearfull disease, so that she lost the power

---

* Deuteronomy 18: 10–12 There shall not be found among you any one that maketh his son or his daughter to pass through the fire, or that useth divination, or an observer of times, or an enchanter, or a witch, or a charmer, or a consulter with familiar spirits, or a wizard, or a necromancer. For all that do these things are an abomination unto the LORD: and because of these abominations the Lord thy God doth drive them out from before thee.

** Leviticus 20:27 A man also or woman that hath a familiar spirit, or that is a wizard, shall surely be put to death: they shall stone them with stones: their blood shall be upon them.

*** 1563 Scottish Witchcraft Act

of her tongue! because she paying the said Agnes two dollars owing hir by hir father, would not give her annual rent therefor:

The third is, that she laid a grievous sickness upon Jonet Grinton, whom ye threatened that she should never eat more in this world, because she had brought again two herring she had bought from you, they not being caller, and sought back hir eight pennies, and of which she died, without eating or drinking, conforme to your threatening:

The fourth is, that ye came in to visit John Buchannan's bairne, being sick of a palsie, and bad the father and mother go ben the house a whylle, and pray to God for him; and in the man whylle ye staid with him and when they returned, they fand him violently sick that he could neither stir hand nor foot, and that by your devilrie; and fand on his right buttock, about the bridth of one's loofe, the same so sore as if a collop had been tain out of it; and he died within eight days, in great dolour;

The fifth is, that falling a scolding with Bessie Currie, the said bairne's mother, about changing of a sixpence which ye alledged to be ill, ye, in great rage threattned that ye gar the devill tack a bite of hir.

The sixth is, that ye laid a grievous sickness on hir husband, John Buchannan, that he brant a whole night as if he had been in a fure, for taking his wife Bessie Currie's part against you, and boasting to cast you over the stair, and calling you a witch; whereon ye threatened him to make him repent his speeches; and for taking the same off him, he coming the next day and drinking a pint of ail with you, and telling you that if you tormented him so another night; he should make all the toune heir tell of it; whereon he was well.

The seventh is, that the said John being offended at you because ye would not thrist his wife a twelve-pennie caik, ye bad him go his way. And as he had begun with witches, so he should end; after which threatening, he streight contracted a long and grievous sicknesse, whereof he was lyke to melt away in sweiting.

The eight is, that in your scolding with Euphame Kincaid, ye calling hir a drunkard, and she calling you a witch, ye replied, 'that is ye was a witch, she and hir's should have better cause to call ye so;' accordingly a gret just fell on the said Euphame's daughter's leg, being playing near your house, and crushed the same, and that by your sorcerie.

The ninth is, that ye ended a compt with Iso-bell Atchesone, and because ye had the devil ride about the toun with hir and hir's; whereupon the nixt day she brak hir leg by ane fall from a horse, and ye came and saw hir and said 'Sie that ye say not that I have bewitched you, as other neigh-bours say.'

The tenth is, that Robert Wat, deacon of the cordiners, having fyned Robert Pursell, your sone-in-law, for a riot, ye came where he and the rest of the craft was conveined, and cursed them most outrageously, whereon, Robert Wat broke the cap on your head; since which tyme he fell away in his worldly means, till long after, he being in your good-son's house, where ye likeways was, ye asked, 'if he remembered since he broke the cap on your head? and that he had never thriven since, nor should, till you had amends of him'; whereon he being reconciled with you, he prospered in his worldly estate as before.

The eleventh is, the laying on of a grievous sickness on Christian Harlaw, for sending back a plack's worth of salt which ye had sent hir, it being too little; ye having threatened hir that it should be the dearest salt ever she saw with her eyes, and then, at her entreaty ye came to her house and she became presentlie weill; whereon Christian said. 'that is ought ailed hir thereafter, she would wyt you.'

The twelfth is, that Christian Sympson being owing you some money, and because she craved only eight days delay to pay it, ye threatened, in great rage, 'that she should have a sore heart or that day eight days:' according whereto, the said Christian's husband broke his leg within the said eight days.

The thirteenth is, that John Robieson having called you a witch, you in malice, laid a flux on him by your sorcerie.

The fourteenth is, for appearing to John Cockburn in the night, when bothe doors and windows were fact closed, and terrifying him in his sleep, because he had discorded with your daughter the day before.

The fifteenth is, for causing all William Smith's means evanish, to the intent he might never be able to relieve some cloaths he had panded besude you, woth an 100lbs. for fourteen merks Scots onlie.

The sixteenth is, for onlaying a grievous sickness on Janet Walker, lying in childbed; and then ye being sent for, and the said Janet's sister begging her health at you for God's sake, ye assented, and she recovered of hir sicknesse presently by your sorcerie.

The seventeenth is, that ye being disappointed of having Alexander Johnstoune's bairne's name, ye, in a great rage and anger, told him, 'that it should be telling him 40lb, betwixt and that tyme twelfmonth, that he had given you his bairne's name;' whereon he tooke a strange sickness and languished long; and at length, by persuasive of neighbours, he came to your house, and after he had eaten and drunken with you, ye with your sorcerie made him wholle. The child whose name ye got not was past eleven ere she could go.

The eighteenth is, that ye having fallin in a controversie with Margaret Williamsone, ye most outrageously wished the devill to blow her blind; after which, she, by your sorcerie, took a grievous sicknesse, whereof she went blind.

The nineteenth is, for laying a madness on Andrew Wilson, conforme to your threatening, wishing the devil to ryve the saul out of him, (which words, the tyme of his frenzie, ware ever in his mouth) and that because he had fallen in a brauling with your daughter.

The twentieth article is a generall, for beiring companie with the devil these twenty-eight years bypast; for consulting with him for laying on and taking off diseases, als weill on men as women and bestiall, which is nottourly known. Item, it is

confest by herself, that she has been commonlie
called a rank witch these many years bygane, and
has been sua diffamed, repute and halden.[123]

Although the court was called on Sunday 11 December, it did
not sit on that day. After the formal reading of the charges,
the trial had to be immediately postponed because the defence
advocates had not yet spoken to Agnes about her case.
Although Agnes had managed, through her daughter, to gain
the services of the lawyers, they had only been able to see their
client twice when they had lodged their summonses. In most
criminal trials, advocates would meet with their clients relatively quickly. However, in witchcraft cases the advocates were
only allowed to see the accused when the Commission were
finished with their investigation and the formal list of charges
was finalised. Once an accusation was made, the Commission
had to find the evidence and there was no time limit set for
how long that might take. Most Commissions took their time
in order to uncover all of the witchcraft that was happening
in their area, but even so most investigations were concluded
within two or three weeks. Some took only a few days. Most
accusations were followed rapidly by further proofs and usually an early confession. In Agnes' case, the Commission's
investigations had taken some 21 weeks. This was exceptional.
The trial actually got underway on 18 December.

The Commission had had 21 weeks in which to undertake
their investigations which then became the prosecution case. In
contrast, the defence advocates only had the time between the
finalised list of charges being completed on 11 December and the
start of the actual trial on the 18th to prepare their case: a mere
six days. While the advocates knew the gist of the complaints

lodged against Agnes, they did not know the evidence that had been gathered or the formal list of charges against her until the final dittay was completed on 11 December. In addition, Lawtie and Nisbet were barred from asking their own questions in the Potterrow on the grounds that this interfered with the 'lawfull progress of ane Commission'. In criminal trials, this rule was frequently ignored and defence advocates would employ people to ask questions and listen in to the local gossip. However, in witchcraft trials the presupposed guilt was so strong that even the defence advocates were normally fully convinced and mounted a less than robust case. As a result, few bothered to ask around for any details that might help the accused.

Because of the length of time Agnes had spent in prison and the status of George Gillespie as minister at Greyfriars Kirk, the trial had attracted a great deal of public attention. In addition, Edinburgh was a powder keg of tension: the city had seen plague and food shortages, there had been an armed siege at the castle and the Covenanter and Royalist forces were at each other's throats. It appeared as if the worst fears of the Kirk were coming true. Early on the morning of 11 December, a steady stream of individuals walked up to the court in the hope of gaining a place to see the 'foul witch of the Potterrow Port'. Turned away before they even got in the building, they returned in even greater numbers the next week. It was a mixed crowd. Some were members of Gillespie's congregation. Genuinely religious, they came to see one of the Devil's own brought to face justice. Shocked, no doubt, that Agnes resided in the same parish as themselves, their malice was based on a genuine fear of the Devil and all his works. They were joined by many others. Some were fervent Covenanters who knew little or nothing of Agnes or the Potterrow, but were fanatical in their hatred of witches. The most zealous among them were actually dismissive of the court system and wished that the Kirk had the authority to deal with witches without all this nonsense of lawyers and judges. As far as the Kirk was concerned, an accusation of witchcraft was an admission of guilt and a death sentence was the only conclusion. Then there were the usual suspects; those with nothing to do and who fancied the fun of a witch trial with the added appeal of being inside out of the winter weather. Not particularly religious, they enjoyed the thrill of hearing all about the activities of witches from the safety of the public benches. There were also some from the Potterrow in the long line waiting to enter the court, but they were by far the smallest group standing in the cold December morning. They were poor, they needed to work, they did not have the luxury of being able to take the day off to go and see what the whole town was talking about. There was also danger in attending the trial. What if Agnes spotted you and laid a curse on you for coming to watch her ordeal? Perhaps her daughter, Margaret, might see you and come and 'get' you after the trial was over. Nevertheless, there were still some, the unemployed and the bored, who stood in line hoping to get a seat.

After the hiatus of the previous week, the trial finally got underway on Sunday 18 December. Agnes was brought into the courtroom and she did not disappoint those on the public benches looking for some excitement. After several months of poor food, bad sanitation, rough treatment from the guards and hours of interrogation, Agnes looked emaciated, unkempt, dirty and smelly, with her grey hair loose and unwashed. In effect, she was the very picture of a witch.

The jury was already in place when Agnes arrived and her appearance may have convinced some of her guilt even before the trial began. There are multiple academic papers detailing how appearance can influence, to a degree, the jury and the judge in modern trials. This is known as 'attractiveness bias'.[124] More attractive defendants receive higher acquittal rates and lower sentences. As few biases are conscious today, it is doubtful that a jury in the 17th century would have been any different. They had been sworn in as 'guid men and true' and each was admonished by the Chancellor of the court to be 'guided by their true Christian hearts'.

Just as the Commissioners had been chosen by George Gillespie, so too the jury was selected by the minister. To find 15 'guid men and true', who else could the courts turn to but the local minister to guide them? The jury consisted of 15 men of 'guid repute', indwellers of the Potterrow. Agnes would have been known to the jury, if not personally then at least by reputation. Did the trial provide an opportunity to settle old scores? Several of those on the jury were cordiners who would, no doubt, listen particularly intently to the accusation of causing poverty to their Deacon. Sitting alongside the cordiners were several tailors. Members of another of the city's corporations, their natural sympathy would lie with the cordiners rather than with a female shop owner and moneylender. Or had their wives frequented Agnes' shop? Had their children been cared for by Agnes through an illness? Would that make them sympathetic? Despite the neighbourhood meeting that had been held and the multiple complaints against Agnes, there must have been some in the Potterrow that she had helped over the years.

The alleged crimes had been numerous and serious enough for the Privy Council to have immediately granted the Commission to investigate Agnes. The full trial also reflected the severity of the case in the number of allegations levelled against Agnes and the composition of the prosecution team, which comprised Sir Thomas Hope of Craighall and John Oliphant, both senior and experienced advocates. Agnes had her two advocates: John Lawtie and John Nisbet.

Thomas Hope was a knight baronet and an advocate in the Lord Advocate's office. During his long and distinguished career, in addition to Agnes' case, he was involved in 21 witchcraft trials, all of which returned a guilty verdict. His junior was John Oliphant, another extremely experienced prosecutor. He was also an advocate in the Lord Advocate's office and had successfully prosecuted four previous witchcraft cases.

While the jury had been selected and given notice of the trial date, the prosecution and defence teams had prepared their cases. The prosecution team listed the authorities they would draw upon to prove their case and the names of the expert witnesses they intended to call. The authorities cited were Jean Bodin and William Perkins, both demonologists; they would also use the book of Moses and the works of Ormlandis.

Jean Bodin was a 16th century French jurist, political philosopher and law professor at Toulouse. Despite being a Catholic, he was a recognised expert of demonology in Scotland. His main work was *De la demonomanie des sorciers* (*On the Demon mania of the sorcerers*).[125] Convinced of the dangers posed by Satan, Bodin's writing encouraged authorities to be ever vigilant. In trials of those accused of consorting with the Devil, he urged the courts to aim for prosecution at all times and to disregard the proper legal procedures, if necessary, to gain a conviction.[126] It was this last point that recommended him to many in the Scottish Kirk despite his Catholicism.

William Perkins was a 16th century English Puritan and Demonologist, and a Fellow at Christ's College in Cambridge. Perkins' book, *A Discourse on the Damned Art of Witchcraft*,[127] was published posthumously in 1608 and surpassed even James I's book *Daemonologie* to become the leading treatise on witches. Disagreeing with Bodin about legal procedures, Perkins nevertheless advocated the widespread use of torture in order to obtain a confession and to find out the nature of the relationship between the accused and the Devil. Perkins' work was another favourite with the Kirk.

Ormlandis was a legal jurist from the early church who wrote in his book *De Sortilegis Ubique* on the ubiquitous nature of witches and witchcraft. His work was frequently cited by the Kirk as proof of the reality of witches and witchcraft, as had been noted even by the early church.

The expert witnesses were: Alexander Colville; Patrick Henderson; physicians MacClure and Sibbet and surgeon Patrick Trotter. What is interesting to note is the inclusion of Colville and Henderson as expert witnesses despite the fact that they were both part of the investigating Commission. A modern court case would not call a member of the investigating team to also act as an expert witness, as the testimony from such a witness would be instantly called into question by the defence council citing a lack of impartiality on the part of the individual. The prosecution team could be accused of persuading their witness to give a favourable testimony. The modern concept of the impartiality and independence of witnesses would have made no sense to the 17th court. The fact that Colville and Henderson had investigated the accusations against Agnes made them the 'perfect' expert witnesses in the court's opinion because they knew what they were talking about. Their familiarity with the case was a positive rather than a negative attribute and made their testimony more reliable in the eyes of the court.

Witchcraft cases were complicated because of the supernatural nature of the crimes involved. The average person might not understand or recognise the significance of the actions of the accused because they were not an expert. Moreover, as each 'witch' could be sneaky and devious in their own way, a knowledge of the accused's behaviour and personality gained through an investigation was a definite asset. In this way, it made perfect sense in certain cases to use investigating Commissioners as expert witness. What is unusual is how few cases were considered to be so complicated that this became necessary. Even in the notorious Bargarran witch trial of 1697 that took place in Paisley, none of the Commissioners were called as expert witnesses. Eleven-year-old Christian Shaw claimed she was bewitched and produced hair, straw, coal, gravel, chicken feathers and cinders out of her mouth which she said had been put there by the 'witches'. Thirty-five local people were accused. The defence claimed Shaw was faking, the prosecution claimed the defence doctors had been bribed. Accusations of bewitchment and cursing, of faked fits and attention seeking behaviour, raged back and forth before a final guilty verdict was delivered on seven individuals.[128] In comparison, Agnes' case was merely that of one individual accused of harming others through witchcraft. This was a standard witchcraft case, like so many before and after. It was not complicated; it was simply weak. Colville and Henderson were required as expert witnesses to bolster the prosecution's assertion that Agnes had caused that harm.

The chancellor of the court was John Dickson, a baillie from the Potterrow who was also a colleague of baillie Eleis and a parishioner of George Gillespie. As a result of that familiarity, Dickson had no qualms about allowing Colville and Henderson to be expert witnesses in the trial.

After the jury was in place, the full list of charges was read out. For those not familiar with exactly what Agnes was accused of, the recital of charge after charge must have reinforced everything they had thought and feared: cursing her neighbours into poverty, causing grown men to sweat in their beds, breaking legs, leaving people blind and crippled, haunting people in their houses and bewitching them to death. It could not get much worse, until the court clerk read out the last article: that she had conspired with Auld Nick and that she had confessed to having done so.

What is interesting in Agnes' trial dittay is that no mention is made of her directly communing with the Devil. As all witches and witchcraft came from Auld Nick and the Kirk was obsessed with him, it is curious that this charge was *not made* against Agnes. In comparison with the other trial records for the period, this is very unusual. Later commentators on the witchcraft trials of the 17th century, such as those collected in *The Spottiswoode Miscellany* written in the 19th century, even commented upon the lack of contact with the Devil in this case. At the same time, however, Agnes was described as a 'vindictive old lady'.[129] The Victorian Antiquarians wrote extensively about the 17th century witchcraft trials and the comment about the lack of contact with the Devil is a curious rarity.

This lack of evidence of Agnes' relationship with the Devil, that fact that no one had seen her with the Devil and that she had never confessed to meeting the Devil or making a pact with him in any way allowed the defence team to challenge the charge of sorcery. Was the charge relevant? If it could not be proved that she had met and formed a pact with the Devil, how could she have any powers of sorcery? Her screaming at a neighbour that she would get the Devil to 'rive the saul out of them' was just a curse said in anger – it had no meaning behind it. Her advocates explained that it sounded worse than it really was. This was typical behaviour from women in the poorer parts of the city. There was no force behind her words. If Agnes had not met Auld Nick, then that must mean her powers came from herself. That was ridiculous; everyone knew women did not have power. Therefore, the charge of sorcery must fall.

This was a clever argument. It was not a question of whether or not Agnes was guilty, but whether or not the court had the evidence to substantiate the article being on her dittay in the first place. According to Lawtie and Nisbet, the prosecution had not proved there was a case to answer. There were no grounds for the sorcery charge.

The prosecution countered this argument by turning it on its head. That she had power was obvious; she had broken legs, laid illness, caused deaths. The fact that women cannot hold power except through the Devil was also obvious. Therefore, Agnes must have met Auld Nick, even if no one had seen her. Furthermore, if she had not been seen then that merely proved what a tricksy witch she was, with the power to hide her meetings. No doubt one of the gifts she was given as part of her 'pact wi' the De'il'. The prosecution insisted that the charge of sorcery stood.

In the Elizabeth Bathgate case of 1634, the defence advocates had also challenged the legality of some of the charges against her on the dittay. In that case, they had been successful and several of the charges were withdrawn. In a similar argument to Lawtie and Nesbitt, Elizabeth's advocates argued simply: if she had had no contact with the Devil and was not a witch as the Crown had originally stated then how, and why, would she murder? In Elizabeth's trial the defence arguments were accepted and she was acquitted of all charges against her.[130] In Agnes' case, Chancellor Dickson listened to both arguments and then agreed with the prosecution advocates. If the defence team had won their point, then almost all of the charges against Agnes would have fallen. More worryingly, in addition to the earlier Bathgate case, this might have set a precedent and meant that other cases involving witchcraft would never make it to the court. The potential ramifications to Calvinist Scotland were incalculable.

The difference between the Bathgate case and that of Agnes was the growing political and religious chaos that was engulfing the country. 1634 had seen a rise in political tension due to the King's economic policies and a widening gulf developing between the nascent Royalist and Covenanter camps. By 1644, the National Covenant had been signed, the Scottish Covenanters had formed the alliance of the Solemn League and Covenant with the English Parliamentarians and the Scottish Civil War had started. The Calvinist Kirk had ample proof of the presence of the Devil. With this background and the pressure that was brought by Gillespie, it is little wonder that Dickson agreed with Hope and Oliphant. The charge of sorcery remained firmly on the dittay.

All of these legal arguments had been disputed by the defence and prosecution before the chancellor. These were points of law and not a matter for the jury. Despite this, the argument had been held in open court and had been heard by all the jurors. They may not have understood all the nuances of the legal reasoning, but the result was clear: Agnes had consorted with the Devil. Given the level of import the Kirk gave to such a charge, the jury, who were all parishioners of Gillespie, would have been left in no doubt of the seriousness of Agnes' crimes.

Once the legality of the sorcery charge was established, the prosecution started to lay out its case. The case against Agnes was complicated, due in part to the evidence against her. The prosecution argued that Agnes was in 'cumpany with the Devill, in consulting wi him'. If she had done what was alleged then, she had power. As a woman, power was unnatural to her and so had to come from a man – the Devil. If her power came from the Devil, she was a witch. The prosecution had the statements from the witnesses proving she had done what was alleged. Even one or two such allegations would have been enough to bring someone to trial, but with Agnes there were 19 different charges against her involving her neighbours. The prosecution had the report from their investigations that showed her quarrelsome nature: the first of the classic four proofs. They had the expert witnesses who could explain why power was unnatural to women; although that was self-evident in the court it had to be proved. With unnatural power Agnes was, therefore, a witch. Lastly, and most damning, the prosecution had her confession.

The prosecution concluded its case at the end of the first day and Agnes was returned to her cell in the Tolbooth and the jury were sent home. Unlike in modern trials where a jury is told not to discuss anything they have heard with anyone, Dickson reiterated his instruct for them to 'search their hearts to know God's truth', but did not instruct them not to discuss the case. Given the nature of the trial, the fact that it was someone from their own neighbourhood and that there were multiple charges involving so many victims, it is unlikely that the jury did not discuss the case.

The trial opened the next day with the case for the defence. After having tried, unsuccessfully, to have the sorcery charge dropped, the defence had three main points on which to attack the prosecution. Rather than defending each charge against her in detail, Lawtie and Nisbet attacked the prosecution's main accusation: that Agnes was a witch in the first place. This was a risky strategy. By not addressing whether or not she had caused illness or blindness, they could ignore most of the witness testimony and attack the central charge of witchcraft and sorcery. Lawtie and Nisbet argued that when Agnes' house was searched no witch's paraphernalia such as a familiar or poppet had been found. No 'such thing (was) found therein, which ever any witch in the world was used to practize'. They stated, correctly, that no one had seen her with the Devil or heard her say she was ever with the Devil. They then explained that for the previous 20 years or so several 'witches' at Edinburgh and Leith had been interrogated, but not one of them had delated

Agnes as a witch. No record existed in which she had been named as a witch.

Time and again the defence argued that Agnes' actions were not diabolical in nature. Telling John and Bessie to pray for their son was not demonic. The prosecution countered that Agnes' prayer or any that she commanded be said were indeed demonic as they were used as a devilish charm. This was a difficult argument for the defence to counter. For an ordinary individual to say their prayers or for them to instruct their child to say their prayers was to be commended, but prayer involved both act and intention. Had the instruction come from Gillespie, the prayer would be sanctioned as the prayer would be from a Christian to God, but as it came from Agnes as part of her magic practices it was instantly tainted. She was a woman with alleged magical powers, but as a woman she could not possess power: that power must have come from her master, the Devil, and thus the prayer must be to the Devil.

The overall defence was that the accusations by Harry Moriesoun were malicious lies concocted by Agnes' neighbours. Did the women of the Potterrow want her out of the way because they still owed her money? Did the men want rid of her because she did not know her place as a woman? The general overall defence sidestepped the issue of questioning the veracity of individual witness statements. None of Agnes' alleged victims was accused of being a liar. The only person whose truthfulness was challenged was Moriesoun, who had not been one of Agnes' victims. Why, the defence argued, had he been the official complainant rather than one of those who had suffered Agnes' wrath?

Despite all these arguments, the defence still had one serious problem with Agnes' case. The last article on her dittay; that of having confessed to being a witch. That alone should have produced a guilty verdict. Yet the wording is curious. The article is described as being 'a generall', that is, an article that was laid on every 'witch' brought to trial. The part which quotes Agnes is even more interesting. Agnes' confession of being a witch had troubled the Commission from the beginning and the wording on this dittay bears out that concern. Agnes stated that she had been called a witch by others but *not* that she had called herself a witch. She had, in truth, *not* confessed. Given Agnes' personality, this statement makes perfect sense. When questioned by Gillespie and the others at the Kirk Session, Agnes may have replied angrily something like 'others call me a witch' and that was as much as they could get out of her. It was probably accepted by the Kirk Session because they thought they had heard a confession. She was a woman, women were witches, they had asked her if she was a witch and she *must have* said she was. For the few who heard what she actually said, they may have assumed that other evidence would come forward – that she would be delated by another witch or be found to have the Devil's Mark. However, the statement that others had called her a witch was not a confession, but rather a sly complaint from Agnes which hid the truth behind the gossip and slander she had endured over the years. It was a good counter to the confession which the prosecution had always known was weak. But weak or not, the ministers were adamant: it was a confession.

Agnes was not allowed to speak during the trial and so any explanation she might give as to what she had actually said and meant by her 'confession' had to be relayed by her advocates. The denial that she was a witch or indulged in witchcraft which the defence had started their reasoning with was, obviously, the right thing to say: an admission in court was an instant guilty verdict and death sentence. However, it was difficult to maintain this denial when Gillespie stood in the witness box and swore that she had confessed. To argue against the minister was tantamount to calling him a liar. Agnes may have meant her admission was what others said of her, but if the minister believed it was a confession who were the jury to believe: a man of God or a woman, an accused witch?

After the defence case rested, Chancellor Dickson called two witnesses for the prosecution. Colville and Henderson came back into court to testify as to the nature of witches, their confessions and how slippery and tricky they would be in denying them. It was, more or less, the same evidence they had given on the previous day, but served to undermine Lawtie and Nisbet's defence argument about Agnes' confession. Lawtie and Nisbet argued that, as the prosecution case had rested, the recall of Colville and Henderson was improper, indeed extrajudicial. However, this was asking Dickson to rule himself as having acted extrajudicially and the argument was lost before it began.

In the late afternoon of 19 December, Chancellor Dickson gave his instructions to the jury. Reminding them of their Christian duty, he sent them away to consider their verdict. Agnes was taken back to the Tolbooth and the public benches were cleared of the spectators. The jury went home in a town that was awash with the story of Agnes' witchcraft and the breech with the English Parliamentarians, which every minister reminded them was the work of the Devil. As if to drive the point home, the unseasonal outbreak of plague was running rampant across the city. Whichever disease it actually was, the illness ran out of control through all of the poorer district in Edinburgh. The ports were closed and the baillies stopped all unnecessary movement within the city. Agnes was lying in the Tolbooth waiting for her verdict and was completely reliant on her daughter for food. If the guards' treatment of accused witches before their trial was bad, it was unbearable afterwards. The assumption, which was usually correct, that this was now definitely a witch removed any and all constraints on their behaviour. The basic supply of bread and water was not given. Why should the guards feed someone due to be executed? Most 'witches' were found guilty and executed within a few days of their trial, but, with the plague raging across the city, the jury were unable to meet and discuss Agnes' case. Agnes was, therefore, left starving in her cell, unless her daughter was allowed to bring her some food, until the plague restrictions were lifted and the jury returned a verdict.

13

Verdict and Sentence

THE TRIAL HAD lasted for only two days when Chancellor Dickson brought matters to a close by charging the jury with their duty. In a modern trial, judges instruct the jury to consider only the evidence that had been presented to them. In witchcraft trials, what a juryman might know about the accused witch was considered an advantage. Modern juries are told to put aside any prejudices they may have. Juries in witchcraft trials were constantly reminded of general preconceptions about witches. Modern juries are warned against discussing the trial with anyone else and to avoid any reporting of the trial in the media. Things were somewhat different in the 17th century. At the end of the first day, the jurors were sent home to the Potterrow after Dickson told them to search their hearts to know God's truth. When the trial finished the jury was left to consider its verdict. At the same time, the jury members were attending Greyfriars Kirk to hear Gillespie preach; the same minister who had led the investigation and appeared as an expert witness. Everyone in the neighbourhood had complained about Agnes, the local baillie had investigated her activities, the prosecution had clearly stated that Agnes had confessed: the verdict should have been a foregone conclusion. George Gillespie and the other Commissioners 'knew' Agnes to be guilty; all that was needed before she faced the flames was the confirmatory verdict from the jury. By the Sunday following the trial, Gillespie and Mungo Law may well have been puzzled by the apparent inability of the jury to deliver a guilty verdict. When they preached their sermons that day, did they quote scripture? *Thou shalt not suffer a witch to live.*[131] Were the jury listening as they sat in the pews? Greyfriars had certainly seen an increase in the size of the congregation since Agnes' arrest and again now that her trial had taken place. Whatever the theme of his sermon, Gillespie must have felt certain that a verdict would be delivered soon, but in that he was to be proved wrong.

As Agnes lay in her Tolbooth cell waiting her verdict, William Laud, whose advice to the King on religious matters in Scotland had been so contentious, faced execution. On 10 January, the old Archbishop was taken out to Tower Hill in London and beheaded. The old man had been in gaol since the spring, after his trial had failed to reach a verdict. The Parliament had passed a bill of attainder which allowed for him to be executed as a traitor. Montrose and his rebels were still eluding Argyll as they roamed the Highland glens. More clansmen were rallying to his cause, as well as that of the King, and the Parliament in Edinburgh raged at his traitorous activities, but could do little else.

After the first Royalist victories in the Scottish Civil War, the fighting had deteriorated into clan warfare as the Royalists rampaged through Campbell country. In retaliation, Argyll assembled his men and trapped Montrose in the Great Glen. Montrose turned his troops and set them on a flanking march through the mountains of Lochaber and surprised Argyll at the battle of Inverlochy on 2 February 1645. The Covenanters and Campbells were heavily defeated. The victory gave Montrose control over the western Highlands and many other clans and noblemen were attracted to the Royalist cause. The danger to the Covenanting cause seemed to grow weekly while the talks between Charles and the English Parliamentarians went round in circles and achieved nothing.

The victory at Inverlochy had far-reaching consequences for the Scots. As a result of their defeat, the Scottish Covenanter army in England sent several hundred troops home to bolster the Covenanter forces in Scotland which weakened the Scottish army in England. With fewer numbers present, the Scots were less able to resist the rising leadership of Oliver Cromwell, who had always disliked and disregarded the Solemn League and Covenant. Cromwell's vision for Great Britain would lead to the Protectorate being imposed on Scotland in 1653.

In the meantime, Agnes was being treated as a convicted witch. The baillies on guard duty knew she was guilty and so were simply awaiting the execution date. Her daughter Margaret may have been allowed one last visit to say goodbye. And so, everyone waited, and waited. One week passed, then two. Christmas came and went. Margaret continued to walk up to the Tolbooth as many times as she could carrying food for her mother, who was now sitting in legal limbo in her filthy cell. Neither guilty nor innocent, she had to endure what must have seemed like endless days and nights in her freezing cold cell knowing that she would ultimately be found guilty, but when? The New Year arrived. Everyone in the Potterrow celebrated and still Agnes sat in her cell. January arrived with heavy snowfall. Margaret trudged up the hill with hot food that was cold by the time she got there. Her long skirt soaked with snow, cumbersome and heavy, it must have been tiring to walk up and down to the Tolbooth. There was still no word from the jury. January turned into a cold and icy February and even then there was no verdict.

Finally, on 8 February 1645, Agnes was taken out of her cell and returned to the courtroom to hear the verdict. The courtroom was packed. Many of the better-off parishioners of Greyfriars who had sat, probably terrified, listening to the wicked goings-on down in the Potterrow during the trial now returned to hear Agnes' fate. Fewer of the Potterrow inhabitants would have been present – most could guess what the verdict would be and could not spare the time – but it is very likely that Margaret sat on the public benches in support of her mother.

After everyone was sworn in, Chancellor Dickson called on the jury foreman to deliver the verdict. The foreman rose and the verdict was read out. Agnes was convicted of being 'in continual society and company of the Devil'. The foreman sat down and Chancellor Dickson repeated the verdict to the open court: she was guilty, she was a witch. He then stared at Agnes and condemned her to be worriet to death outside Edinburgh Castle and her dead body to be then burned at the stake.

At that point the court should have risen. There was no more to be said. There was no appeal. The matter was resolved. Agnes had previously repeatedly and loudly denied any suggestion of having confessed to being a witch, a sound strategy at the beginning of her trial, but as the verdict and sentence was now declared, she had nothing to lose. She was not allowed to, and was not supposed to, speak. Agnes was expected to hear her fate in silence. She did not. Agnes had one last outburst to make. Standing tall in the courtroom, she yelled out that she had often consulted with the Devil and that she was indeed 'ane rank witch', a term used to describe a witch who is 'noble, proud and powerful'. Agnes was dragged out of the courtroom and taken back to her cell in the Tolbooth.

Why had the jury taken so long to come to their verdict? Most trial records show guilty verdicts delivered within a day or two of the trial finishing, with some juries convicting on the day of the trial itself. Many show guilty verdicts where the accused faced far fewer charges on their dittay than Agnes. It could be argued that the jury in Agnes' case was already prejudiced against her as they were from the neighbourhood and knew of her behaviour. Most of them no doubt knew or were related to those who had complained about her. There were members of the Cordiners Corporation on the jury who would hear of Agnes' attack on the previous Deacon. Equally, they were parishioners of Greyfriars Kirk which made it unthinkable to contradict the minster in his belief of Agnes' guilt. All of this would tend to lead to a swift and guilty verdict, but in Agnes' case this did not happen. The jury, despite the pressure from the Kirk to convict quickly, did take their time to consider the evidence and the counter arguments put forward by Agnes' defence advocates. She had a bad temper and cursed people in the street. What woman in the Potterrow did not? She cut the Buchannans' child and yet they had approached her for help with young John in the first place, and despite having had previous arguments wither her on several occasions. She cursed people and then their legs were broken, but had that been her witchcraft or possibly that of another witch? Or had those legs simply been broken due to an accident?

While the 17th century court system may be open to criticism for allowing an investigator to also be an expert witness for the prosecution and for the local minister to head up the Commission to try Agnes in the first place, the jury does seem to have carefully weighed the evidence against her. They did not rush to judge. After delivering the verdict, the jury returned to their lives in the Potterrow and Agnes returned to her cell in the Tolbooth. Execution was surely only a day or two away. Most 'witches' were executed within a few days or a week of a guilty verdict. Yet again, Agnes did not follow the usual timetable. After another week in her cell, Agnes was still waiting to be executed. A second week passed, then a third. Only after 25 more days in the Tolbooth was Agnes taken to be executed.

Over her remaining time in the Tolbooth, it is not known if her daughter Margaret visited. Margaret's support had been unusual and Agnes had been very fortunate, as many families abandoned accused witches to their fate. But that previous support had been for an accused witch, not for one who had been found guilty by the court and had shouted out for all of Edinburgh to hear that she was 'ane rank witch'. Did Margaret still walk up the hill with food and what little comfort she could? If she was reviled previously, with her mother's confession now the talk of the town it must have been even harder for her to endure the abuse that was now aimed at her. If Margaret did not visit, or was not allowed to, then it is likely that the guards were careful to ensure that Agnes did not die before she was due to be worriet. Twenty-five days is a long time to survive with no food, and Agnes was middle-aged and had already endured several months of ill-treatment. It is possible that the guards gave her just enough food to stop her from dying and to avoid any punishment of themselves if she did so.

While Agnes had been sitting waiting, the General Assembly of the Kirk had met and discussed improving education in the schools, the ordination of ministers, control of drunkenness at weddings and recommendations on their ongoing relationships with the English Parliamentarians and the King. Gillespie and Law had attended the Assembly and been preaching thrice weekly about the usual practices of Auld Nick; no doubt using Agnes as an example of his evil deeds. The formal execution of a witch was purely a matter for the secular authorities. It was Edinburgh Town Council that had to buy the wood and rope, set a date, employ an executioner and post the public notices. It was the Council that instructed John Eleis and the other baillies about the time and date in order that they could control any crowds. The Kirk never sullied its own hands with the practicalities of a witch execution. The Kirk did not pay for the executioner or the wood to burn the 'witch'. The Kirk did not pay for the guards who brought the witch from her cell to the execution site. The Kirk did not compensate the street-traders or shopkeepers whose business was disrupted by a witch's execution. The Kirk did not even pay for the public notices, although they did in many cases oversee the wording to ensure it was as strongly condemnatory as possible.

On 6 March 1645, Agnes was brought out of her cell for execution on Castle Hill. It was a bitterly cold Monday morning and Agnes was wakened at dawn. Dressed in thin hair shifts, barefoot and bare-headed, 'witches' walking to their execution were expected to show contrition. They were supposed to be penitent. They were supposed to be scared as they were about to meet their Maker and, under the Calvinist doctrine of predestination, were set to enter Hell for all eternity. Did Agnes submit meekly to her final walk? After she was wakened by the baillies, her hair would have been cut to ease the strangulation. Her hands would have been bound behind her back and a noose placed around her neck, the loose rope of which would be used to pull her along the street. The execution of a witch was always a public affair. George Gillespie, Mungo Law and the other Commissioners would follow as the baillies led Agnes from the Tolbooth up to the castle to where a pyre of wood, with some coal and tar to aid the burning, was waiting. Despite the entire occasion being overseen by the Kirk, an undercurrent of superstition still underpinned the day. The wood required for a witch burning was always freshly cut, as it was generally believed that anyone selling wood for a burning would be haunted by the witch thereafter.

The procession from the Tolbooth to the castle execution site was supposed to be followed by everyone from the parish. Again, superstition dictated that Auld Nick might appear at the last minute and 'rescue' his witch. To contradict this belief and to prove that the Devil was the prince of lies, the Kirk ministers required everyone to attend the execution to see God's justice done. It is doubtful if everyone from the Potterrow would have left their work to watch Agnes be put to death, but many would. Some, no doubt, because they truly thought her wicked and deserving of punishment. Others, frightened by the whole affair and who may even have given evidence against her, like the Buchannans, perhaps wanted to make sure she really was dead and would not come back to haunt them. Then there were the those who were just there for a day out. A witch execution was not over quickly and, although a macabre spectacle, could provide an entire day's entertainment for those so inclined. Drinking ale and following Agnes on her walk from cell to death, the crowd entertained itself by cat-calling and throwing muck at 'the witch'.

Agnes was a strong personality, but she was still a middle-aged woman who had spent over nine months in a cold, damp cell. The path from the Tolbooth up towards the castle is not a great distance to walk in good weather, but in a biting March wind after weeks of imprisonment, rough treatment and filthy conditions, Agnes may well have struggled to walk barefoot on the cold, Edinburgh cobbles with her hands bound. There are several records of 'witches' falling on their way to execution and being dragged along on their hands and knees, much to the delight of the crowd. Whether or not Agnes fell, this was only the start. Before the 'witch' was worriet she might do or say something exciting. This was, after all, the 'witch' that had screamed and yelled in the court when her verdict and sentence had been read out. She might admit again that she was a witch, or perhaps yell a curse at someone. Then there was the actual worrieting as the executioner did his work and then there were the several hours it took for the body to burn. Modern cremation in a clean, controlled, enclosed environment may take between two and three hours to burn a body completely. Burning a body in the open air, with wood that may not be perfectly dry and with the early spring weather of Edinburgh which could include wind and rain, would take considerably longer. All the while the rougher elements in the crowd could sit around eating and drinking and swapping stories.

Once the baillies had dragged Agnes to the pyre, Gillespie, as the lead Commissioner, would repeat the sentence and then preach a sermon reminding the townsfolk of the wickedness of witches and of the damnation and hellfire that awaited them. This was Gillespie's big moment. He had triumphed over the Devil. He had outwitted Auld Nick. The work of the courts, the lawyers, the witnesses and the jury were forgotten about. The execution of a witch was always declared as a triumph for the Kirk, with the contributions of all others ignored. Although the 'witch' was not allowed to speak, in Agnes' case it is doubtful she would remain quiet. Did she scan the crowd hoping for a last glimpse of her daughter and shout out a final farewell? Did she yell abuse at George Gillespie or curse Harry Moriesoun? The official records did not normally note any final words. In some instances, however, the last words of a 'witch' were recorded. A final confession would prove their guilt, a curse would demonstrate their wickedness and a declaration of innocence would show the world their stubborn arrogance and blatant disregard for the authority of the Kirk. Unfortunately, there is no record of any last statement from Agnes, although she may well have repeated her declaration that she was indeed 'ane rank witch'.

After the minister had said his last exhortation, the executioner stepped forward. Two of the baillie's men held Agnes' arms and forced her into a kneeling position, facing the crowd. Once she was held fast, the executioner approached and tightened the noose around her neck. Agnes' natural reaction would have been to struggle as best as she could. To counter this, the executioner might have put one of his knees in the small of her back to get a better purchase, or he might have used her bound hands as a resting place for his foot. As Agnes was held by the baillie's men, if the executioner pushed down too hard on her hands her arms would be forced back, pulling both shoulders out of their joints. Once he was in a comfortable position, the executioner would start to twist the noose around her neck. Sometimes a small piece of wood was slipped between the noose and the witch's neck which could be twisted, worrieting the victim. It could take several minutes for a witch to die depending on the strength of the executioner, his experience and the amount of 'give' in the rope. Most were unconscious within one or two minutes and inexperienced executioners or, in the case of multiple executions, those who were tired, might then suppose the witch to be dead and deliver them onto the pyre. It is not known how long Agnes took to die, but the executioner at the castle was, at least, experienced and she would presumably be spared accidental death by burning.

While Agnes was being worriet, she was facing the watching crowd. Gillespie was watching his parishioners. Although they were the people that had complained to him in the first place, few of them bothered to attend the Kirk on a Sunday as they should. These were not the nice, respectable parishioners that lived near Greyfriars. They were the damned who lived in the spider's nest of the Potterrow, the sort of place that bred witches. As the execution continued, Gillespie noted his parishioners' behaviour. Who looked visibly shocked, who turned their faces away and who was enjoying the day's entertainment far too much with their ale, crude jokes and lack of proper Calvinist piety?

The entertainment that was on offer was a truly gruesome one. As the rope tightened about her neck, Agnes' face would have started to swell and her lips, nose and the tips of her ears would have taken on a blueish tinge as the blood supply was cut off. Her eyes would have bulged in their sockets and her tongue protruded from her mouth. By this time, a frothy mucus would have been streaming from her mouth and nostrils, and the gurgling in her throat would have been loud enough for some in the crowd to hear. Despite being held fast by rope and baillie's men, Agnes would still have struggled. Her fingers and hands would have twisted and turned, chafing themselves on the rope. As unconsciousness and death approached, Agnes would have lost control of her body and would probably have urinated and defecated. Many records note the crowd's delight at the smell of a 'stinking witch' as the simple hair shift became befouled: the final humiliation. After Agnes had finally died, her body would have been tied onto the pyre and a few extra licks of tar were probably applied to the shirt to aid the fire.

The execution of a witch was a public affair for two very important and interlinked reasons. Firstly, it consigned an evil-doer to the flames. Agnes' death was a stark warning to others who might think of following her wicked ways exactly what would happen to them if they did so. Gillespie, and the other Greyfriars' ministers over the years, had shown scant regard for the inhabitants of the Potterrow and had routinely ignored what went on in the neighbourhood as long as it remained there. Agnes' gruesome death was a practical, if macabre, demonstration of what would happen if their filth and super-stition overflowed into decent Edinburgh. The moment Harry Moriesoun arrived at the minister's door to complain, the

Potterrow could be ignored no longer and its transgressions had to be punished. For Margaret, watching as her mother choked to death, this was a sombre warning.

Just as importantly, however, Agnes' death demonstrated the power of the Kirk and the true faith in combination with the false nature of the Devil. He had promised his followers everything they wanted, he had sought them out and then, at the last moment, he had abandoned them to their fate. Agnes and her ilk were forced to endure an horrific and painful death to expose the wicked deceit of Auld Nick. It was for this reason that the Kirk demanded everyone's presence at an execution. The painful death of the witch was just the beginning of their punishment as they were then cast into the fires of Hell for all eternity. The doctrine of predestination might have been a difficult theological concept for some, but the agonised death of a witch served as a warning to the likes of the inhabitants of the Potterrow. They were all already damned, as Gillespie knew, but to keep them in order they needed to be confronted by the falsity of the Devil. Moreover, the diabolical nature of witches, like Agnes from the Potterrow, confirmed the righteousness of Gillespie and the rest of the Calvinist Kirk.

14

Aftermath

AFTER AGNES' EXECUTION, life returned to normal in the Potter-row. Margaret and her husband still lived in the area although she had stood by her mother throughout her imprisonment and trial. Was she eyed suspiciously by her neighbours as she went about in the street? Or was it more than suspicion; was it also fear? Hadn't she been involved in haunting Cockburn? And if her mother was a witch, did that mean she was one also? Wasn't she known throughout the neighbourhood as a witch's gett? What about those who had complained about Agnes? Would she haunt them from beyond the grave? Would Margaret come after them in some way, seeking revenge for her mother's death? Neither of the Greyfriars ministers appear to have visited the Potterrow any more frequently than before. If the residents were looking for some comfort or reassurance from their religious leaders, it was sadly lacking. In cases such as this, neighbourhoods that had produced a witch were often damned by association and merely left to their own devices.

What is curious is the lack of action taken against Agnes' daughter. Margaret was named in at least two of the charges against Agnes: the incidents with John Cockburn and Andrew Wilson had both involved her. In both situations she, and not Agnes, had initiated the arguments and in the case with John the weaver, Margaret was surely as culpable as her mother in haunting him in his home. What was going on? Why did Gillespie not bring a Commission against Margaret as a suspected witch? Was he quite content that a named witch was still living in his parish? What had happened to the Calvinist zeal to battle the Devil? What of the baillie? Was John Elies comfortable that a named witch was in the Potterrow? Were both too distracted by the increasingly fraught political situation, despite neither being a soldier or actively involved in any fighting? Or was it the flimsy excuse that no one from the neighbourhood had formally complained about Margaret? And why not? Why had the Potterrow not taken the opportunity of complaining about Margaret too and being rid of the witch's gett as well as the witch?

Even though no one had formally complained, Margaret should, by the laws of that time, have been arrested. Those individuals named as witches in other trials very quickly found themselves locked up to face trial and execution, so why not Margaret? Was it, perhaps, that Gillespie and Elies were left feeling, at the very least, uncomfortable with what had been happening in the Potterrow? Although never officially censured for their apparent lack of knowledge about what was happening in the neighbourhood, their ignorance had nevertheless been exposed for all to see. Was a further trial involving Margaret considered yet another public embarrassment? Or was it actually more callous than that? If no one in the Potterrow officially complained about Margaret, well, hell mend them. Both officials had shown unconcern about what happened in the tenements of the Potterrow. Admittedly, Gillespie had only been at Greyfriars Kirk since 1642, but between then and Agnes' trial had been a rare visitor to the Potterrow. His predecessor, Andrew Ramsay, had ministered to the Potterrow, on paper at least, from 1614 to 1641 but had also been noted for his absence in the area, as had James Fairlie for the seven years of his tenure. Mungo Law was proving to be no better. The destitute, poor and middling folks of the Potterrow consistently had ministers who appeared to care little for them, visiting only rarely and for basic ministry care such as funerals. These men of the cloth, Calvinist to the core and members of God's Elect, had other things on their minds. The position at Greyfriars Kirk was seen as a political stepping stone to greater things – it was not a ministry for the care of ordinary people. All of the Greyfriars ministers were charged with the care of their parishioners; none of them cared for the Potterrow. All of them were housed and well-fed with a fat stipend from the public purse, while neglecting the Potterrow. Ripened by their own corruption, all of them gained promotion and an increase in status while the inhabitants of the Potterrow saw no improvement in their lot. All of them had failed to see the violence, poverty and neglect that was in their parish while they set their sights on higher things. George Gillespie and Mungo Law were happy to tell the world of their battles against the Devil: proof of their own godliness. Once Agnes' trial was over and she had served her purpose in their rise to the leadership of the Covenanters, the Potterrow was no longer of any concern. Margaret may well have been her mother's daughter, a witches gett, capable of curing or causing illness and haunting people in their own homes, but if no formal complaint was made then the Potterrow could be conveniently forgotten about.

It was not just the actions, or rather inactions, of the minister and the baillie that were ignored after the trial. All of those who had originally complained about Agnes were equally dismissed. The Witchcraft Act of 1563 was quite specific: it outlawed both witches and those who consulted with witches. The Kirk's Condemnatory Act of 1642 had been equally clear: those who consulted with witches were to be dispatched to God's judgement. Why had the likes of John Buchannan and Bessie Currie not been arrested? The families of those who had been cursed by Agnes had merely chosen to beg her to remove their relative's illness. They had not called in a doctor and then reported Agnes as they should. Why was Gillespie not initiating investigations into them? Why was baillie Eleis not knocking at their doors? And what of the others in Gillespie's parish who were obviously consulting with witches – what was happening to them? Just as with Margaret, the Calvinist zeal for witch-hunting was demonstrably absent. This is all the more curious given Gillespie's behaviour in his previous Fife parish where he had initiated and presided over investigations into multiple witch accusations.

By the time the spring of 1645 arrived, the port was busy again. The traders came and went, the middling sorts worked in their shops, the working poor scratched a living and the destitute begged on the streets. The background tension of the war was all around and Agnes was all but forgotten. For the various people left injured by Agnes and her alleged activities, no help was forthcoming. The Kirk might root out witches, but showed little or no charity for those left in the aftermath of a witch trial. Euphame Kincaid had a crippled daughter; Christian Sympson had a crippled husband; Christian Dickson's daughter was limping; Jonet Grinton's family had no mother; Margaret Williamson was blind: in each case, no charity from Greyfriars Kirk's poor fund appears to have been made. Those who could not work were supported as best they could by their families, or else fell into dire poverty very quickly. In contrast, the four members of the Commission were paid for their time and any expenses they had accrued by the end of March. In addition, all four were commended for the work they had undertaken.

The Kirk had also been quick to take over Agnes' estate. What, if anything, was left of her savings, her possessions and her shop were forfeit. The cost of witchcraft trials was borne by the public purse, but as witchcraft was a crime against God the estate of guilty 'witches' fell to the Kirk. There are numerous records where families were left penniless after the 'witch' was executed and the Kirk took possession of the deceased's estate. Some individuals were left destitute and homeless. In the case of accused male witches there is a higher rate of suicide than with female witches. Although there are many factors at play in any act of suicide, it may be that caring for one's family was a consideration. Death by suicide was a sin and a scandal, and the dead, in most cases, were not allowed a Christian burial, but at least their families were provided for by the retention of the suicide's estate.

No blame was ever laid at the minister or the baillie's door for what had been happening in the Potterrow under their noses. It was the sneaky nature of the Devil and his witches that deceived honest men, not their own neglect. The fact that Gillespie had seldom visited his parishioners in the Potterrow was not mentioned, despite the fact that absence in the neighbourhood had rendered him remote and thus unapproachable for the ordinary people. When Bessie and John's child was ill and needed prayers said, it never crossed their mind to approach the minister. When Agnes was terrorising her neighbours with threats, no one thought to seek him out. Equally, John Eleis and the other baillies seemed to have policed the Potterrow on a daily basis without seeing Agnes the moneylender and her threatening ways. Every public slanging match, every open argument, every yelled curse only seems to have happened when John was 'not there' to see it. Despite being a constant presence at the port ensuring the safety of the city, John, as well as every single one of his men, failed to see or hear anything Agnes said or did. There are numerous entries in the Council and Kirk Session records of individuals arrested and admonished for their behaviour: arguing in the street or cursing their neighbours. Despite the fact that Agnes was convicted of acts of 'witchcraft and sorcerie' spanning *28 years*, no one in authority had seen anything.

After Agnes' execution Gillespie remained minster of the first charge at Greyfriars Kirk for a further two years until he was promoted to the ministry at St Giles in 1647.[132] In the two years from Agnes' execution until he moved to St Giles, he was seldom, if ever, seen in the Potterrow.

Mungo Law remained as minister of the second charge at Greyfriars Kirk. An unrepentant Covenanter, he was captured by the English Army at Alyth on 28 August 1651 and was kept prisoner until January 1653. On his release, he resumed his charge at Greyfriars and continued there until his death in February 1660.[133] Like Gillespie, he considered most of the inhabitants of the Potterrow to be already damned by God and thus did not take the trouble to visit the area.

While the attitudes of both Gillespie and Law seem harsh to modern eyes, it must be remembered that they were devout Calvinists who firmly believed in the theology of predestination, as did all of the men of the Kirk in the 17th century. They also genuinely believed that they were under attack by the Devil which was 'proved' by the famine, plague and war through which they lived. They were neither particularly cruel, nor more overly zealous than any other Kirk minister of their time. Their treatment of Agnes was equally informed by the time in which they lived. The political, religious and physical chaos of the mid-17th century was a perfect storm of events that created fear in almost everyone and led many in the Scottish Kirk into the religious frenzy that saw Auld Nick and all his works in every aspect of their lives.

Alexander Colville continued in his legal career and was involved in three witchcraft trials in 1661 involving 19 accused witches and then a further two trials in 1662. In these later trials, he sat solely as a Commissioner and did not take on the dual role of investigator and Commissioner as he had in Agnes' case. In fact, the only other time in which he took on the dual roles was earlier in 1629, in the case of Alexander Drummond. The Drummond case was a particularly contentious one and Colville was initially sent to Perth as an investigator before being asked to also sit as a Commissioner. Although Drummond was convicted and executed for witchcraft, there was a posthumous campaign to clear his name as he was said to be 'ane notable Christian and did all his wondrous cures by lawfull meanes'.[134] A search of the records indicates that the only times when an individual was asked to undertake the dual roles of investigator and Commissioner were in difficult or controversial cases where the evidence was weak. In most of the cases, a guilty verdict was the outcome.

John Eleis, the baillie who had worked in the Potterrow all of his adult life but failed to see or hear anything of Agnes' temper before her trial, disappeared from the records, as did Patrick Henderson.

Agnes' two lawyers, John Lawtie and John Nesbitt, also disappeared from the records after her trial. There is no note of them appearing as defence advocates in any further witchcraft trials or in any other court cases. The records may have been lost over the years, or their defence of Agnes and summoning of the Lord Provost may indeed have proved to be career suicide and the two men were either forced to leave Edinburgh or to leave the legal profession.

Agnes' case had been curious from the start. The amount of time she sat in gaol awaiting trial while evidence was gathered, the fact that she was not brodded for the Devil's Mark, the length of time the jury took to reach a verdict: all of these are at odds with the normal course of justice in a witchcraft trial. These differences even caused comment shortly afterwards. Alexander Seton joined the faculty of advocates on 10 December 1641, almost three years before Agnes' case came to trial. He was knighted by Charles II and became Lord Pitmeddin in 1677 when he was appointed as a Lord of Session, the highest Scottish court. He opposed the repeal of the Test and Penal Laws proposed by King James VII and, as a result, was removed from his seat on The Bench and the Court of Justiciary. In 1688, King William III offered to reinstate him as one of the Lords of Session, but Sir Alexander declined, feeling it inconsistent with his previous Oaths of Allegiance to

James VII. He then retired from professional life. During his retirement, he wrote treatises and commentaries on numerous court cases. Despite being retired, many of his writings were studied by young legal students and advocates as part of their training, most notably, *The laws and customs of Scotland, in matters criminal*, published in 1699. In his writings on Agnes' trial, Pitmeddin makes careful note of the composition of the jury with its several members of the Cordiner's Corporation and people from the Potterrow. He acknowledges that the evidence against Agnes, although strong on first reading, did not stand up to scrutiny and commented that the final sentence was harsh.[135]

One final curiosity surrounds the records of the summons of the Lord Provost of Edinburgh, Sir John Hay: they are missing. Again, these records may simply have disappeared over the years, but it is noticeable that in many witchcraft trials the records pertaining to the great and the good always seem to go missing, while those of ordinary people and the 'witches' themselves can be much more readily found. The records of life in 17th century Scotland are remarkably full, but it is curious that certain documents are conspicuous by their absence. Within witchcraft trials, the names of male accused frequently disappear: in the case of the Stow 'witches' of 1649, the male accused is merely the 'man from Lauder', while the women are identified and named. In some witchcraft trials, names have been deliberately scored out or physically ripped out of the document. In a case where officials are at fault, any judgement against them is often missing or recorded with little detail. The admonition from the Privy Council against Sir Archibald Douglas of Kelso for his treatment of two underage girls in

1662 has vanished. In all of the records concerning Agnes' case, Sir John's reply to his summons is missing. On the other hand, Agnes' trial records are in the National Library of Scotland in full.

After the difficulties that had been encountered in Agnes' trial, it is noticeable that Edinburgh did not have another witchcraft trial until 1649. This was despite the city being the capital with a relatively large population and a shipping coastline with all the attendant potential accidents due to bad weather. In addition, many important witch trials from across the country were frequently held in Edinburgh. In that same time period, around 55 'witches' were brought to trial across various other parts of the country.[136]

Two of the key elements in Agnes' story were the rise of the Covenanters and their battles with the King and the fact that she lived in Edinburgh. Living in the capital city put Agnes and the other residents of the Potterrow at the heart of the religious and political upheavals of the 17th century. They may well have only been the poor and middling sorts of the Potterrow who cared little for politics, but the religious fervour that swept the country was intensified in Edinburgh, the site of the drafting and signing of the National Covenant. Agnes and her neighbours could not escape the rising tension. Every leading Covenanter minister was preaching hellfire and damnation from every pulpit in the city. Every street corner saw groups of Covenanters vowing to die for the Covenant or Royalists pledging their loyalty to the King. Armed men roamed the Potterrow Port, rumours of atrocities by Catholics were widespread and daily reports of Auld Nick abroad in the land meant that anyone suspected of witchcraft was instantly arrested.

A witch living in a remote village in the Highlands might remain undetected by the minister: Agnes could not. A 'quarrelsome dame' on one of the islands might not be reported by her community: Agnes was. Agnes had been known as a witch for almost 30 years before the Potterrow had finally had enough of her. Agnes was one of the early casualties of the rising tension and eventual war between King and Covenanter.

The phrase 'the rising tension' barely does justice to what life must have been like in the Potterrow. Life was lived on the edge for most of the population of Scotland. The harvest failed frequently and there were subsequent food shortages, as well as famine in some years. There were regular occurrences of 'plague' which killed indiscriminately, whatever its actual nature. The Kirk kept everyone in a constant state of fear and anxiety with weekly sermons about the pervasive nature of sin and the presence of Auld Nick, and the country was at war with its own King. The Potterrow Port with its constant flow of people (some of whom were strangers), its misinformation from rumours and stories and its lack of care from its ministers lived with 'rising tension' on a daily basis on a scale difficult to comprehend today.

The Covenanters were strongly represented in the west of Scotland. Due to the geography of Scotland, however, most gravitated to the east as any attack from King Charles was expected from Berwick-upon-Tweed rather than Carlisle. During this period, Glasgow was around half the size of Edinburgh, but, combined with the other towns along the Clyde and in Lanarkshire and Ayrshire, had a much greater population. It is noticeable that between 1638 and 1645 there were ten witchcraft trials in Glasgow and the western shires of

Scotland. During that same period, there were 18 in Edinburgh alone, including Agnes'. The overheated atmosphere in Edinburgh gave the likes of Agnes nowhere to hide. When the politics and religion of the day combined such that the squabbles of the Potterrow became a matter for the Privy Council itself, Agnes the shopkeeper entered the historical records.

After Agnes' death, Edinburgh continued to cope with the religious and political turmoil of the struggles between Covenanters and Royalists, Presbyterians and Episcopalians and King Charles and the English Parliamentarians. The wars intensified and culminated in the execution of the King in 1649. Proof, if it was needed, that the world was turned upside down and that Auld Nick must indeed be stalking the land. The Cromwellian Commonwealth was imposed on Scotland, to be followed by the Restoration while the Kirk continued to see witches everywhere it looked. The Commonwealth, which had acted as a brake on the authority of the Kirk, had seen a significant reduction in the frequency of witchcraft trials, but the numbers soon rose with the Restoration.[137]

By the end of the century, the weather had improved and there were fewer harvest failures and fewer instances of plague. The restoration of King Charles II in 1660 started the process by which the previous political upheavals were soon resolved, although these would not be fully determined until after the reign of William and Mary. The Anglican church in England was finally and fully established in England while the form of worship followed in Scotland was more or less left to the Scots to decide for themselves. With fewer stresses and strains in daily life, the need for a scapegoat reduced. As the century came to a close, the courts and philosophers, although not the

Kirk, were increasingly questioning the whole notion of witch-craft and the ability of women to work magic. Or at least the reliability of accusations based on the gossip of women. The advocates wanted stronger proof and so fewer Commissions were granted. The requirement for stronger proofs in court saw acquittals rise and accusations of witchcraft fell away.

Universal belief in the existence of witches and witch-craft had been a necessary prerequisite for the trials that took place in the 17th century. Whether emanating from the Devil or from magic, the practices of women were inherently suspi-cions. For every woman, and man, accused of witchcraft, there was a female or male accuser who genuinely believed that their misfortune had been caused by witchcraft. Within the Kirk's obsession with Auld Nick, no other explanation was possible. Within the Kirk's authority, trial and execution were the only solution. With the rise in rational thought, the universal belief in magic started to be undermined. Superstition could not withstand the intellectual challenge.

The last 'witch' tried in Edinburgh was Margaret Myles. Delated by another accused witch, Margaret was brought to trial, found guilty and was executed on 20 November 1702 at Castle Hill. The records of her trial are incomplete and the detail of the initial accusation against her is not known. The name of her accuser is also not known. Margaret was brought out of prison and the minister, George Andrew, begged her to renounce the Devil. It was reported that she would not do so, but then said, 'Lord, take me out of the Devil's hands and put me in Gods.'[138] Unusually for a 'witch', Margaret was not wor-riet and her body was not burned but was hanged.

By the 18th century, the new town of Edinburgh saw the birth of the Enlightenment. Clubs such as the Easy Club, the Political Economy Club and the Select Society were formed where men could discuss the latest thinking in philosophy, economics and politics. In the Potterrow, nothing much had really changed: the destitute and poor muddled along with the few middling folks in their midst. The tenements were still dark, rat- and flea-infested buildings with no sanitation and no heating in the winter. The minister at Greyfriars still seldom visited and the families that needed help with an ill child continued to seek out the local witch for help. The Kirk of Scotland reaffirmed their belief in witches and witchcraft in 1773.

15

Epilogue

AGNES FINNIE WAS a widow struggling to get by in an era when women had few rights; a time of fear and chaos when war, famine and pestilence threatened individuals every single day and when the Kirk saw Auld Nick round every corner. She lived in a part of Edinburgh that received little help from that Kirk. Agnes was a shopkeeper and moneylender, two professions that require a degree of mettle in dealing with those who would not pay. Was all this the reason for her temper, or was something else going on?

Huntington's disease is a condition that progressively stops parts of the brain working properly. It is also a heritable disease. The condition worsens over time and is usually fatal after a period of up to 20 years. Those with Huntington's experience physical and behavioural changes as a result of the disease. These behavioural changes vary, but may include irritability which can then develop into verbal aggression. Outbursts of screaming, swearing, slamming doors and hitting walls can also occur.[139] Did Agnes have Huntington's? Her behaviour does appear to have become more extreme as the years went on. Did Margaret inherit Huntington's from her mother? The same temper seems to have been present in both women. The current estimated prevalence of Huntington's disease in North

Western Europe is approximately six to 14 cases per 100,000 population.[140]

Of course, there is no way of knowing if Agnes and Margaret had Huntington's disease or any other conditions which may have influenced their actions. They may simply have been two women with bad tempers who were struggling to survive and reacting to circumstances that were becoming increasingly out of their control.

The image that is conjured up by the word 'witch' has changed over the centuries. Agnes was not the stereotypical healer, collecting herbs in the fields and forests of the Scottish countryside. Neither was she a cackling hag bent over a cauldron in a lonely cottage. She was a real person, with all the faults and flaws that this entails. Although not noted as a regular in Greyfriars, Agnes was a Christian, but she also believed in and practised magic. Was she bewildered and angry about what was happening in the world around her and the seeming inability of her magical practises to protect her from famine, pestilence and war? Given her temper and the way she conducted business around the Potterrow, did she deserve to be arrested? Perhaps. Did she deserve to be found guilty? Also, perhaps. But did she deserve to be executed?

In the 17th century, the Kirk was genuinely fearful of the Devil and witches. Areas like the Potterrow, with their continued acceptance of and reliance on witches and their magic, lived an almost parallel existence where Auld Nick was a familiar, albeit somewhat ambiguous, figure. When, however, matters in the Potterrow spilled out into the wider parish, then previously unknown individuals like Agnes became the focus of all of that societal anxiety. For the likes of George Gillespie and the rest of the Edinburgh Covenanters, 'witches' like Agnes Finnie came along at just the right time and in just the right place to become the lightning rod for those anxieties. Agnes frightened people just as all of those societal problems were frightening people. Agnes, like all witches became the physical embodiment of all of those anxieties. If a witch could step across the border from the poverty-stricken, superstitious inhabitants of the Potterrow and infect the rest of decent Edinburgh, then all those other nebulous fears could also spill across and bring about a whole world of social unrest. She was the embodiment of the apocalypse to the clergy, while remaining a flesh and bone part of the city's poor. Witches and their activities were an uncomfortable reminder in the 17th century that, beneath the facade of their 'modern' Presbyterian image of Scotland, belief in superstition and magic continued. The authority of Kirk and Council were merely the outer cloak of the life of the city. The certainty of God's Elect had always been precarious. No one could know God's mind with complete conviction and the presence of witches and witchcraft exposed that frailty. Witches and their beliefs penetrated the consciousness of the people in a way that, with a few exceptions like Burke and Hare, ordinary crimes had not done in the past and arguably would not do in the future.

With the chaos of war, famine and plague all around them, the Kirk of Scotland tried to forge a common purpose and cleave the nation together to fight the Devil. What it actually did was to turn people against one another and cleave the Kirk away from the ordinary women and men living in places like the Potterrow. The harsh simplicity of predestination and the brutal, fixed notion of good and evil alienated the Kirk from the poor and left women like Agnes dangerously exposed. Practitioners of magic, when exposed, died in their thousands.

Agnes' story mirrored the rising tension of religion and politics in the country. From basic nastiness and yelled curses to the death of a child; from discontent with the King's command to civil war. Much has been written about Scotland and Great Britain in the 17th century. One key element of that century, and especially of the period between 1637 and 1647, is the sheer confusion of daily life. The interplay between politics and religion; the arguments between Charles and the English Parliamentarians; the fighting of the Scottish Highland clans; the claims and religious certainty of the Covenanters and the differences between the Presbyterians, the Episcopalians and the Puritans rendered daily life for ordinary people like Agnes a chaotic place, even without the spectre of witches. The politics of the elite always has unintended consequences for ordinary people. When those politics are themselves confused, those unintended consequences can be devastating. This uncertainty alone would have given rise to stresses and strains for those living in the Potterrow. The Kirk's obsession with the Devil was the added element that took those stresses and strains and elevated them into the terrors that saw Agnes, and those like her, face the rope and the flames. Violence, or at the very least the threat of violence, became endemic across Edinburgh. The tension between the Covenanters and Royalists was relentless and on a scale that is difficult for the modern mind to comprehend. No one could feel completely secure about their physical or spiritual safety.

This was an all-consuming state of terror that appeared endless.

Witches were not pagans. Everyone in 17th century Scotland, with a few, very few exceptions, was Christian. Witches were Christians who practised magic; that use of magic lay alongside their Christianity. Magic was used in an everyday sense to help you negotiate the world of illness, loss, etc. Everyone knew there were people who used magic. When the Kirk conflated their belief in the works of Auld Nick with those magical practitioners, it may have served to 'prove' their godliness and explain the chaotic world of the 17th century but it was to have a lasting legacy.

Witches have captured the public imagination in a way that few other 'beings' have. Is it because they were, and in some cases are still, perceived as women with power? Within the patriarchal society of the 17th century, men were supposed to have power and women were not. Witches were perceived as empowered women at that time, but, not only that, they were women with power that came from magic – not from physical strength, political power, status, money or titles, but from some nebulous entity called magic. However, despite that power they were still caught and executed – by men – and order was restored. After the 17th century, witches entered folklore as a cautionary tale – see what happens if women get power – but also as a 'safe scare'. Witches might attain power and perform their foul deeds, but, ultimately, they will be caught and punished. Much like the thrill of a ghost story that may set the pulse racing yet is, ultimately, just a story, witches may perform magic but will always get caught.

But there are other elements that add to the appeal of witches: the ordinary and the extraordinary, and the combination of the two. Despite the caricatures in 17th and 18th century wood-cuts, witches were ordinary women. They looked just like your sister or your mother. You might pass them in the street totally unaware of their true nature. And these ordinary women had extraordinary magical powers. Somehow, they could command forces to help heal a sick child or find some lost property: power that was beyond the learned men of the Kirk. In the humdrum world of the 18th century, magical stories held a mystical charm that could lift you out of the day-to-day life as a rural farm worker or town weaver. The industrial revolution of the 19th century forced people into the mechanised world of machines and rigid working days. Stories of magic relieved the reality of life. For artists, these magical stories gave them the inspiration for their romanticism. The Brothers Grimm collected folktales and found witches aplenty. Nineteenth century male fears over female power echoed back to those of their 17th century breth-ren. In the 21st century, witches have evolved into various differ-ent forms, allowing different people to recreate them into what works for them. Whatever form they take, their power to fasci-nate remains.

Acknowledgements

THIS BOOK WAS written to illustrate the life of Agnes Finnie, a widow living in the Potterrow Port in Edinburgh who was accused, tried and executed as a witch in the 17th century. Her life and trial shed light on the dark corners of the tenements of Edinburgh; how the political arguments between King and parliament affected ordinary people and how the Kirk's obsession with the Devil that held sway in the century led to the deaths of so many women and men. But mostly her story illustrates the reality behind the stereotype of the witch. Agnes was no wise woman gathering herbs in the countryside, but a real person with all the usual human flaws, as were all those accused of being a witch.

The records held at the National Records of Scotland and the National Library of Scotland have proved invaluable in compiling this book, as has the University of Edinburgh's *Survey of Scottish Witchcraft*. I wish to especially thank the National Library of Scotland for supplying me with all of Agnes' trial records, as well as large amounts of other background material. Further thanks are due to Mike and Jessica Troughton for their photographs. Finally, thanks are due to the editorial team at Luath Press for their help in producing this book.

Bibliography

Annals of Auchterarder.

Baillon, Le Comte de, *Henriette-Marie de France, reine d'Angleterre: étude historique suivie de ses lettres inédites* (Paris: Librairie Academique, 1872).

Black, G.F., *Calendar of Cases of Witchcraft in Scotland 1510 to 1727* (New York: The New York Public Library, 1938).

www.british-history.ac.uk/church-scotland-records/acts/1638-1842/pp73-96.

Brown, N.P., *Pagans and Priests* (Oxford: Lion Hudson, 2006).

Bryce, W. Moir, *History of the Old Greyfriars' Church Edinburgh* (Edinburgh: William Green and Sons, 1912).

Burnet, *Lives and Actions of the Dukes of Hamilton* (London: 1677).

www.bvh.univ-tours.fr/Consult/index.asp?numfiche=221.

Calendar of State Papers Ireland.

Calvin, Jean, *Institutes of the Christian Religion* (1536).

Camden Miscellany, VIII, A letter from the Earl of Manchester.

Cantor, N.F., *In the Wake of the Plague* (London: Simon & Schuster, 2001).

Cawthorne, N., *Witch Hunt* (London: Arcturus Publishing Ltd, 2002).

Chambers, Robert, *Domestic Annals of Scotland* (Edinburgh and London: Chambers, 1859–61).

Circuit Court Books.

Clarendon State Papers, II.

Commons Journal, III.

Culross Kirk session records in *Stirling Natural History and Antiquarian Society Transactions*, 1984–5, pp 84–101.

Cunningham, T., *Journal of Thomas Cunningham* (Scottish History Society, 1928).

Davidson, T., *Rowan tree and red thread* (Edinburgh: Oliver and Boyd, 1949).

—— 'The cure of Elf-Disease in Animals', in *Journal of the history of medicine*, Volume XV, Issue 3, (1960).

Dalyell, J.G., *The Darker Superstitions of Scotland: Illustrated From History and Practice* (Andesite Press, 2017).

Dingwall, H., *Physicians, Surgeons and Apothecaries: Medicine in Seventeenth-Century Edinburgh*, (East Linton: Tuckwell Press, 1995).

Dunlop, A.I., *The Kirks of Edinburgh: 1560–1984* (Edinburgh: Scottish Record Society, 1988).

Edinburgh Burgh Records, 1635–42.

eprints.whiterose.ac.uk/103389/1/PrevalenceofHD-SystematicReview-BAIG.pdf.

Ewan, E., and Meickle, M. (eds), *Women in Scotland, c.1100–c.1750* (East Lothian: Tuckwell Press, 1999).

Forbes-Leith, *Memoirs of Scottish Catholics* (London: 1909).

'The Fraser Manuscript', *A Collection of Providential Passages Antient and Modern Forreign and Domestick* (Edinburgh: 1670).

Froud, B., and Lee, A., *Faeries* (New York: Peacock Press, 1978).

Gibson, Marion, 'Witchcraft in the Courts', in Marion Gibson, ed, *Witchcraft And Society in England And America, 1550–1750* (Continuum International Publishing Group, 2006).

Goodare, J., *The Scottish witch-hunt in context* (Manchester: Manchester University Press, 2002).

Greenham, R., *Works* (1601).

Guthry, 'History', in *Scottish Historical Review*, XXII.

Harris, T., *Rebellion: Britain's First Stuart Kings, 1567–1642* (Oxford: Oxford University Press, 2014).

Henderson, E., *Annals of Dunfermline* (Alpha Edition, 2019).

Hickes, G., *Ravillac Redivivus* (1678).

Hopkins, M., *The discovery of witches* (1649).

Hume Brown, P., *The Register of the Privy Council of Scotland*, 2nd series, Vol VIII (Edinburgh: General Register House, 1908).

Jillings, K., *Scotland's Black Death* (Stroud: Tempus Publishing, 2003).

Justiciary Court, 26/9.

Kaplan, L., 'Charles I's Flight to the Scots', *Albion: A Quarterly Journal Concerned with British Studies*, Volume 11, Issue 3 (1979), pp 207–23.

Knox, J., *The First Blast of the Trumpet against the Monstrous Regiment of Women* (1558).

Kors, A.C., and Peters, E., *Witchcraft in Europe 400–1700* (Philadelphia: University of Pennsylvania Press, 2001).

Kramer, H., *Malleus maleficarum* (1486), ed P.G. Maxwell-Stuart (Manchester: Manchester University Press, 2007).

Lamont-Brown, R., *Scottish Witchcraft* (Edinburgh: Chambers, 1994).

Larner, C., *Enemies of God* (London: Chatto & Windus, 1981).

—— Hyde Lee, C., and McLachlan, H., *Source book of Scottish Witchcraft* (Glasgow: The Grimsay Press, 2005).

Linton, E.L., *Witch Stories* (London: Chapman and Hall, 1861).

MacKenzie, Kirsteen M., *The Solemn League and Covenant of the Three Kingdoms and the Cromwellian Union, 1643–1663* (London: Routledge, 2017).

Mackie, Lenman and Parker, *A History of Scotland* (New York: Hippocrene Books, 1986).

Marshall, K., *John Knox* (Edinburgh: Birlinn, 2000).

Mason, Roger A., 'National Covenant and Solemn League and Covenant', in Michael Lynch, ed, *The Oxford Companion to Scottish History* (Oxford: Oxford University Pres, 2007).

Maxwell-Stuart, P.G., *An Abundance of Witches* (Stroud: Tempus Publishing Limited, 2005).

—— *Satan's Conspiracy* (East Lothian: Tuckwell Press, 2001).

—— *Witchcraft: A History* (Stroud: Tempus Publishing, 2000).

—— *Witch Hunters* (Stroud: Tempus Publishing, 2003).

Munro, R., *A true relation of the Proceedings of the Scottish Army in Ireland* (London: 1642).

www.nhs.uk/conditions/huntingtons-disease/.

www.nhs.uk/conditions/stroke/causes/.

Normand, L., and Roberts, G., *Witchcraft in Early Modern Scotland* (Exeter: University of Exeter Press, 2000).

Pearce, D., *Henrietta Maria* (Stroud: Amberley Publishing, 2015).

Pennethorne, H., *Witchcraft* (Stroud: The History Press, 2004).

Perkins, W., *Discourse on the Damned Art of Witchcraft* (Puritan Publications, 2016).

Presbyterie book of Kirkcaldie.

Presbyterie book of Peebles.

Presbyterie book of Perth.

Presbyterie book of Strathbogie.

Ramsay, *Elminthologia* (London: 1688).

Royle, T., *Civil War: The Wars of the Three Kingdoms 1638–1660* (London: Abacus, 2006).

Scott, Hew, *Fasti ecclesiae scoticanae; the succession of ministers in the Church of Scotland from the reformation* (Edinburgh: Oliver and Boyd, 1915).

Scot, R., *Discoverie of witchcraft proving the common opinions of witches contracting with divels, spirits, or familiars* (1584).

Shapiro, A.K., and Shapiro, E., *The Powerful Placebo: From Ancient Priest to Modern Physician* (Baltimore: John Hopkins University Press, 2006).

Sharpe, C.K., *A historical account of the belief in witchcraft in Scotland* (Glasgow: Thomas Morrison, 1884).

Smout, T.C., *A history of the Scottish people 1560–1830* (London: Fontana Press, 1998).

Spalding, *Memorials of the Troubles* (Aberdeen: Spalding Club, 1850).

Spottiswoode Society, *The Spottiswoode Miscellany, A collection of original paper and tracts illustrative chiefly of the civil and ecclesiastical history of Scotland,* Vol II (Edinburgh: Spottiswoode Society, 1844).

Stafford MSS X, *Wentworth to Northumberland.*

Stewart, J.E., *Defendant's Attractiveness as a Factor in the Outcome of Criminal Trials: An Observational* Study (1980).

Stuart, J., *Daemonologie* (Edinburgh: 1591), eds L. Normand and G. Roberts (Exeter: University of Exeter Press, 2000).

Thomas, K., *Religion and the decline of magic* (London: Penguin Books, 1991).

Warriston, A., *Diary* (Edinburgh: Scottish History Society, 1911).

Wedgewood, C.V., *The King's Peace, 1637–1641* (London: Penguin Books, 2001).

—— *The King's War, 1641–1647* (London: Penguin Books, 2001).

—— *The thirty years war* (New York: New York Review of Books, 2005).

Whyte, I.D., 'Population and mobility in early modern Scotland', in R.A. Houston and I.D. Whyte, eds, *Scottish Society, 1500–1800* (Cambridge: Cambridge University Press, 2005).

Young, J.R., 'The Covenanters and the Scottish Parliament, 1639–51: the rule of the godly and the 'second Scottish Reformation", in E. Boran and C. Gribben, eds, *Enforcing Reformation in Ireland and Scotland, 1550–1700* (Aldershot: Ashgate, 2006), pp 131–58.

Manuscript sources:

Books of Adjournal JC2/8

Register of the Privy Council 2nd Series

Calendar of State Papers Domestic Series

References

1   Sharpe, C.K., *A historical account of the belief in witchcraft in Scotland*, pp 53–8.

2   Dunlop, A.I., *The Kirks of Edinburgh: 1560–1984*, p 28.

3   Hickes, G., *Ravillac Redivivus*, p 73.

4   Whyte, I.D., 'Population and mobility in early modern Scotland', in *Scottish Society, 1500–1800*, p 41.

5   1 Corinthians, 14:34.

6   Greenham, R., *Works*, p 554.

7   Shapiro, A.K., and Shapiro, E., *The Powerful Placebo: From Ancient Priest to Modern Physician*, p 2.

8   www.nhs.uk/conditions/stroke/causes/.

9   *Register of the Privy Council,* 2nd series, vol 1, p 258.

10 Ibid, p 275.

11 *Presbyterie Book of Perth*, p 307.

12 *Register of the Privy Council*, 2nd series, vol 1, pp 297–8.

13 Ibid, p 425.

14 Ibid, p 469.

15 Sharpe, C.K., *A historical account*, p 113.

16 *Register of the Privy Council,* 2nd series, vol 1, p 607.

17 Ibid, vol 2, p 410.

18 Wedgewood, C.V., *The King's Peace*, p 153.

19 Ibid, p 154.

20 Ibid.

21 *Register of the Privy Council of Scotland, 1633–35*, p 126.

22 Wedgewood, C.V., *The King's Peace*, p 162.

23 Trial record, *Books of Adjournal,* JC2/8.

24 Trial record, *Books of Adjournal,* JC2/8.

25 *Register of the Privy Council of Scotland, 1633–35*, p 537.

26 Ibid, 2nd series, vol 4, pp 405, 423, 426, 435.

27 Murmuring a judge or clergyman was the criminal offence of publicly criticising an authority figure.

28 *Register of the Privy Council of Scotland, 1637*, p 509.

29 Ibid, pp 223–4, 258–60.

30 *Register of the Privy Council,* 2nd series, vol 2, p 437.

31 Dingwall, H., *Physicians, Surgeons and Apothecaries: Medicine in Seventeenth-Century Edinburgh*, pp 85–6.

32 Gibson, Marion, 'Witchcraft in the Courts', pp 1–9.

33 Bryce, W. Moir, *History of the Old Greyfriars' Church Edinburgh*, p 52.

34 Ibid, p 55.

35 *Register of the Privy Council of Scotland, 1638*, pp 4, 15–16.

36 Mason, Roger A., 'National Covenant and Solemn League and Covenant'.

37 Spalding, *Memorials*, p 97.

38 Trial record, *Books of Adjournal,* JC2/8.

39 Bryce, W. Moir, *History of the Old Greyfriars' Church Edinburgh*, p 52.

40 Burnet, *Lives*, pp 50–1.

41 Ibid.

42 Ibid, p 52.

43 Forbes-Leith, *Memoirs of Scottish Catholics*, pp 202–3.

44   Warriston, A., *Diary*, pp 393,
      395, 397.
45   *Presbyterie book of Kirkcaldie*,
      pp 131–2.
46   Ibid, p 135.
47   Ibid, pp 135–6.
48   Harris, T., *Rebellion: Britain's First
      Stuart Kings, 1567–1642*, p 372.
49   Ibid.
50   Pearce, D., *Henrietta Maria*,
      pp 145–7.
51   *Calendar of State Papers Domestic
      Series*, 1638–39, pp 101, 120, 152.
52   Mackie, Lenman and Parker, *A
      History of Scotland*, pp 205–6.
53   *Register of the Privy Council*,
      1638–9, pp 96–102.
54   *Calendar of State Papers Domestic
      Series*, 1638–39, pp 405–10.
55   Revelation of John of Patmos, 6:8.
56   *Presbyterie book of Strathbogie*,
      p 15.
57   *Presbyterie booke of Kirkcaldie*,
      p 141.
58   Ibid, p 113.
59   *Presbyterie book of Peebles*,
      pp 160–1.
60   *Register of the Privy Council*, 2nd
      series, vol 7, pp 474–7.
61   *Calendar of State Papers Domestic
      Series*, 1639, p 198.
62   Ibid, p 355.
63   Stafford MSS X, *Wentworth to
      Northumberland*.
64   *Calendar of State Papers Ireland*,
      1633–47, pp 223–51.
65   *Calendar of State Papers Domestic
      Series*, 1639–40, pp 263–6.
66   *Register of the Privy Council*, 2nd
      series, vol 2, p 122.
67   Harris, T., *Rebellion: Britain's First
      Stuart Kings, 1567–1642*,
      p 342.
68   Guthry, 'History', in *Scottish
      Historical Review*, XXII, p 65.
69   *Register of the Privy Council*, 1639,
      p 142.

70   *Calendar of State Papers Domestic
      Series*, 1640, p 472.
71   Ibid, p 558.
72   Ibid, pp 144–5.
73   www.british-history.ac.uk/church-
      scotland-records/acts/1638-1842/
      pp44-45.
74   *History of Peeblesbire*, p 160.
75   www.british-history.ac.uk/church-
      scotland-records/acts/1638-1842/
      pp49-50.
76   *Calendar of State Papers Domestic
      Series*, 1640, pp 99–100.
77   *Calendar of State Papers Domestic
      Series*, 1640–41, p 111.
78   Royle, T., *Civil War: The Wars of the
      Three Kingdoms, 1638–1660*, p 108.
79   *Edinburgh Burgh Records*, 1635–42,
      pp 86–7.
80   *Register of the Privy Council*, 2nd
      series, vol 7, pp 198–211.
81   Munro, R., *A true relation of the
      Proceedings of the Scottish Army in
      Ireland*, p 9.
82   *Register of the Privy Council*, 2nd
      series, vol 2, p 165.
83   Ibid, pp 288–96.
84   Scot, R., *Discoverie of witchcraft
      proving the common opinions of
      witches contracting with divels,
      spirits, or familiars*, chap XXIV.
85   www.british-history.ac.uk/church-
      scotland-records/acts/1638-1842/
      pp52-73.
86   Scott, H., *Fasti Ecclesiae Scoticanae*,
      p 15.
87   *Journal of Thomas Cunningham*,
      pp 64–8.
88   *Register of the Privy Council*, 2nd
      series, vol 7, p 373.
89   *Clarendon State Papers*, II, p 183.
90   Ibid, V, p 1359.
91   Ibid, VI, pp 1335, 349.
92   *Register of the Privy Council*, 2nd
      series, vol 7, pp 429–33.
93   *Edinburgh Burgh Records*, 1642–55,
      pp 28–9.

94 Baillon, *Henriette Marie de France*, p 487.

95 Kaplan, L., 'Charles I's Flight to the Scots,' p 207.

96 *Register of the Privy Council*, 2nd series, vol 7, pp 442–4.

97 www.british-history.ac.uk/church-scotland-records/acts/1638-1842/pp73-96.

98 *Register of the Privy Council*, 2nd series, vol 7, pp 595–6.

99 Dalyell, *Darker Superstitions*, pp 253–6, 492–3, 514.

100 Henderson, *Annals of Dunfermline*, p 309.

101 'Culross Kirk session records' in *Stirling Natural History and Antiquarian Society Transactions*, 1984–5, p 81.

102 *Annals of Dunfermline*, p 310.

103 Dalyell, *Darker Superstitions*, pp 373, 665.

104 *Annals of Auchterarder*, p 208.

105 Sharpe, C.K., *A historical account of the belief in witchcraft in Scotland*, p 113.

106 *Commons Journal*, III, pp 219–20.

107 *Edinburgh Burgh Records*, 1642–55, pp 33–5.

108 *Calendar of State Papers Domestic Series*, 1643–7, pp 25, 30.

109 Froud, B., and Lee, A., *Faeries*, pp 28–9.

110 Davidson, T., 'The cure of Elf-Disease in Animals', p 282.

111 *Register of the Privy Council*, 3rd series, vol 1, p 243.

112 Ramsay, *Elminthologia*, p 71.

113 Kramer, H., *Malleus maleficarum* (1486).

114 *Register of the Privy Council*, 2nd series, vol 8, p 101.

115 Spottiswoode Society, *Spottiswoode Miscellany*, vol 2, p 271.

116 *Register of Privy Council*, 2nd series, vol 3, p 135.

117 Hopkins, M., *The discovery of witches*, pp 24–5.

118 SRO, JC2/14, pp 259–60.

119 *Commons Journal*, November 1644.

120 Harris, T., *Rebellion: Britain's First Stuart Kings, 1567–1642*, pp 53–4.

121 *Camden Miscellany*, VIII, A letter from the Earl of Manchester.

122 Spalding, *Memorials*, II, p 425.

123 *Register of the Privy Council*, 2nd series, vol 8, pp 134–5.

124 Stewart, J.E., *Defendant's Attractiveness as a Factor in the Outcome of Criminal Trials: An Observational* Study (1980).

125 www.bvh.univ-tours.fr/Consult/index.asp?numfiche=221.

126 Pennethorne, H., *Witchcraft*, p 181.

127 Perkins, W., *Discourse on the Damned Art of Witchcraft* (Puritan Publications, 2016).

128 *Circuit Court Books*, JC10/4 fo 1r–81r second pagination and Privy Council PC1/51 pp 136–9.

129 Spottiswoode Society, *The Spottiswoode Miscellany*, p 53.

130 *Register of Privy Council*, 2nd series, vol 5, pp 176–7, 572.

131 Exodus 22:18.

132 Dunlop, A.I., *The Kirks of Edinburgh: 1560–1984*, p 81.

133 Ibid.

134 *Justiciary Court*, 26/9 item 5.

135 Ibid, p 53.

136 Black, G.F., *Calendar of Cases*, pp 53–6.

137 Ibid, pp 65–74.

138 Chambers, R., *Domestic Annals*, vol 3, p 217.

139 www.nhs.uk/conditions/huntingtons-disease/.

140 eprints.whiterose.ac.uk/103389/1/Prevalence%20of%20HD%20-%20Systematic%20Review%20-%20BAIG.pdf.

Luath Press Limited

committed to publishing well written books worth reading

LUATH PRESS takes its name from Robert Burns, whose little collie Luath (*Gael.*, swift or nimble) tripped up Jean Armour at a wedding and gave him the chance to speak to the woman who was to be his wife and the abiding love of his life. Burns called one of the 'Twa Dogs' Luath after Cuchullin's hunting dog in Ossian's *Fingal*. Luath Press was established in 1981 in the heart of Burns country, and is now based a few steps up the road from Burns' first lodgings on Edinburgh's Royal Mile. Luath offers you distinctive writing with a hint of unexpected pleasures.

Most bookshops in the UK, the US, Canada, Australia, New Zealand and parts of Europe, either carry our books in stock or can order them for you. To order direct from us, please send a £sterling cheque, postal order, international money order or your credit card details (number, address of cardholder and expiry date) to us at the address below. Please add post and packing as follows: UK – £1.00 per delivery address; overseas surface mail – £2.50 per delivery address; overseas airmail – £3.50 for the first book to each delivery address, plus £1.00 for each additional book by airmail to the same address. If your order is a gift, we will happily enclose your card or message at no extra charge.

Luath Press Limited
543/2 Castlehill
The Royal Mile
Edinburgh EH1 2ND
Scotland
Telephone: +44 (0)131 225 4326 (24 hours)
Email: sales@luath.co.uk
Website: www.luath.co.uk